Health Communication and Sport

Health Communication and Sport

Connections, Applications, and Opportunities

Edited by Jimmy Sanderson
and Melinda R. Weathers

LEXINGTON BOOKS
Lanham • Boulder • New York • London

Published by Lexington Books
An imprint of The Rowman & Littlefield Publishing Group, Inc.
4501 Forbes Boulevard, Suite 200, Lanham, Maryland 20706
www.rowman.com

86-90 Paul Street, London EC2A 4NE

Copyright © 2022 by The Rowman & Littlefield Publishing Group, Inc.

All rights reserved. No part of this book may be reproduced in any form or by any electronic or mechanical means, including information storage and retrieval systems, without written permission from the publisher, except by a reviewer who may quote passages in a review.

British Library Cataloguing in Publication Information Available

Library of Congress Cataloging-in-Publication Data

Names: Sanderson, Jimmy, editor. | Weathers, Melinda R., 1980- editor.
Title: Health communication and sport : connections, applications, and opportunities / edited by Jimmy Sanderson and Melinda R. Weathers.
Description: Lanham, Maryland : Lexington Books, 2022. | Includes bibliographical references and index.
Identifiers: LCCN 2022014261 (print) | LCCN 2022014262 (ebook) | ISBN 9781793649751 (cloth) | ISBN 9781793649775 (paper) | ISBN 9781793649768 (ebook)
Subjects: LCSH: Communication in sports. | Communication in public health. | Sports—Health aspects. | Sports—Safety measures. | Health promotion.
Classification: LCC GV567.5 .H43 2022 (print) | LCC GV567.5 (ebook) | DDC 363.14—dc23/eng/20220506
LC record available at https://lccn.loc.gov/2022014261
LC ebook record available at https://lccn.loc.gov/2022014262

Contents

Introduction	vii
Chapter One: Media Framing and Athlete Mental Health *David Cassilo*	1
Chapter Two: Media Framing, Sport, and Public Health *Travis R. Bell and Janelle Applequist*	15
Chapter Three: Developing a Rhetoric of Mental Health from a Communication and Sport Perspective *Katherine L. Lavelle*	31
Chapter Four: Corporate Social Responsibility and Health Promotion Campaigns among Major U.S. Professional Sporting Leagues *Adam Rugg*	47
Chapter Five: Parent and Child Communication and Health Risks in Sport *Joseph McGlynn*	63
Chapter Six: Coach-Athlete Communication and Implications for Health *Gregory A. Cranmer, Rikishi T. Rey, and Sai Datta Mikkilineni*	79
Chapter Seven: Why Kinesiology and Athletics Departments Should Collaborate to Advance Health Equity *Larry D. Proctor, Sarah Stokowski, Danielle H. McArdle, and C. Keith Harrison*	95
Chapter Eight: Health Policymaking in Organizations *Nicole Butterbaugh and Blair W. Browning*	107

Chapter Nine: Sport and Health Risk Culture 125
Jennifer McMahon, Kerry R. McGannon, and Chris Zehntner

Chapter Ten: The U.S. Center for SafeSport: Preventing Abuse and
  Misconduct in Sport 139
Erin McConnell and Nicole Johnson

Chapter Eleven: Athletes, Social Media, and Health 155
Ellen MacPherson, Erin Willson, and Gretchen Kerr

Chapter Twelve: Athletes, Mental Health, and the COVID-19
  Pandemic 171
Carly Perry, Ali Bowes, and Alex Culvin

Chapter Thirteen: Athletes, Wearable Technology, and Health 187
Roth Smith

Index 201

About the Editors 215

Introduction

Health communication is a prominent topic in the communication studies discipline and sport represents a particularly compelling yet understudied area of inquiry. Communication around health choices and information in sport contexts can be seen in diverse areas including how parents manage health risks related to their children's athletic participation in sports like tackle football (McGlynn, Boneau, & Richardson, 2020), athletes' willingness to speak up and advocate for mental health (Cassilo, 2020), sport organizational policies related to health and safety (Cranmer & Sanderson, 2018), sexual abuse enacted by youth sport coaches through social media platforms like Snapchat (Sanderson & Weathers, 2020), and more recently, parents managing health needs of their children resulting from the loss of sports due to the COVID-19 pandemic (Sanderson & Brown, 2020).

Historically, sport has been a domain where the physical, mental, and emotional health of participants has been subjugated under the guise of toughness. As a result, organizations ranging from the National Football League (NFL) to the National Collegiate Athletic Association (NCAA), have enacted rule changes in recent years to promote health and safety among participants. These organizational decisions align with increasing societal dialogue around health and safety, parents growing concerns about their children playing contact sports, and enhanced media advocacy around the health impacts of sport participation. These outcomes also have initiated social resistance, as some individuals perceive that health and safety are compromising toughness and the "American" value systems (Sanderson & Cassilo, 2019). Understanding these discursive elements is crucial to learning more about why people make the health decisions they do. Said differently, perceived social norms and pressures and how those are enacted and perpetuated ideologically across sport and national cultures function as persuasive agents that may influence decisions made about sport and health (see chapter 5 in this volume).

The intersection of sport and health further represents a fertile area of study given how many individuals participate in sport over the lifespan. For many people, sport participation begins at a young age, and as athletes matriculate through the domains of sport participation such as recreation leagues, to club/

travel teams, to interscholastic sport, and ultimately high-level intercollegiate and professional sport, communication around health issues and decisions are important to understand and assess. That is, information, choices, and decisions around health have significant consequences for sport participants and other stakeholders (e.g., coaches, families). Parents play a major role in determining what kind of sports their children will play, and what kinds of risk are acceptable to incur through that participation (see chapter 4 in this volume). For instance, one family may allow their child to play high-contact sports such as tackle football or ice hockey, while another family may only allow their children to play less contact-oriented sports such as tennis or golf. Sometimes children do not participate in sport at all.

Additionally, how coaches and other athletic administrators communicate health policies and respond to health concerns impacts athletes' experiences with sport. Some coaches may stigmatize athletes who report health concerns or may pressure athletes to engage in excessive training regiments that can exacerbate mental and physical health issues (see chapters 8, 9, and 10 in this volume). Sport organizations, sport participants policies, and decision-making are also impacted by events out of their control, such as with the global COVID-19 pandemic. The pandemic not only disrupted sport activity, but has required increased protocols governing safe participation, all of which has implications for athletes' physical and mental health (see chapter 12 in this volume). Media also plays a prominent role in how people understand issues of health and sport (see chapters 1 and 2 in this volume). Moreover, how media organization and sport journalists talk about health issues and how they portray athletes who experience mental health issues contributes to how audiences may perceive these topics, and these perceptions can influence health decisions made in sport contexts (e.g., fear of stigmatization that may prompt an athlete to play through injury). Finally, health communication does not solely reside in athletic contexts. How athletes engage with and are affected by social media can have profound effects on their mental well-being (see chapter 11 in this volume).

As the preceding examples illustrate, there is much we can learn about health communication through its manifestation in sport contexts. We are excited to offer this volume as a resource for advancing understanding and scholarship at the intersection of sport and health. This collection brings together an international group of scholars along with sport organization practitioners to outline previous and current efforts with sport and health (connections), how health communication topics and issues manifest in sport settings (applications), and the potential for further research to strengthen our understanding in this area (opportunities). We are most grateful for our collaborators and the expertise they have brought to this project. This volume features work from scholars analyzing health issues in sport from interpersonal, organizational, and media perspectives. This diversity helps illuminate how health communication plays out in a variety of sport settings.

In chapter 1, David Cassilo examines the rising importance of athlete mental health and how mass media influences portrayals of athletes navigating mental health challenges, such as Simone Biles, Naomi Osaka, and Michael Phelps. Cassilo examines constructs such as media framing and how journalists and mass media organizations over time have portrayed athletes' mental health challenges, including how portrayals are becoming more supportive of athletes who are dealing with mental health challenges. Cassilo observes that more diversity in health and sport research is needed, as previous efforts are largely single-case studies focused on one athlete, sport, or country. Cassilo also argues for longitudinal research approaches that will help to better understand media portrayals of athlete mental health, along with encouraging researchers to adopt more diverse methods including autoethnography .

In chapter 2, Travis Bell and Janelle Applequist examine media portrayals of public health and how those influence sport contexts. They examine media framing around public health issues such as cancer and HIV/AIDS and then analyze contemporary settings where media framing of public health issues has become very salient. Specifically, they analyze topics such as concussions and Chronic Traumatic Encephalopathy (CTE), along with the impacts of COVID-19, and how media coverage tends to focus more on economic impacts before eventually looking at health-related outcomes. They also discuss how athletes utilize social media to initiate conversations about mental health by sharing their own narratives and experiences. They conclude by arguing for more attention to diversity, and how race, gender, ethnicity, and other identity elements may contribute to how media frames public health issues in sport. They also suggest that cases related to COVID-19, such as Washington State University terminating head football coach Nick Rolovich for not taking the COVID-19 vaccine, offer important case studies that will help illuminate the role of media framing and public health in the future.

In chapter 3, Kate Lavelle provides a compelling analysis of the role of rhetoric in understanding sport and health issues, particularly communication from athletes surrounding challenges of mental health. Lavelle notes that taking a rhetorical approach to understanding mental health and/or illness discourses help to both better understand conditions and experiences of athletes and how they function as persuasive acts inside particular contexts. Lavelle proposes a "rhetoric of mental health" that is derived from linkages with Burke's notion of identification as persuasion and the rhetorical ecology approach. Lavelle advocates that such an approach offers benefits related to providing a richer understanding of disclosure, and how disclosure operates as persuasive argument. Lavelle discusses these and other rhetorical elements through an examination of contemporary mental health disclosures by athletes including National Basketball Association (NBA) players Kevin Love and DeMar DeRozan. Lavelle advances directions for future research including focusing attention on hegemonic masculinity, looking at constructs such as hyperfemininity, particularly for female athletes, and female athletes of color. Lavelle notes that analyzing intersectional pressures may help to understand the role they play in contributing to mental health and other illness disclosures.

In chapter 4, Adam Rugg analyzes health promotion campaigns, and the ways in which sport organizations utilize campaigns to support health and fitness programming. Rugg discusses how such efforts tend to fall under the umbrella of corporate social responsibility, and notes that while such campaigns do have worthy goals, the motivations for such campaigns are suspect. More specifically, Rugg observes how such campaigns tend to operate as more covert forms of public relations and may be more aligned with image repair as opposed to altruistic motivations to improve health. Rugg analyzes campaigns targeted to areas of youth health and fitness such as the National Football League's (NFL) "Play 60" initiative and also looks at how sport organizations engaged these audiences during the COVID-19 pandemic, such as with Major League Baseball's (MLB) "Play Ball at Home" campaign. Rugg also discusses how sport organizations utilize campaigns to align with public health efforts, particularly those related to COVID-19 and vaccination. Rugg argues that more work is needed to investigate sport organizations' efforts related to health practices and how those intertwine with public/private initiatives. Rugg further suggests the need to examine both holistically and independently, player-led and organizational-led campaigns.

In chapter 5, Joseph McGlynn examines the role of health in youth sport by discussing how family communication influences decision-making in this context. McGlynn discusses parent motivations for youth sports, family dynamics, and the role of parent-child communication around risk in sport. McGlynn also analyzes how these topics influence communication around sport participation and health risks, such as willingness to report or manage concussion symptoms. McGlynn evaluates challenges to productive health conversations in family settings through analysis of parental bias, parental uncertainty, and the quality of parent-child relationship. Of particular interest, McGlynn notes how parents often face a "double bind" as they must manage safety risks for their child's welfare, but also have to avoid risks that may come from their child not participating in physical activity. McGlynn observes the need for future research to focus more on dyadic investigations that involve both parent and child accounts, along with looking at the quality of parental messaging around health risks in sport, and the ways in which compliance functions to impact health and sport (e.g., parent telling child the family will be disappointed if the child ceases playing a sport).

Introduction xi

In chapter 6, Greg Cranmer, Rikishi Rey, and SaiDatta Mikkilineni examine the role of coach-athlete communication and how it influences health. They note that coaches hold considerable influence over athletes and their health and health decision-making. As one example, they observe that coaches hold power over an athlete's training regimen, including rehabilitation, and note that how a coach communicates with athletes can impact athletes' emotional distress and anxiety. They analyze how coaches' communication can influence athletes reporting injuries, how athletes rehabilitate from injuries, along with how coaches' communication and interaction may contribute to dietary and eating disorders. The authors note that a need exists for researchers to examine how coach-athlete communication contributes to athletes' injuries related to overuse, traumatic brain injuries, along with how discourse may initiate or exacerbate mental health issues for athletes. They also call attention to the need for more diverse and rigorous methodologies to examine this topic, including creating specific measures to specifically analyze coach-athlete relationships and the use of more phenomenological and social-psychological approaches to guide investigations in this area.

In chapter 7, Larry Proctor, Sarah Stokowski, Danielle McArdle, and Keith Harrison examine health equity in sport. They note how important health equity is and the impact it can have on life satisfaction outcomes, along with how these inequities intersect with other social inequities. They discuss how advocacy related to social justice and diversity can help bring about change in sport-related contexts to promote more health equity outcomes. They share a particular focus on how health equity can be achieved in sport-and kinesiology-based classroom settings in programs such as motor learning and development, data analytics, and general curricula and instructional models. They also analyze existing models to address this area and propose a new Holistic-Kinesiology-Athletic Model. They observe how this model may be particularly useful in attending to mental health issues within intercollegiate athletics to help bring about outcomes related to strength, social determinants of health, and cultural competency.

In chapter 8, Nicole Butterbaugh and Blair Browning investigate the role of health policymaking in sport. They observe how sport organizations have historically used policies to strengthen organizational outcomes and analyze how health policymaking can be utilized to bring positive results for organizational stakeholders such as athletes and fans. They situate their analysis of sport organization and health policymaking through sport organization's COVID-19 policies with a specific examination of the NBA's "Bubble" for the 2020 playoffs and MLB's use of specific ballparks for the 2020 playoffs, the use of proximity tracking devices, and policies related to the COVID-19 vaccine. They asses how these polices have impacts for sport organizations recruiting athletes, athletes' mental health, and financial results. They conclude by proposing directions for future research related to looking more individually at sport organizations internal processes and methods for implementing health policy.

In chapter 9, Jennifer McMahon, Kerry McGannon, and Chris Zehntner examine health risk culture. They discuss how sport is, unfortunately, often a context ripe for abuse and exploitation that is justified in the name of enhanced performance. They rightly note that there is a need to investigate how athletes experience these issues while participating and how they manage these issues post-sport. They examine a variety of accounts from athletes participating in diverse sports to illustrate the breadth and depth of this issue. Their analysis also investigates the role that coaches and staff members play in enacting these abuses and how these behaviors may be linked to larger cultural ideologies. Their chapter provides an illuminating reminder of how sport can exert a heavy toll on athletes both during and post-athletic career. They advocate for more research related to health consequences for athletes subjected to abuse and how such investigations may help enhance athlete standard of care. They also suggest the need for more evidence-based education tied to athletes' narrative experiences and how these may help prevent abuse in the future.

In chapter 10, Erin McConnell and Nicole Johnson from the United States Center for SafeSport provide a discussion of athlete maltreatment, connecting the topic to Safe Sport's mission to ending all forms of abuse in sport. Their chapter provides an informative summary of prevailing abuse and maltreatment in sport, including sexual maltreatment, physical maltreatment, and emotional maltreatment. Their chapter also provides an insightful look into SafeSport and their programming and policy initiatives. They discuss how the Center operates each of these areas, along with a compelling look at response and resolution of abuse and maltreatment cases. McConnell and Johnson provide directions for future research, including developing more holistic approaches to athlete protection and incorporating more efforts to magnify athletes' voices and empower athletes to bring about cultural change.

In chapter 11, Ellen MacPherson, Erin Willson, and Gretchen Kerr examine the health implications connected to athletes' social media consumption. They discuss that while social media may offer some positive outcomes for athletes, it also comes with a number of challenges that possess significant effects for mental and physical health (e.g., being victimized by cyberbullying, engaging in social comparison). They discuss health implications for athletes related to using social media to build personal brands, interact with fans, and to engage in advocacy, particularly around mental health challenges. They further analyze areas where social media may create health-associated challenges and risks for athletes including hostile interactions with fans and organizational conflict. They suggest that future research will benefit from more investigations into athletes' lived experiences with social media and more investigations examining how athletes are individually and uniquely impacted by social media.

In chapter 12, Carly Perry, Ali Bowes, and Alex Culvin investigate the health impacts for athletes associated with the global COVID-19 pandemic. They note that during the COVID-19 pandemic, there has been increased concern for athletes' mental well-being and they discuss the challenges and unique stressors faced by athletes (e.g., uncertainty related to competition, lack of motivation). They analyze multiple factors such as gender, sport type, sport level, in-career and out-career transitions, and help-seeking behaviors; and they observe how each of these influence mental health effects stemming from the COVID-19 pandemic. They further address ways that mental health was managed during the pandemic and note the need for more research in this area, including looking at factors such as mental health literacy and the role of parents, support staff, and mental health officers. They also suggest that sport organizations need to adopt more holistic approaches to caring for athletes and bettering the sport environment.

Finally, in chapter 13, Roth Smith analyzes health implications related to athletes and wearable technology. Smith chronicles the rise of wearable technology and other forms of fitness and health tracking both in professional and recreation sport settings. Smith discusses how the intersection of sport and wearable technology poses compelling implications for mobile health (mHealth); specifically, Smith considers outcomes related to social community both offline and online. Smith notes how social community functions may contribute to retention and sustained use of devices. Smith also observes how this community of users provides a compelling corpus to study topics such as health information seeking and social support. He also notes challenges related to people utilizing these devices more for fashion than health purposes and individuals who may not take advantage of the data produced by these devices. Smith concludes by offering directions for future research including how these devices specifically contribute to health-related outcomes in sport along with implications for privacy and surveillance.

As these chapters demonstrate, health communication plays a significant role in diverse sport contexts and will continue to do so in the future. Indeed, health information and decision-making begin early in life, continue through more competitive realms of sport, and are influenced by interactions between parents, athletes, coaches, administrators, and media, among others. The growth of social media and wearable technology also hold significant implications for sport and health moving forward, including policymaking and support for athletes with their physical and mental health. We hope this volume inspires scholars and practitioners to advance scholarship and understanding of health communication and sport. We also hope that such work will strengthen sport experiences and athlete health and well-being, and help sport organizations' policies and programming to evolve and adapt (e.g., increased attention to athlete mental health).

Jimmy Sanderson
Texas Tech University
Melinda Weathers
Sam Houston State University

REFERENCES

Cassilo, D. (2020). Royce White, DeMar DeRozan and media framing of mental health in the NBA. *Communication & Sport.* Advance online publication. doi: 10.1177/2167479520933548.

Cranmer, G. A., & Sanderson, J. (2018). "Rough week for testosterone": Public commentary around the Ivy League's decision to restrict tackle football in practice. *Western Journal of Communication, 82,* 631–647.

McGlynn, J., Boneau, R. D., & Richardson, B. K. (2020). "It also might be good for your brain": Cognitive and social benefits that motivate parents to permit youth tackle football. *Journal of Sport & Social Issues, 44,* 261–282.

Sanderson, J., & Cassilo D. (2019). "I'm glad I played when the country still had gonads": Bottom-up framing around Pop Warner's kickoff policy change. *Journal of Sports Media, 14,* 1–22.

Sanderson, J., & Brown, K. (2020). COVID-19 and youth sports: Psychological, developmental, and economic impacts. *International Journal of Sport Communication, 3,* 313–323.

Sanderson, J., & Weathers, M. (2020). Snapchat and child sexual abuse in sport: Protecting child athletes in the social media age. *Sport Management Review, 23,* 81–94.

Chapter One

Media Framing and Athlete Mental Health

David Cassilo

Simone Biles, Naomi Osaka, and Michael Phelps are three of the most accomplished athletes in the world. They possess unique talents that have allowed them to rise to the top of their respective sports. However, they also all possess something far more common—mental health concerns. Biles, Osaka, and Phelps are a part of the 51.5 million Americans suffering from mental illness (Mental Illness, 2021). Unlike most of those Americans, these athletes have a very visible platform to speak publicly about their mental illness and bring awareness to it. Biles withdrew from several events during the 2020 Summer Olympics due to mental health concerns (Lewis, 2021), Osaka pulled out of the 2021 French Open due to her anxiety concerns (Carayol, 2021), and Phelps has openly discussed his depression and suicidal thoughts (Scutti, 2018). Together they are a part of a growing movement within sport to raise awareness about athlete mental health. This trend is a relatively new one, as athlete mental health in the United States was a relatively taboo subject (Kaier et al., 2015), as a stigma was created around athletics that revealed mental health concerns clashed with having mental toughness (Bauman, 2016). Thus, for most of American sports history, admissions like the ones made by Biles, Osaka, and Phelps were nearly non-existent. Prior to the 2010s, perhaps the only notable case of an athlete publicly discussing his mental health was former Major League Baseball player Jimmy Piersall, who was admitted to a mental hospital in 1952 and later diagnosed with bipolar disorder (Fedorocsko & Bishop, 2019).

MEDIA FRAMING AND ATHLETE MENTAL HEALTH

The sudden increase of athletes openly discussing their mental health has also led to an increase in the media covering such issues. Media coverage of mental health is an important area of examination due to the media framing implications. In short, the media can shape how the public discusses health issues (Hayes et al., 2007). As described by Entman (1993), media framing is to "select some aspects of a perceived reality and make them more salient in a communicating text, in such a way as to promote a particular problem definition, causal interpretation, moral evaluation, and/or treatment recommendation for the item described" (p. 52). Media framing organizes content by providing a context, thus specifying the most salient issue of the news coverage through the writer's news-making practices of selection, emphasis, exclusion, and elaboration (Tankard et al., 1991). Through this process, the way the news story is portrayed influences how it is understood by the audience (Scheufele & Tewksbury, 2007), and these effects on the audience can last weeks after initial exposure (Tewksbury et al., 2000). In essence, the frames create a map for the audience of how they should understand the story as well as the issues within it (Terkildsen & Schnell, 1997).

Collectively, the repetition of the same frames by different media outlets can lead to these frames being interpreted as fact (Billings & Eastman, 2003). These types of framing effects have been seen in a variety of areas related to health. Recent research has examined different elements related to the media framing of the COVID-19 pandemic. Findings indicate, for instance, that frames heightened fears about the pandemic (Ogbodo et al., 2020) and that there have been mental health concerns among athletes during this time (Reardon et al., 2020). Other research found that news frames about the virus created stereotypes and stigmatization of people from China (Mutua & Ong'ong'a, 2020). Framing research also focused on issues of health within specific coverage areas, including sport and physical injuries. Cassilo and Sanderson (2018) examined the digital media coverage of the retirement of National Football League player Chris Borland due to fears about health issues and head injuries. Their research found that most media coverage was largely supportive of Borland and of putting his health first, thus normalizing the behavior. The researchers elaborated that prioritizing health issues within football coverage can shape how the public views football. Elsewhere, White et al. (2020) examined the media framing of concussions in European soccer, finding a lack of awareness of the issues and thus, the lack of significance given to the issues within the frames of coverage. Several frames used concussions as an excuse for poor performance, thus downplaying to the audience the health-related importance of sustaining such an injury.

While mental health is receiving more attention in sports media coverage within the last decade, it has previously been covered in other ways. When examining past research on mental health, media portrayals have received criticism due to their influence on the stigmatization of different forms of mental illness. That stigma can lead to many issues, including stereotypes, discrimination, and unwillingness to seek help (Corrigan, 2004), as well as cause feelings of shame, self-blame, and secrecy for people with mental health issues (Benbow, 2007). Negative media depictions of mental health can even override any personal experience that may be positive (Philo et al., 1994). Such media stigmatization includes connecting mental health to criminal behavior (Coverdale et al., 2002). This is problematic in many areas, but most notably because media coverage is the most common source of knowledge for the public about mental health issues (Myrick et al., 2014) and often these portrayals are inaccurate (Cutcliffe & Riahi, 2018). Such coverage rarely includes the perspective of mental health professionals (Salter & Byrne, 2000) and often those who experience the mental health concerns are left without a voice (Wahl et al., 2002). Coverage does often include links between mental illness and biological factors, which creates an interpretation by the audience that patients can never recover from their ailments (Slopen et al., 2007).

Other common links within mental health media coverage include a connection between mental illness and dangerousness (Wahl, 2003) as well as violence. For instance, McGinty et al. (2016) found in their research of 400 news stories from 1995–2014 about mental illness concerns of non-public figures that more than half of the coverage they examined included a reference to violence. Another study by McGinty et al. (2014) saw a particular link within media coverage between mental health and gun violence. Linking mental illness and violence creates a stigma that those with mental illness are dangerous and should be avoided (Stout et al., 2004). That trend is shifting in some areas, though. In their own media analysis, Chen and Lawrie (2017) found that while violence was still a common element within mental health media coverage, there was a growing trend of coverage that included giving a voice to those portrayed with the mental health concern. This progress may be attributed to the recent rise of citizen journalism, as research has shown that mental health portrayals by these types of journalists tend to be more positive and hopeful (Carmichael et al., 2019). Yet even progress in this area can be diminished, as prior research has shown that it takes just one significant or dramatic media portrayal of mental illness by any type of journalist to dominate all other forms of media coverage about the issue (Anderson, 2003).

These sorts of negative mental health media depictions can have an impact on the individuals who suffer from these illnesses. As previously mentioned, many instances of media coverage about mental health connect it to dangerousness and violence, despite the reality being that most of those diagnosed with mental illness are not criminals (Wahl, 2003). Negative stigmas such as these can negatively influence self-esteem, help-seeking behaviors, medication adherence, and the overall recovery of those who suffer from mental illness (Stuart, 2006). Such coverage also influences others. Individuals who receive their information about mental illness primarily from electronic media have lower tolerance of people with mental illness than those who get their information from other areas such as people who work with those who have mental illness and classes that included mental health topics (Granello et al., 1999). Additionally, inaccurate patterns of coverage may influence public opinion and policy regarding mental health (Wahl, 2003). Wahl adds that one area where this influence may be seen is how communities provide care and support for those with mental health concerns.

For reasons like these, it is essential that the stigma is reduced through coverage of successful treatment and recovery from mental illness (McGinty et al., 2016). One such way to do this is to use human interest stories about those who suffer from mental illness, as this type of coverage can defy stigmas created by negative mental health coverage (Stuart, 2006). To do this, journalists can use tactics like first-person accounts of mental illness to humanize the coverage (Whitley & Berry, 2013). Another type of news content that would help erase stigmatization would be mental health informational coverage, as prior research has shown that it can lead the audience to support others and seek their own mental health treatment (Hoffner et al., 2017). And finally, in cases in which mental health is actually connected with violence, proper contextualization is vital. Such coverage should include research as well as expert interviews which can accurately describe the frequency that mental health and violence are related (Wahl, 2003).

Sport is an area of coverage in which health issues are more often discussed due to their public disclosures. In recent years, this has included instances of mental health disclosures and, accordingly, media coverage about these disclosures and research about media coverage. Elsey et al. (2020) examined the different types of those disclosures finding they mostly fall into two categories—team-led or player-led disclosures. Additionally, they found that the need for players to account for their absence from the team can accelerate these types of mental health disclosures, which may not always align with the timeline the player would like to disclose on. The researchers added that being as accurate and truthful about these disclosures as possible can minimize scrutiny and normalize the mental health concerns. During the 2017–18 NBA season, DeMar DeRozan and Kevin Love both publicly expressed their mental health ailments. A content analysis of the media coverage of those disclosures found that the athletes were framed as having strength for making these statements (Parrott et al., 2021). Both DeRozan and Love were portrayed as mental health advocates, and the coverage called to end the mental health stigma by letting the athletes share their own story, while also stressing the commonality of such experiences.

In a follow-up study (Parrott et al., 2020), the researchers examined the social media commentary surrounding the disclosures by DeRozan and Love. As the media coverage did, the social media comments were largely supportive and accepting of the athletes for their disclosures. Social media messages from fans included advice, encouragement, and the sharing of personal experience, all of which show forms of support to the athletes. Cassilo (2020) took a similar approach to examining media coverage of athlete mental health disclosure by examining the cases of DeRozan and fellow NBA player Royce White. In White's case, his disclosure came during the 2012–13 season and ultimately, he played just three games in the NBA despite being a first-round pick. Unlike DeRozan, the coverage surrounding White had frames that were critical of him and his situation, which could be attributed to a few areas. One being the method of disclosure, as DeRozan addressed the matter in a more subtle way through social media and interviews, while White was a more vocal and frequent communicator about mental health through both those channels. Often, White would publicly challenge both the league and his team, the Houston Rockets. The other being that while DeRozan had the credibility of being an NBA All-Star at the time of expressing his concerns, White had yet to play an NBA game. Such types of media coverage present a significant difference from prior coverage about mental health in sports.

Lavelle (2020) provided an additional study on Love's public mental health disclosures by conducting a critical discourse analysis of both his disclosure and his mental health advocacy. Her analysis particularly examined the role race played in Love's ability to make such a disclosure, suggesting that because Love was White he had a greater capability to not only express his concerns publicly but also to be praised for doing so. Still, despite the role that race played, the researcher stated that Love, like other athletes, is still subject to the limitations of the athlete that arise from the hegemonic masculinity that surrounds male sport. While it is important to study mental health communication of professional athletes, their experiences differ greatly from those of the college athlete.

Cassilo and Kluch (2021) examined the media framing of D.J. Carton, a former Ohio State men's basketball player who stepped away from his team during the 2019–20 season to focus on his mental health. Eventually, Carton left the university and transferred to Marquette University. Media frames were largely positive of Carton's experience, including showing support for Carton, positioning him as a mental health advocate, and shedding the stigma related to mental health. However, a major difference from similar studies examining professional athletes was the commodification of Carton. Many frames within the coverage focused predominately on Carton's athletic value rather than his personal mental health experience. This coverage examined what Ohio State was losing with Carton gone and what other teams could gain by having him transfer to their university. These frames became more common the further away from his announcement to step away from the team, thus suggesting that there was a sort of time limit on coverage devoted to his mental health. In the 20th century, perhaps the most well-known athlete to publicly discuss his mental illness was Jimmy Piersall, a Major League Baseball Player from 1950–67 who suffered from bipolar disorder. To understand how he was covered in the media, Fedorocsko and Bishop (2019) conducted a narrative analysis of obituaries and tributes written about Piersall, finding that such coverage presented a very limited view of the experience of mental illness.

CONTEMPORARY SETTINGS FOR MEDIA FRAMING AND ATHLETE MENTAL HEALTH

Due to the relative newness of open conversations in sport about mental health, many aspects of the athlete experience and the demands they put on the athlete are beginning to be questioned. One such case arose in May 2021 when women's tennis player Naomi Osaka expressed her concerns about how press conferences that she would be required to take part in at the French Open would impact her mental health, specifically her anxiety (Carayol, 2021). Osaka, who at the time was considered the top athlete in her sport, announced on Twitter that she would not be attending those press conferences during the tournament. Her announcement included:

> "I've often felt that people have no regard for [athletes'] mental health and this rings very true whenever I see a press conference or partake in one," Osaka wrote. "We're often sat there and asked questions that we've been asked multiple times before or asked questions that bring doubt into our minds and I'm just not going to subject myself to people that doubt me." (Osaka, 2021a)

In the wake of her announcement, the four Grand Slam tournaments officials fined Osaka $15,000 and threatened to suspend her from future tournaments (Goel, 2021). Shortly after, Osaka announced that she was withdrawing from the French Open to focus on her mental health (Carayol, 2021). Again, she took to Twitter for that announcement, and within it, she included, "I announced it preemptively because I do feel like the rules are quite outdated in parts and I wanted to highlight that" (Osaka, 2021b). This particular statement is important to examine because of the questions it raises in relation to mental health and sport. Perhaps most essential among them is, knowing what we do know about mental health, would we construct sports and the practices that have become a part of them in the same ways?

Just a few months later, Simone Biles, who was expected to win several gold medals at the 2020 Summer Olympics, withdrew from many events due to her mental health concerns (Lewis, 2021). Competing in the all-around gymnastics competition qualifications stage, Biles suffered several mishaps yet still qualified for the final with the top score. While warming up for the team competition, she continued to experience mishaps, and ultimately withdrew from that competition as well as several individual competitions that were scheduled to follow. Biles cited mental health concerns for her withdrawal, saying:

> I say put mental health first. Because if you don't, then you're not going to enjoy your sport and you're not going to succeed as much as you want to. So it's OK sometimes to even sit out the big competitions to focus on yourself, because it shows how strong of a competitor and person that you really are—rather than just battle through it. (Chappell, 2021)

Elite athletes are vulnerable to a wide range of mental health problems (Rice et al., 2016). Aside from the pressures associated with their sports, other mental health triggers can include the amount of travel, time away from their family, time-related demands, and press conferences. As elite athletes like Osaka and Biles continue to express their concerns about mental health, it becomes important for the officials of these sports to listen so that they can address the specific elements of the athletics structure that are impacting the mental health of their competitors.

While athletes like Osaka or Biles may have the financial resources to skip competitions and seek help on their own for mental health concerns, not all athletes are as fortunate. Specifically, college athletics has been a growing area of concern related to mental health. Although the college athlete faces many issues that contribute to psychological stress (de Souza et al., 2019), prior research has shown that they are less willing to seek help than their peers (Edwards & Froehle, 2021). The levels of stress have only been heightened in recent years, as the COVID-19 pandemic increased stress and mental health concerns for college athletes (Bullard, 2020), as many of these athletes were isolated from their peers. A lack of seeking help in any setting can be partly because of knowledge barriers, as young people in general have poor mental health literacy (Gulliver et al., 2012), financial barriers (Sheffield et al., 2004), or logistical barriers, like getting to mental health treatment facilities (Aisbett et al., 2007). College athletes also fear any sort of negative reaction from coaches and administrators (Proctor & Boan-Lenzo, 2019).

In particular, young men can be less likely to seek mental health support due to how the behavior could be portrayed as weakness, and thus call into question that individual's masculinity (Moreland et al., 2018). Some of the mental health challenges that college athletes specifically face include depression, anxiety, substance abuse, and eating disorders (Ryan et al., 2018). Female athletes in particular are more likely to experience depression (Wolanin et al., 2016). Other research has examined student-athletes with suicidal thoughts (Gross et al., 2020). There are ways to support all these athletes. Kern at el. (2017) found that Athletes Connected, a program that combined anecdotal mental health videos with informational presentations, increased awareness of mental health problems as well as help-seeking behaviors of college athletes. The researchers found that brief contact and education-based interventions like these can lessen the stigma surrounding mental health. Stigmas like these can prevent student-athletes from seeking help (Gulliver et al., 2012). Elsewhere, Hilliard et al. (2020) examined the stigma connected with mental illness in Division II and III athletics, and as part of their findings, suggested that sports counselors and psychologists with different areas of expertise should be readily available to college athletes.

DIRECTIONS FOR FUTURE RESEARCH

Mental health research in the sports communication field is in its relative infancy with the majority of those studies coming since 2019. Thus, it is hard to suggest just a few areas of research within this subject matter because there is so much need for growth and depth. Any research project will help grow the understanding of mental health and sports communication. Media framing is one area where some attempts have already been made to better understand athlete mental health (Parrott et al., 2019; Cassilo, 2020; Cassilo & Kluch, 2021). Yet, this research is rather limited at this point. The athletes within those studies mostly come from the NBA, and one athlete, DeMar DeRozan, is examined in two studies. These studies also only examine athlete mental health disclosures and the media framing around them. And with only male athletes examined, the scope of such research is very limited to this point. Therefore, research that examines different genders, sports, races, and levels of competition (e.g., student-athletes) is needed. As the Cassilo (2020) study showed in regard to DeRozan and White, factors such as professional experience and method of mental health disclosure may play a role in how the media frames athlete mental health, making it important to consider other factors and how they may erase or perpetuate long-existing stigmas in mental health coverage. Also, with such limited research in this area, it is hard to determine if there are any trends within how these athletes are covered. It is also necessary to examine media portrayal of athlete mental health in other countries. While the United States has become more accepting of mental health in recent years, it does not represent the attitudes of every country. Both countries with more progressive and more conservative national attitudes toward mental health are worthy of exploration.

While media framing may be the focus of this chapter, there are other methods of inquiry that are necessary to grow the understanding of athlete mental health as it relates to communication. For instance, interview-based studies like the autoethnography of a former college athlete's mental health struggles (Gross et al., 2020) are excellent ways to grow this line of research. First-person accounts of mental illness help humanize the subject matter (Whitley & Berry, 2013), making them not only an essential part of media coverage but also of research. Interview projects should not only focus on the mental health struggles of athletes but also on the communication strategies that create a supportive culture within a sport organization and the communication barriers that help prolong the stigma. Understanding the experiences of having a mental illness is important, but to truly change any sort of stigmas that exist as part of an athletic setting, it is imperative that we understand how those stigmas are created. Therefore, a focus on the culture of sport, both in a team-setting and individual-setting, will help grow our knowledge of mental health issues. Interview research should also be focused on an athlete support system beyond the locker room, particularly examining the roles of parents and other family members in supporting athletes with mental health issues. Under-reporting of concussions has been linked to parent pressure (Kroshus et al., 2015), thus making it an intriguing area of research to understand whether the same is seen with mental health issues.

The role of fans in the athlete mental health dynamic is an important area of inquiry as well. In other realms, social media users have created counter frames to what is seen in media coverage. For instance, while concussion media coverage has focused on health issues, social media response to such coverage can be less supportive and more critical of the athletes or safety measures being reported on (Cassilo & Sanderson, 2019). To this point, research has suggested that social media users discussing mental health have challenged traditional stigmas (Parrott et al., 2020). However, having just one examination from one specific point in time is not enough to draw broad conclusions from. There are other social media platforms and other athlete characteristics (e.g., gender, sport, etc.) that have yet to be explored. For instance, initial examination of social media reaction to Osaka and Biles and their decisions related to mental health suggest that the audience was more conflicted in support for them than they were for Love and DeRozan. It is impossible to determine why that may be the case without a research project focused on this area. Understanding and contextualizing those differences as well as grasping the impact of social media discourse on mental health stigmas remain worthy areas of examination. Additionally, it seems certain that cases like Osaka's and Biles' will only become more prevalent. Thus, there is a need to understand their media portrayal quickly, especially as attitudes toward mental health in the United States become more progressive by the day.

However, to return to an earlier point, there is such limited research on athlete mental health that all inquiries are welcomed and encouraged to grow the field. There are a lot of unknown and notable cases worthy of examination arising on a frequent basis. Many of the inquiries to this juncture have used media framing as a tool, and such studies have helped grow our understanding of how athlete mental health is discussed in this new era of openness and support. Gone seem to be the days of sport rooted in hegemonic masculinity where athletes sacrificed their health, both physical and mental, for the sake of winning. There are new ways to discuss the "toughness" of an athlete. While Osaka, Biles, and Phelps may be the largest names on the athletic stage talking about their mental health, they are surely not alone with hundreds, if not thousands, of athletes following suit. Such openness is a growing trend within sport and society, making the communication of mental health an essential area of study for sports communication moving forward.

REFERENCES

Aisbett, D. L., Boyd, C. P., Francis, K. J., Newnham, K., & Newnham, K. (2007). Understanding barriers to mental health service utilization for adolescents in rural Australia. *Rural Remote Healing, 7*(1), 624. doi: 10.22605/RRH624

Anderson, M. (2003). "One flew over the psychiatric unit": mental illness and the media. *Journal of Psychiatric and Mental Health Nursing, 10*(3), 297–306. doi: 10.1046/j.1365-2850.2003.00592.x

Bauman, N. J. (2016). The stigma of mental health in athletes: Are mental toughness and mental health seen as contradictory in elite sport? *British Journal of Sports Medicine, 50*(3), p. 135–136. doi: 10.1136/bjsports-2015–095570

Benbow, A. (2007). Mental illness, stigma, and the media. *Journal of Clinical Psychiatry, 68*(Suppl 2), 31–35.

Billings, A. C., & Eastman, S. T. (2003). Framing identities: Gender, ethnic, and national parity in network announcing of the 2002 Winter Olympics. *Journal of Communication, 53*(4), 569–586. doi: 10.1111/j.1460-2466.2003.tb02911.x

Bullard, J. B. (2020). The impact of COVID-19 on the well-being of division III student-athletes. *The Sport Journal, 41*(2).

Carayol, T. (2021, May 31). Naomi Osaka withdraws from French Open amid row over press conferences. *The Guardian.* https://www.theguardian.com/sport/2021/may/31/naomi-osaka-withdraws-french-open-press-conference-fines-tennis

Carmichael, V., Adamson, G., Sitter, K. C., & Whitley, R. (2019). Media coverage of mental illness: A comparison of citizen journalism vs. professional journalism portrayals. *Journal of Mental Health, 28*(5), 520–526.

Cassilo, D. (2020). Royce White, DeMar DeRozan and media framing of mental health in the NBA. *Communication & Sport*. doi: 10.1177/2167479520933548

Cassilo, D., & Kluch, Y. (2021). Mental health, college athletics, and the media framing of D.J. Carton's announcement to step away from his team. *Communication & Sport*, doi: 21674795211041019.

Cassilo, D., & Sanderson, J. (2019). "I'm glad I played when the country still had gonads": Bottom-up framing around Pop Warner's kickoff policy change. *Journal of Sports Media*, 1–22.

Cassilo, D., & Sanderson, J. (2018). "I don't think it's worth the risk": Media framing of the Chris Borland retirement in digital and print media. *Communication & Sport, 6*(1), 86–110. doi: 10.1177/2167479516654513

Chappell, B. (2021, July 31). Read what Simone Biles said after her withdrawal from the Olympic final. *NPR*. https://www.npr.org/sections/tokyo-olympics-live-updates/2021/07/28/1021683296/in-her-words-what-simone-biles-said-after-her-withdrawal

Chen, M., & Lawrie, S. (2017). Newspaper depictions of mental and physical health. *BJPsych Bulletin, 41*(6), 308–313. doi: 10.1192/pb.bp.116.054775

Corrigan, P. (2004). How stigma interferes with mental health care. *American Psychologist, 59*(7), 614. doi: 10.1037/0003-066X.59.7.614

Coverdale, J., Nairn, R., & Claasen, D. (2002). Depictions of mental illness in print media: A prospective national sample. *Australian & New Zealand Journal of Psychiatry, 36*(5), 697–700.

Cutcliffe, J. R., & Riahi, S. (2018). A systematic perspective of violence and aggression in mental health care: Toward a more comprehensive understanding and conceptualization. In J. C. Santos & J. R. Cutcliffe (Eds.), *European Psychiatric/Mental Health Nursing in the 21st Century* (pp. 453–477). Cham: Springer. doi: 10.1007/978-3-319-31772-4_33

de Souza, N. L., Esopenko, C., Conway, F. N., Todaro, S. M., & Buckman, J. F. (2019). Patterns of health behaviors affecting mental health in collegiate athletes. *Journal of American College Health*, 1–8. doi: 10.1080/07448481.2019.1682591

Edwards, B., & Froehle, A. (2021). Examining the incidence of reporting mental health diagnosis between college student-athletes and non-athlete students and the impact on academic performance. *Journal of American College Health*, 1–7. doi: 10.1080/07448481.2021.1874387

Elsey, C., Winter, P., Litchfield, S. J., Ogweno, S., & Southwood, J. (2020). Professional sport and initial mental health public disclosure narratives. *Communication & Sport*. doi: 10.1177/2167479520977312

Entman, R. M. (1993). Framing: Toward clarification of a fractured paradigm. *Journal of Communication, 43*(4), 51–58. doi: 10.1111/j.1460-2466.1993.tb01304.x

Fedorocsko, M., & Bishop, R. (2019). Running the bases backward: Journalists mark the death of Jimmy Piersall. *Communication & Sport*, doi: 2167479519867084.

Goel, V. R. (2021, May 31). Naomi Osaka fined $15,000 and threatened with suspension for avoiding media at French Open. *CBS News*. https://www.cbsnews.com/news/naomi-osaka-french-open-fined-media/

Granello, D. H., Pauley, P. S., & Carmichael, A. (1999). Relationship of the media to attitudes toward people with mental illness. *The Journal of Humanistic Counseling, Education and Development, 38*(2), 98–110. doi: 10.1002/j.2164-490X.1999.tb00068.x

Gross, K. D., Rubin, L. M., & Weese, A. P. (2020). College athletes and suicide prevention: A collaborative autoethnography. *Journal of Issues in Intercollegiate Athletics*, Winter 2020 Special Issue, 82–97.

Gulliver, A., Griffiths, K. M., & Christensen, H. (2012). Barriers and facilitators to mental health help-seeking for young athletes: A qualitative study. *BMC Psychiatry, 12*(157), 1–14. doi: 10.1186/1471-244X-12-157

Hayes, M., Ross, I. E., Gasher, M., Gutstein, D., Dunn, J. R., & Hackett, R. A. (2007). Telling stories: News media, health literacy and public policy in Canada. *Social Science & Medicine, 64*(9), 1842–1852. doi: 10.1016/j.socscimed.2007.01.015

Hilliard, R. C., Watson, J. C., & Zizzi, S. J. (2020). Stigma, attitudes, and intentions to seek mental health services in college student-athletes. *Journal of American College Health,* doi: 10.1080/07448481.2020.1806851.

Hoffner, C. A., Fujioka, Y., Cohen, E. L., & Atwell Seate, A. (2017). Perceived media influence, mental illness, and responses to news coverage of a mass shooting. *Psychology of Popular Media Culture, 6*(2), 159. doi: 10.1037/ppm0000093

Kaier, E., Cromer, L. D., Johnson, M. D., Strunk, K., & Davis, J. L. (2015). Perceptions of mental illness stigma: Comparisons of athletes to nonathlete peers. *Journal of College Student Development, 56*(7), 735–739. doi: 10.1353/csd.2015.0079

Kern, A., Heininger, W., Klueh, E., Salazar, S., Hansen, B., Meyer, T., & Eisenberg, D. (2017) Athletes Connected: Results from a pilot project to address knowledge and attitudes about mental health among college student-athletes. *Journal of Clinical Sport Psychology, 11,* 324–336. doi: 10.1123/JCSP.2016–0028

Kroshus, E., Garnett, B., Hawrilenko, M., Baugh, C. M., & Calzo, J. P. (2015). Concussion under-reporting and pressure from coaches, teammates, fans, and parents. *Social Science & Medicine, 134,* 66–75.

Lavelle, K. L. (2020). The face of mental health: Kevin Love and hegemonic masculinity in the NBA. *Communication & Sport*. doi: 10.1177/2167479520922182

Lewis, S. (2021, July 30). Simone Biles opens up about withdrawal from Olympic competitions: "I don't think you realize how dangerous this is." *CBS News*. https://www.cbsnews.com/news/simone-biles-olympics-gymnastics-withdrawal-twisties/

McGinty, E. E., Frattaroli, S., Appelbaum, P. S., Bonnie, R. J., Grilley, A., Horwitz, J., ... & Webster, D. W. (2014). Using research evidence to reframe the policy debate around mental illness and guns: process and recommendations. *American Journal of Public Health, 104*(11), e22–e26. doi: 10.2105/AJPH.2014.302171

McGinty, E. E., Kennedy-Hendricks, A., Choksy, S., & Barry, C. L. (2016). Trends in news media coverage of mental illness in the United States: 1995–2014. *Health Affairs, 35*(6), 1121–1129. doi: 10.1377/hlthaff.2016.0011

Mental illness. (2021). *NIMH.* https://www.nimh.nih.gov/health/statistics/mental-illness

Moreland, J. J., Coxe, K. A., & Yang, J. (2018). Collegiate athletes' mental health services utilization: A systematic review of conceptualizations, operationalizations, facilitators, and barriers. *Journal of Sport and Health Science, 7,* 58–69. doi: 10.1016/j.jshs.2017.04.009

Mutua, S. N., & Oloo Ong'ong'a, D. (2020). Online news media framing of COVID-19 pandemic: Probing the initial phases of the disease outbreak in international media. *European Journal of Interactive Multimedia and Education, 1*(2), e02006.

Ogbodo, J. N., Onwe, E. C., Chukwu, J., Nwasum, C. J., Nwakpu, E. S., Nwankwo, S. U., . . . & Ogbaeja, N. I. (2020). Communicating health crisis: a content analysis of global media framing of COVID-19. *Health Promotion Perspectives, 10*(3), 257.

Osaka, N. [@NaomiOsaka]. (2021a, May 26). Image. [Tweet] Twitter. https://twitter.com/naomiosaka/status/1397665030015959040?s=20

Osaka, N. [@NaomiOsaka]. (2021b, May 31). Image. [Tweet] Twitter. https://twitter.com/naomiosaka/status/1399422304854188037?s=20

Parrott, S., Billings, A. C., Buzzelli, N., & Towery, N. (2021). "We all got through it": Media depictions of mental illness disclosures from star athletes DeMar DeRozan and Kevin Love. *Communication & Sport, 9*(1), 33–54. doi: 10.1177/2167479519852605

Parrott, S., Billings, A. C., Hakim, S. D., & Gentile, P. (2020). From #endthestigma to #realman: Stigma-challenging social media responses to NBA players' mental health disclosures. *Communication Reports, 33*(3), 148–160. doi: 10.1080/08934215.2020.1811365

Philo, G., Secker, J., Platt, S., Henderson, L., McLaughlin, G., & Burnside, J. (1994). The impact of the mass media on public images of mental illness: media content and audience belief. *Health Education Journal, 53*(3), 271–281. doi: 10.1177/001789699405300305

Proctor, S. L., & Boan-Lenzo, C. (2010). Prevalence of depressive symptoms in male intercollegiate student-athletes and nonathletes. *Journal of Clinical Sport Psychology, 4*(3), 204–220. doi: 10.1123/jcsp.4.3.204

Reardon, C. L., Bindra, A., Blauwet, C., Budgett, R., Campriani, N., Currie, A., Gouttebarge, V., McDuff, D., Mountjoy, M., Purcell, R., Putukian, M., Rice, S., & Hainline, B. (2021). Mental health management of elite athletes during COVID-19: A narrative review and recommendations. *British Journal of Sports Medicine, 55,* 608–615. doi: 10.1136/bjsports-2020-102884

Rice, S. M., Purcell, R., De Silva, S., Mawren, D., McGorry, P. D., & Parker, A. G. (2016). The mental health of elite athletes: a narrative systematic review. *Sports Medicine, 46*(9), 1333–1353.

Ryan, H., Gayles, J. G., & Bell, L. (2018). Student-athletes and mental health experiences. *New Directions for Student Services, 163,* 67–79. doi: 10.1002/ss.20271

Salter, M., & Byrne, P. (2000). The stigma of mental illness: how you can use the media to reduce it. *Psychiatric Bulletin, 24*(8), 281–283. doi: 10.1192/pb.24.8.281

Scheufele, D. A., & Tewksbury, D. (2007). Framing, agenda setting, and priming: The evolution of three media effects models. *Journal of Communication, 57*(1), 9–20. doi: 10.1111/j.1460-2466.2006.00326_5.x

Scutti, S. (2018, January 20). Michael Phelps: "I am extremely thankful that I did not take my life." *CNN.* https://www.cnn.com/2018/01/19/health/michael-phelps-depression/index.html

Sheffield, J. K., Fiorenza, E., & Sofronoff, K. (2004). Adolescents' willingness to seek psychological help: Promoting and preventing factors. *Journal of Youth and Adolescence, 33,* 495–507. doi: 10.1023/B:JOYO.0000048064.31128.c6

Slopen, N. B., Watson, A. C., Gracia, G., & Corrigan, P. W. (2007). Age analysis of newspaper coverage of mental illness. *Journal of Health Communication, 12*(1), 3–15. doi: 10.1080/10810730601091292

Stout, P. A., Villegas, J., & Jennings, N. A. (2004). Images of mental illness in the media: identifying gaps in the research. *Schizophrenia Bulletin, 30*(3), 543–561. doi: 10.1093/oxfordjournals.schbul.a007099

Stuart, H. (2006). Media portrayal of mental illness and its treatments. *CNS Drugs, 20*(2), 99–106. doi: 10.2165/00023210-200620020-00002

Tankard, J., Hendrickson, L., Silberman, J., Bliss, K., & Ghanem, S. (1991). *Media frames: Approaches to conceptualization and measurement.* Paper presented to the Association for Education in Journalism and Mass Communication, Boston.

Terkildsen, N., & Schnell, F. (1997). How media frames move public opinion: An analysis of the women's movement. *Political Research Quarterly, 50*(4), 879–900. doi: 10.1177/106591299705000408

Tewksbury, D., Jones, J., Peske, M. W., Raymond, A., & Vig, W. (2000). The interaction of news and advocate frames: Manipulating audience perceptions of a local public policy issue. *Journalism & Mass Communication Quarterly, 77*(4), 804–829. doi: 10.1177/107769900007700406

Wahl, O. F. (2003). News media portrayal of mental illness: Implications for public policy. *American Behavioral Scientist, 46*(12), 1594–1600. doi: 10.1177/0002764203254615

Wahl, O. F., Wood, A., & Richards, R. (2002). Newspaper coverage of mental illness: Is it changing? *Psychiatric Rehabilitation Skills, 6*(1), 9–31. doi: 10.1080/10973430208408417

White, A. J., Parry, K.D., Humphries, C., Phelan, S., Batten, J., & Magrath, R. (2020). Duty of Karius: Media framing of concussion following the 2018 UEFA Champions League Final. *Communication & Sport.* doi: 10.1177/2167479520948048

Whitley, R., & Berry, S. (2013). Trends in newspaper coverage of mental illness in Canada: 2005–2010. *The Canadian Journal of Psychiatry, 58*(2), 107–112. doi: 10.1177/070674371305800208

Wolanin, A., Hong, E., Marks, D., Panchoo, K., & Gross, M. (2016). Prevalence of clinically elevated depressive symptoms in college athletes and differences by gender and sport. *British Journal of Sports Medicine, 50,* 167–171. doi: 10.1136/bjsports-2015-095756

Chapter Two

Media Framing, Sport, and Public Health

Travis R. Bell and Janelle Applequist

Media framing of health-related topics has an interesting and sometimes muddied history that must consider journalistic autonomy, evolving science, and misinformation (Wallington et al., 2010). This complexity has been influenced by diminishing news media outlets, rapid development and availability of scientific data, and the resulting challenge of who shares these details and how with multiple publics informed across fragmented sources. Health is an emerging sub-discipline within sport communication studies because "sport is intricately linked with health" (Coombs & Harker, 2021, p. 142) through athletic competition, medical implications, and consideration of risks and benefits. Further, the impact of social media on each of these intersecting points of source, data, and access to information is important to consider throughout this chapter to conceptualize the re-shaping of what defines "media" and what defines "health" within the context of sport.

This chapter is organized to offer a brief explanation of media framing and largely to consider case studies across historical and contemporary media settings that overlap sport and public health. Before doing so, it is helpful to recognize a critical distinction between health and public health. Health is generally considered at clinical and individual levels of interpretation via the World Health Organization (WHO) constitution definition set forth in 1948 defined as "a state of complete physical, mental, and social well-being and not merely the absence of disease or infirmity" (n.d.). Public health has many moving parts, but Turnock (2015) provides a defined lens whereby public health "is a broad social enterprise, more akin to a movement, that seeks to extend the benefits of current knowledge in ways that will have the maximum impact on the health status of a population" (p. 11). Turnock includes media as a critical social constituent within this network of information. Specifically, this chapter highlights how individual stories of health emerge and develop into sports public health crises that media help shape and mold within the public sphere.

Media Framing of Public Health

Media framing is a conceptual and theoretical understanding of how media influence stories through selection of details, salience of appearance, and omission of people and ideas (Entman, 1993; Reese, 2001). At its core, framing introduces stories, centralizes themes, and develops and enhances storylines that shape a narrative around an issue, with politics, sports, health, and economics as framing mechanisms that remain consistent in the media engine (Carter, 2013; Druckman, 2001). The traction that storylines garner can remain in a near incubation stage with a brief mention (e.g., laws that never pass), can develop through repeated attention (e.g., election coverage), and if considered a grand enough scope can achieve a media lifecycle where storylines may shift but are likely to never disappear (e.g., smoking effects). This does not mean that media construct stories nor can media conjure up people. Instead, media help mold framing effects that impact the social construction of stories and people to influence public opinion about them (Carter, 2013; Gamson, 1989).

The conceptualization of framing within this chapter leans on a social constructionist standpoint that recognizes value and merit in facts and empirical needs to examine them, but that must first consider how facts come to be. Gamson (1989) provides that lens: "Facts have no intrinsic meaning. They take on their meaning by being embedded in a frame or story line that organizes them and gives them coherence, selecting certain ones to emphasize while ignoring others" (p. 157). In a public health context, cancer is deadly and requires early detection to fight it. Cancer of all types are also guided by, as Murray et al. (2021) outline, nine framing schemas that facilitate cancer literacy. For example, breast cancer receives billions of dollars in research funding, extensive media coverage, and a dedicated month of publicly-engaged awareness campaigns compared to all other forms of cancer. Research explains this was a time-intensive and mediated shift in the 1990s from individual storylines toward gender equity and impact on families to a collective public health frame of gender equity, impact on family dynamic, economics, and government oversight (Andsager & Powers, 1999; Kolker, 2004). This process served to amplify, frame, and redefine breast cancer from a private and individual concern to a public health problem (Kolker, 2004).

Consideration of public health and sport together in media studies developed primarily in the 1980s around two central topics: performance-enhancing drugs and HIV/AIDS. Interestingly, both developed through individual storylines that exploded into public health crises. Drugs were framed in media coverage as rampant in sport culture largely around three factors: (1) quick recovery, (2) fairness, and (3) addiction. Specifically, doping scandals in Olympic track and field and cycling (Denham, 2004a; Waddington, 2000), steroid use in baseball (Denham, 2004b; Quick, 2010; Rutecki & Rutecki, 2010), and painkillers in football (King, 2014) exemplify storylines that exploded into mainstream media narratives about public health concerns in sport. Collectively, drug use in sport centered on its illegality within the context of sport more so than the health implications for the individual that illuminate how sporting governing bodies adapted from accommodating cheaters for self-serving financial interests to self-regulating agencies who now made drug use a punitive act through enhanced drug policies (Denham, 2004b; King, 2014). News media were especially culpable in driving storylines of athletic achievement under the guise of rapid success that looked past doping only to help tear down the individual athletes who thrived during that same heralded time when league or organizational oversight was missing (Waddington, 2000).

HIV/AIDS was (and remains) a pandemic that vaulted into U.S. mainstream media in the 1980s that framed the disease as one that primarily infected drug users and gay men (Dearing & Rogers, 1992). News media was considered the primary source of HIV/AIDS information for more than 70 percent of the U.S. population (Brodie et al., 2004). Thus, the framing principles from emerging development to moral panic to crisis management positioned HIV/AIDS as a deviant act in problematized communities that misaligned with heterosexual morals and values (Jonsen et al., 1986; Weeks, 1989). What developed in the 1990s in sport followed a similar pattern with triggering events that applied fear of spreading the disease where competitors could not avoid contact in team sports (Swain, 2005). Interestingly, the framing of three famous athletes constructed the narrative of HIV/AIDS in sport: NBA hall-of-famer Magic Johnson, tennis star Arthur Ashe, and Olympic diver Greg Louganis. Johnson and Ashe each announced they were HIV-positive in 1991, with Johnson from what he emphasized as heterosexually transmitted and Ashe from a blood transfusion. Ashe died in 1993. Louganis, who is gay, announced in 1995 that he was positive and had competed in the 1988 Seoul Olympics while positive, which was amplified since he hit his head on the diving board and some blood ended up in the pool (Nair, 2000). Thus, the mediated narratives of sexuality and cover-up fueled how HIV/AIDS was considered as more deviant for Louganis, unfortunate for Ashe, and qualified for Johnson as a sexual misstep (Bell, Applequist, & Dotson-Pierson, 2019; Cole & Denny, 1994; Wachs & Dworkin, 1997).

Prescription drugs and HIV/AIDS in media serve as two examples of how mass media can drive and shape public understanding by shifting individual storylines into collective framing mechanisms that influence public understanding. Long-term effects of media attention around public health issues can impact individual health behaviors but also serve to normalize the issue as acceptable within sport culture (Bell, Applequist, & Dotson-Pierson, 2019). These historical examples of public health concerns in sport offer necessary context for contemporary examples that often start in individual social media stories that develop into mediated public health crises.

CONTEMPORARY SETTINGS

Three current examples serve to showcase the ways in which media framing, sport, and public health intersect: (1) concussions in sport and the prominence of chronic traumatic encephalopathy (CTE) in the National Football League (NFL), (2) athletes' use of social media platforms to create public awareness and destigmatize mental health, and (3) the role that COVID-19 played in halting global sports. Each primary example merits consideration within the globalization of sport and health in media discourse. Additionally, these brief case studies illustrate a shifting and challenging dynamic within media framing of health regarding who influences the message.

Concussions, CTE, and Sport

Sports-related concussions (SRC) can be positioned as arguably the largest public health concern ever related to sport because SRCs impact athletes in youth, club, collegiate, and professional sport as well as recreational activities (Bryan et al., 2016; Giza et al., 2017; Martin et al., 2017). Interestingly, SRC in media translated from benign (e.g., athlete went to the sideline for a play) to catastrophic (e.g., athlete died from second impact syndrome) and every point on the spectrum of journalistic inquiry (McLendon et al., 2016; Mirer & Mederson, 2017). As Kuhn et al. (2017) noted, "media play a crucial intermediary role in providing information to the public" (p. 1732). Thus, the impact of media reporting on concussions in contact sport has influenced how parents, athletes, and coaches disclose concussion-related symptoms (Tallapragada & Cranmer, 2020) while simultaneously recognizing the long-term implications this information could have on future earning potential in the lucrative world of sport. All this was before concussions were mediated alongside degenerative brain diseases that threatened the long-term stability of sport and the masculine and gendered identity embedded within media framing of concussions (Bell, Applequist, & Dotson-Pierson, 2019; Cranmer & Sanderson, 2018).

In 2002, Dr. Bennet Omalu conducted an autopsy on former Pittsburgh Steelers player Mike Webster, finding the first recorded case of CTE in an NFL player (Omalu et al., 2005). CTE, a degenerative brain disease that causes paranoia, memory loss, aggression, depression, anxiety, suicidal ideations, and dementia, is linked to instances of repeated brain trauma (Concussion Legacy Foundation, 2021). While not scientifically correlated with concussions, Omalu et al.'s (2005) seminal findings linked the long-term outcome of CTE with being an NFL player. Media reporting conflated concussions and CTE into the same context that elevated the NFL into a media blitz centered on brain injuries (Bell, Applequist, & Dotson-Pierson, 2019). Rather than publicly acknowledge Omalu's findings and champion a solution to the problem, the NFL staged an extensive cover-up, claimed there was no known risk to players, raised concerns about Omalu's research, and refused to share data on player concussions until 2012 (Fainaru-Wada & Fainaru, 2013).

A *New York Times* story in 2007 following the suicide of former Philadelphia Eagles safety Andre Waters one year earlier stoked a media firestorm that publicly connected Omalu's work surrounding CTE with the NFL and shifted the narrative from individual player deaths by suicide to a larger, sociocultural risk of long-term brain injuries in contact sport, primarily centered on football (Bell, Applequist, & Dotson-Pierson, 2019; Karimipour, 2016; Schwarz, 2007). Many of the NFL's tactics to avoid responsibility for player health have been compared to Big Tobacco's creation of faulty science that cigarettes were not harmful for consumers (Bell, Applequist, & Dotson-Pierson, 2019; Brandt, 2007, 2012). It was not until 2016 that the NFL acknowledged a link between football and CTE (Fainaru, 2016). The CTE crisis that faced the NFL exemplified arguably the most complex intersection of media framing, sport, and public health.

Interestingly, the year 2017 settled CTE and concussions in mediated contradiction and subjectivity. First, former New England Patriots tight end Aaron Hernandez hanged himself in April while in prison serving a life sentence for murder. His 27-year-old brain revealed the worst level of CTE in anyone near his age and offered a journalistic rationale for his actions (Gregory, 2020). The following month, former Patriots teammate and future hall of fame quarterback Tom Brady's concussion history was revealed by his supermodel wife Gisele Bündchen during an interview on "CBS This Morning." She said, "We don't talk about it, but he does have concussions" (Willis, 2017). The media circus that ensued revealed that Bündchen's claims were seriously questioned and taken as a threat to football (Siegel, 2019). The media focused on former players' comments insinuating that rule changes surrounding concussions and CTE were "ruining the game," that it was ultimately Brady's responsibility to reveal his concussions, and that Bündchen's status as a wife and mother did not qualify her to comment on a medical issue pertaining to her husband's profession (Siegel, 2019). Thus, the media narrative surrounding concussions and CTE exposed the effects of football but also illustrated how the public health concern of brain injuries ultimately tired over time and did not matter in life or death because football continues to generate billions of dollars annually by protecting its entity—not its players.

The media narrative surrounding the larger issue of CTE was important, but it was an issue that developed in real time. This parallel example to HIV/AIDS outlined how science evolved as information was being shared with the public (Bell, Applequist, & Dotson-Pierson, 2019; Wachs & Dworkin, 1997; Weeks, 1989). While the media was attempting to understand the science, reporting fixated on sensationalized human-interest stories before shifting to quantified public health statistics. Research of media frames across 12 years of CTE coverage found that media often "missed the mark," underrepresenting CTE as a "football only" issue, presenting it through a hypermasculine lens, and often miseducating the public by linking the diagnosis with concussions rather than the issue of repetitive blows to the head (Bell, Applequist, & Dotson-Pierson, 2019). Sensationalized reporting of suicides connected to posthumous CTE diagnoses further perpetuated the hypermasculine image of football. Instead, media's responsibility in framing the issue should have been to inform the public on the health issue in an effort to educate audiences beyond the sport fan base. For example, parents need to be aware of concussions and CTE in youth sports to ensure that children are adequately protected but that conversation has been largely missed by media. Females in sport have also been absent from the conversation.

ATHLETES' USE OF SOCIAL MEDIA TO HIGHLIGHT MENTAL HEALTH

Mental health provides a second contemporary public health issue in sport perpetuated through media discourse. Media historically has framed mental health negatively and in relation to violent outcomes, which has misinformed the public about the array of mental health conditions (McGinty et al., 2016; Myrick et al., 2014). Interestingly, this concern festered at individual health levels in sport, but by breaking past traditional gatekeeping functions of mass media, athletes have started to shape a narrative *before* traditional media influence the long-term existence of mental health. The three following examples illustrate how athletes have utilized the media, and social media platforms in particular, to spur mainstream mediated narratives.

Kevin Love

In 2018, Cleveland Cavaliers forward Kevin Love revealed he suffered a panic attack during a 2017 game. He did not publicly share this sooner for fear of being seen as "weak" or "less reliable as a teammate" (Love, 2018). What inspired him to speak out, however, was a public announcement via Twitter from the Toronto Raptors' DeMar DeRozan that "the depression got the best of me" and a subsequent interview with *The Toronto Star*. Love's online story for *The Players' Tribune* presents a moment where the athlete became the storyteller by giving inside access into their experience but also providing the story that avoids a sometimes "distortive circuit that journalists fashion" (Schwartz & Vogan, 2017, p. 47) when reporting on sport. Love shared in his first-person account that for 29 years he viewed mental health as a sign of weakness or "someone else's problem" but an in-game panic attack shifted his entire view. Through sharing his experience after DeRozan, Love reiterates that "because just by sharing what he shared, DeMar probably helped some people—and maybe a lot more people than we know—feel like they aren't crazy or weird to be struggling with depression. His comments helped take some power away from that stigma, and I think that's where the hope is" (Love, 2018).

Compassionate media reporting followed that helped to further destigmatize mental health in professional sport and offered a call to action (Parrott et al., 2021). Love, DeRozan, and fellow NBA player Royce White, who had a shorter reach as a first-year player, laid a foundation for talking about an invisible illness deemed difficult to culturally unpack in a masculine sports league such as the NBA (Cassilo, 2022). Fan responses on social media offered encouragement while traditional media communicated to audiences that people with similar experiences are "not alone," allowing media spaces to act as a vehicle for shaping fan attitudes toward future mental health treatment (Parrott et al., 2021). However, Lavelle (2021) noted that Love's revelation was praised by media largely for his social location as a white player yet constrained for what would be expected in a masculine sport.

Naomi Osaka

In May 2021, four-time tennis Grand Slam champion Naomi Osaka released a statement on Instagram explaining her decision to withdraw from the French Open after winning her first round match but not participating in a post-round media availability. Osaka described how she struggled with depression and anxiety surrounding having to participate in post-match news conferences that impacted her mental health (Bagwaiya, 2021). In her post, she addressed the media directly:

> Though the tennis press has always been kind to me (and I wanna apologize especially to all the cool journalists who I may have hurt), I am not a natural public speaker and get huge waves of anxiety before I speak to the world's media. I get really nervous and find it stressful to always try to engage and give you the best answers I can. (Osaka, 2021a)

While the French Tennis Federation president Gilles Moretton deemed Osaka's decision as "unfortunate" during a four-sentence prepared statement, media framed Osaka's decision as an act of bravery, which helped to further legitimize mental health as *health*, and framed her decision as an affront to media access (Yeo, 2021). Osaka clarified in a *Time* cover story that she appreciated the members of the media but struggled with the constructed and controlled press conference (Osaka, 2021b).

Media extended the storyline to include other prominent athletes in the tennis community (Billy Jean King, Serena and Venus Williams), the NBA (Kyrie Irving and Steph Curry), and Olympic sprinter Usain Bolt who publicly supported Osaka (via social media), which validated her argument that the mental health of athletes is an issue that deserves attention (Pretot, 2021). Additionally, medical health educators noted how a shift should follow to remove a perceived taboo of mental health in elite athletes and suggested a call for more holistic forms of athlete training beyond the physical techniques to succeed athletically (Walker et al., 2021).

Simone Biles

On July 26, 2021, U.S. gymnastics and Olympic superstar Simone Biles wrote on Instagram, "I truly do feel like I have the weight of the world on my shoulders at times," adding that "the Olympics is no joke" (Biles, 2021). The next day, she withdrew from the Tokyo Olympic games to focus on her mental well-being, one day after she removed herself from the team final.

Media shared a statement from USA Gymnastics, which fully supported Biles' decision, highlighting her bravery in prioritizing her mental health (Maine, 2021). Media framing included fellow athlete, celebrity, and fan support for Biles shared on social media ("Still our GOAT," 2021). While the encouragement was prominent, criticism of her decision to not "tough it out" existed. Texas Deputy Attorney General Aaron Reitz called Biles a "national embarrassment" on Twitter and retweeted a video from the 1996 Olympics where American gymnast Kerri Strug continued competing even while injured (Mayer, 2021). British TV personality Piers Morgan asked on Twitter if "'mental health issues' are now the go-to excuse for poor performance in elite sport," calling Biles' move a "joke" (Morgan, 2021). Gerald

(2021) provided a different perspective, whereby Biles' "refusal" to compete was a radical form of athlete resistance and self-protection.

By sharing their own experiences in a first-person manner, Biles, Love, and Osaka started conversations about mental health in sport and circumvented journalistic gatekeeping. They serve to educate the public (hopefully with accuracy) on recognizing risk factors, seeking help, and destigmatizing these unseen elements of health. They also exemplify how social media can be a vehicle for athletes' self-presentation to actively engage in creating public health discourse surrounding their profession (Goffman, 1959; Smith & Sanderson, 2015). However, the mediated conversation surrounding mental health, athletes, and sport is in its infancy. Thus, merely mentioning mental health can help normalize the subject for audiences but may be promoting an incomplete version of "mental health" as experienced individually while failing to accurately define it (Lavelle, 2021). Additionally, with Osaka and Biles, both women of color, Gerald (2021) noted backlash based on race and the important aspect that athletes are layered human beings, meaning that issues of race, gender, and privilege must be considered.

COVID-19

The COVID-19 pandemic forced the cancellation, postponement, and shortening of major sporting events (e.g., Tokyo Olympics, Euro 2020, Wimbledon) around the world. Media reported on the economic losses associated with the halt in sport. For example, U.S. sporting leagues lost $13 billion and 1.5 million jobs in 2020 (Drape et al., 2020). Parry et al. (2021) supported that media focused on the financial precariousness of women's sports leagues (British football in particular) and suggested a media shift toward increased coverage and visibility for women's sports. However, certain instances of increased coverage for women's sports, such as the National Women's Soccer League (NWSL), were a result of circumstance, whereby the league was the first U.S. pro sports league to return to play during the pandemic. Herein lies the public health concern of media missing a significant COVID-19 story whereby sports leagues weighed exchanging sponsorship and broadcast deals against the potential health risk of the athletes (Bell et al., 2022).

Initial media framing on ESPN's *SportsCenter* revealed that health context was minimized while the loss frames for economics and fandom shaped the narrative (Bell, 2021). In the case of the NBA, over time media framing of the league's suspension of play in 2020 started with economic and fairness frames before considering health, safety, and quality of life as the pandemic became more widespread (Sadri et al., 2021). Additional research on media coverage of the NBA in the first six months of 2020 found that the league made decisions based on health and safety, but also prioritized economic incentives and competitive advantages (Hindman et al., 2020).

Research on media framing during COVID-19 developed quickly through fragmented coverage but highlighted how sport and public health are inextricably linked (Skinner & Smith, 2021). While not the first pandemic or major global health concern to halt international and local sporting events (e.g., 1918 Spanish flu, SARS in 2003), COVID-19 serves as exemplary rationale that investigating journalistic and social media framing of a worldwide health event through real-time sharing of health information can shape individual behaviors (e.g., players opt out, mandatory testing) within a public health crisis.

DIRECTIONS FOR FUTURE RESEARCH

This chapter provided a broad overview of the historical and contemporary intersection of media framing, public health, and sport. In doing so, a goal was to showcase the expanding definitions of "media" and how public health develops from individual health narratives. Specifically, we recommend that scholars address mental health in future media framing studies to consider its complexity but also its inclusivity across sport(s). Further, Cassilo and Kluch (2021) suggest social media as a critical space to consider health disclosures and fan engagement as witnessed with Love, Osaka, and Biles. Additionally, the revelations from Osaka and Biles during COVID-19 illustrate the complexity needed to analyze public health through a media framing lens in the context of sport. Race and gender, especially, are critical narrative tropes to unpack in relation to stigmatization and normalization of mental health and public perception of why and how athletes publicly reveal these personal disclosures.

The COVID-19 pandemic is of particular interest for future research guided by media framing. Specifically, analysis of individual health decisions and sporting league mandates can facilitate holistic understanding of how COVID-19 developed as a public health crisis within sport. Such examples could include media framing of Washington State firing head football coach Nick Rolovich for refusing to get a COVID-19 vaccine, professional golfer Bryson DeChambeau's misinformed public declaration of not getting vaccinated because he would "take away that ability" from others (Harig, 2021), the mandatory vaccine requirement from the NBA and New York State through the lens of Kyrie Irving, or the gendered impact on injury risk. Seeing how these storylines were framed over time can help assess the impact of media framing on public perception of risk.

Future media framing research should consider shifting technologies that can be defined as "media" and their influence on framing of health in sport. Augmented and virtual reality is being implemented to help properly train athletes, thereby minimizing instances of risk or injury for athletes (Joshi, 2019). Wearable technology (e.g., smart clothing sensors, smart glasses) can provide real-time training data and biometrics to optimize performance and are being implemented into live broadcasts to illustrate player movement and athleticism (Mons, 2020). Additionally, research on commercialization and specialization in youth sport as a public health concern of safety and risk can be considered. This could develop through the physical and financial costs of sport-related injuries in youth sport and the threat of burnout embedded in sport culture (Bell, Distefano, et al., 2019) along with the rise of mediated spaces that rapidly elevate young athletes into celebrity culture. These topics along with the historical foundation and contemporary examples outlined in this chapter illustrate why the intersection of media framing, public health, and sport is critical to consider in an ever-expanding "media" space that allows storylines to develop rapidly in the public sphere.

REFERENCES

Andsager, J. L., & Powers, A. (1999). Social or economic concerns: How news and women's magazines framed breast cancer in the 1990s. *Journalism & Mass Communications Quarterly*, 76(3), 531–550.

Bagwaiya, C. (2021, June 1). Why did Tennis star Naomi Osaka quit French Open? *The Bridge Chronicle*. https://www.thebridgechronicle.com/sports/why-did-tennis-star-naomi-osaka-quit-french-open.

Bell, D. R., DiStefano, L., Pandya, N. K., & McGuine, T. A. (2019). The public health consequences of sport specialization. *Journal of Athletic Training*, 54(10), 1013–1020.

Bell, T. R. (2021). SportsCenter: A case study of media framing U.S. sport as the COVID-19 epicenter. *International Journal of Sport Communication*, 14(2), 298–317. https://doi.org/10.1123/ijsc.2020-0258.

Bell, T. R., Applequist, J., & Dotson-Pierson, C. (2019). *CTE, media, and the NFL: Framing a public health crisis as a football epidemic.* Lexington Books: Lanham, MD.

Bell, T. R., Dotson-Pierson, C., & Applequist, J. (2022). "Big risks, big rewards": Framing the NWSL Challenge Cup amid a pandemic. In A. C. Billings, L. A. Wenner, & M. Hardin (Eds.), *American sport in the shadow of a pandemic: Communicative insights* (pp. 95–109). New York: Peter Lang.

Biles, S. [@simonebiles]. (2021, July 26). "it wasn't an easy day or my best but I got through it. I truly do feel like I have the weight of the world on my shoulders at times" [Photograph]. https://www.instagram.com/p/CRxsq_kBZrP/.

Brandt, A. M. (2007). *The cigarette century: The rise, fall, and deadly persistence of the product that defined America.* New York: Basic Books.

Brandt, A. M. (2012). Inventing conflicts of interest: A history of tobacco industry tactics. *American Journal of Public Health, 102*(1), 63–71.

Brodie, M., Hamel, E., Brady, L. A., Kates, J., & Altman, D. E. (2004). AIDS at 21: Media coverage of the HIV epidemic 1981–2002. *Columbia Journalism Review*, supplement to March/April, 1–8.

Bryan, M. A., Rowhani-Rahbar, A., Comstock, R. D., & Rivara, F. (2016). Sports- and recreation-related concussions in US youth. *Pediatrics, 138*(1), 1–10.

Carter, M. (2013). The hermeneutics of frames and framing: An examination of the media's construction of reality. *Sage Open.* doi: 10.1177/2158244013487915

Cassilo, D. (2022). Royce White, DeMar DeRozan and media framing of mental health in the NBA. *Communication & Sport, 10*(1), 97–123. https://doi.org/10.1177/2167479520933548.

Cassilo, D., & Kluch, Y. (2021). Mental health, college athletics, and the media framing of D. J. Carton's announcement to step away from his team. *Communication & Sport*. Advance online publication. https://doi.org/10.1177/21674795211041019.

Cole, C. L., & Denny, H. (1994). Visualizing deviance in post-Reagan America: Magic Johnson, AIDS, and the promiscuous world of professional sport. *Critical Sociology, 20*(3), 123–147.

Coombs, W. T., & Harker, J. L. (2021). *Strategic sport communication: Traditional and transmedia strategies for a global sports market.* New York: Routledge.

Concussion Legacy Foundation (2021). What is CTE? https://concussionfoundation.org/CTE-resources/what-is-CTE.

Cranmer, G. A., & Sanderson, J. (2018). "Rough week for testosterone": Public commentary around the Ivy League's decision to restrict tackle football in practice. *Western Journal of Communication, 82*, 631–647.

Dearing, J. W., & Rogers, E. M. (1992). AIDS and the media agenda: In T. Edgar, M. A. Fitzpatrick, & V. S. Freimuth (Eds.), *AIDS: A communication perspective* (pp. 173–194). Hillsdale, NJ: Lawrence Erlbaum Associates.

Denham, B. E. (2004a). Hero or hypocrite? United States and international media portrayals of Carl Lewis amid revelations of a positive drug test. *International Review for the Sociology of Sport, 39*, 167–185.

Denham, B. E. (2004b). *Sports Illustrated*, the mainstream press and the enactment of drug policy in Major League Baseball: A study in agenda-building theory. *Journalism, 5*, 51–68.

Drape, J., Chen, D. W., & Hsu, T. (2020, December 13). 2020: The year in sports when everybody lost. *The New York Times.* https://www.nytimes.com/interactive/2020/12/13/sports/coronavirus-sports-economy-wisconsin.html.

Druckman, J. N. (2001). The implications of framing effects for citizen competence. *Political Behavior, 23*(3), 225–256.

Entman, R. M. (1993). Framing: Toward clarification of a fractured paradigm. *Journal of Communication, 43*(4), 51–58.

Fainaru, S. (2016, March 14). NFL acknowledges, for first time, link between football, brain disease. *ESPN*. https://www.espn.com/espn/otl/story/_/id/14972296/top-nfl-official-acknowledges-link-football-related-head-trauma-cte-first.

Fainaru-Wada, M., & Fainaru, S. (2013). *League of denial: The NFL, concussions, and the battle for truth*. New York: Three Rivers Press.

Gamson, W. A. (1989). News as framing: Comments on Graber. *American Behavioral Scientist, 33*(2), 157–161.

Gerald, C. (2021, July 28). Simone Biles and the rise of the "great refusal." *The Guardian*. https://www.theguardian.com/commentisfree/2021/jul/28/simone-biles-naomi-osaka-great-refusal-no.

Giza, C. C., Prins, M. L., & Hovda, D. A. (2017). It's not all fun and games: Sports, concussions, and neuroscience. *Neuron, 94*, 1051–1055.

Goffman, E. H. 1959. *The presentation of self in everyday life*. New York: Doubleday.

Gregory, H. (2020). Making a murderer: media renderings of brain injury and Aaron Hernandez as a medical and sporting subject. *Social Science & Medicine, 244*. https://doi.org/10.1016/j.socscimed.2019.112598.

Harig, B. (2021, August 4). Bryson DeChambeau returns after being COVID-positive, doesn't regret not getting vaccinated. *ESPN.com*. Retrieved from https://www.espn.com/golf/story/_/id/31958173/bryson-dechambeau-returns-being-covid-positive-regret-not-getting-vaccinated.

Hindman, L. C., Walker, N. A., & Agyemang, J. A. K. (2020). Bounded rationality or bounded morality? The National Basketball Association response to COVID-19. *European Sport Management, 21*(3), 333–349. https://doi.org/10.1080/16184742.2021.1879191.

Jonsen, A. R., Cooke, M., & Koenig, B. A. (1986). AIDS and ethics. *Issues in Science and Technology, 2*, 56–65.

Joshi, N. (2019, October 26). Revolutionizing sports with augmented reality. *Forbes*. https://www.forbes.com/sites/cognitiveworld/2019/10/26/revolutionizing-sports-with-augmented-reality/?sh=6db8725c1416.

Karimipour, N. (2016). Suicide on the sidelines: Media portrayals of NFL players' suicides from June 2000 to September 2012. *Journal of Sports Media, 11*(1), 49–80.

King, S. (2014). Beyond the war on drugs? Notes on prescription opioids in the NFL. *Journal of Sport and Social Issues, 38*(2), 184–193.

Kolker, E. S. (2004). Framing as a cultural resource in health social movements: Funding activism and the breast cancer movement in the US 1990–1993. *Sociology of Health & Illness, 26*(6), 820–844.

Kuhn, A. W., Yengo-Kahn, A. M., Kerr, Z. Y., & Zuckerman, S. L. (2017). Sports concussion research, chronic traumatic encephalopathy and the media: Repairing the disconnect. *British Journal of Sports Medicine, 51*(24), 1732–1733.

Lavelle, K. L. (2021). The face of mental health: Kevin Love and hegemonic masculinity in the NBA. *Communication & Sport, 9*(6), 954–971. https://doi.org/10.1177/2167479520922182.

Love, K. (2018, March 6). Everyone is going through something. *The Players' Tribune*. https://www.theplayerstribune.com/articles/kevin-love-everyone-is-going-through-something.

Maine, D. (2021, July 28). Simone Biles withdraws from individual all-around gymnastics competition at Tokyo Olympics to focus on mental well-being. *ESPN*. https://www.espn.com/olympics/gymnastics/story/_/id/31902290/simone-biles-withdraws-individual-all-competition-tokyo-olympics-focus-mental-health

Martin, T. G., Whisenant, W., Agyemang, K. J. A., & Dees, W. (2017). Media exposure of sport concussions. *Journal of Multidisciplinary Research*, *9*(2), 45–56.

Mayer, E. (2021, July 28). Simone Biles is a "National Embarrassment" Texas Deputy AG Tweets, Causing Outrage. *Newsweek*. https://www.newsweek.com/simone-biles-national-embarrassment-texas-deputy-ag-tweets-causing-outrage-1614027.

McGinty, E. E., Kennedy-Hendricks, A., Choksy, S., & Barry, C. L. (2016). Trends in news media coverage of mental health illness in the United States: 1995–2014. *Health Affairs*, *35*(6), 1121–1129.

McLendon, L. A., Kralik, S. F., Grayson, P. A., & Golomb, M. R. (2016). The controversial second impact syndrome: A review of the literature. *Pediatric Neurology*, *62*, 9–17.

Mirer, M., & Mederson, M. (2017). Leading with the head: How NBC's *Football Night in America* framed football's concussion crisis, a case study. *Journal of Sports Media*, *12*(1), 21–44.

Mons, J. K. (2020, January 28). 10 great ways how AR will impact the world of sports. *Sport Tomorrow*. https://sporttomorrow.com/10-great-ways-ar-will-impact-the-world-of-sports/.

Morgan, P. [@piersmorgan]. (2021, July 27). "Are 'mental health issues' now the go-to excuse for any poor performance in elite sport? What a joke. Just admit you did badly." [Tweet]. https://twitter.com/piersmorgan/status/1420027274565390355.

Murray, C., von Possel, N., Lie, H. C., & Breivik, J. (2021). The nine cancer frames: A tool to facilitate critical reading of cancer-related information. *Journal of Cancer Education*. Advance online publication. https://doi.org/10.1007/s13187-021-02062-7.

Myrick, J. G., Major, L. H., & Jankowski, S. M. (2014). The sources and frames used to tell stories about depression and anxiety: A content analysis of 18 years of national television news coverage. *Electronic News*, *8*(1), 49–63.

Nair, Y. (2000). Dead images, live transmissions: Greg Louganis and the construction of AIDS on television. *Discourse*, *22*(1), 53–69.

Omalu, B. I., DeKosky, S. T., Minster, R. L., Kamboh, M. I., Hamilton, R. L., & Wecht, C. H. (2005). Chronic traumatic encephalopathy in a National Football League player. *Neurosurgery*, *57*(1), 128–134. https://doi.org/10.1227/01.NEU.0000163407.92769.ED.

Osaka, N. [@naomiosaka]. (2021a, May 31). "Hey everyone, this isn't a situation I ever imagined or intended when I posted a few days ago" [Photograph]. https://www.instagram.com/p/CPi9kJHJfxO/.

Osaka, N. (2021b, July 8). It's O.K. not to be O.K. *Time*. https://time.com/6077128/naomi-osaka-essay-tokyo-olympics/.

Parrott, S., Billings, A. C., Buzzelli, N., & Towery, N. (2021). "We all go through it": Media depictions of mental illness disclosures from star athletes DeMar DeRozan and Kevin Love. *Communication & Sport, 9*(1), 33–54. https://doi.org/10.1177/2167479519852605.

Parry, K. D., Clarkson, B., Bowes, A., Grubb, L., & Rowe, D. (2021). Media framing of women's football during the COVID-19 pandemic. *Communication and Sport.* Advance online publication. https://doi.org/10.1177%2F21674795211041024.

Pretot, J. (2021, June 2). Japan, sponsors join athletes to support Osaka after French Open withdrawal. *Reuters.* https://www.reuters.com/lifestyle/sports/fellow-athletes-rally-around-osaka-after-french-open-withdrawal-2021-06-01/.

Quick, B. L. (2010). Applying the health belief model to examine news coverage regarding steroids in sports by ABC, CBS, and NBC between March 1990 and May 2008. *Health Communication, 25*(3), 247–257.

Reese, S. D. (2001). Prologue—Framing a public life: A bridging model for media research. In S. D. Reese, O. H. Gandy, Jr., & A. E. Grant (Eds.), *Framing public life: Perspectives on media and our understanding of the social world* (pp. 7–31). New York: Routledge.

Rutecki, J. W., & Rutecki, G. W. (2010). A study of media impact on public opinion regarding performance enhancement in Major League Baseball. *The Open Sports Science Journal, 3*, 140–148.

Sadri, S. R., Buzzelli, N. R., Gentile, P., & Billings, A. C. (2021). Sports journalism content when no sports occur: Framing athletics amidst the COVID-19 international pandemic. *Communication & Sport.* Advance online publication. https://doi.org/10.1177/21674795211001937.

Schwartz, D., & Vogan, T. (2017). *The Players' Tribune*: Self-branding and boundary work in digital sports media. *Journal of Sports Media, 12*(1), 45–63.

Schwarz, A. (2007, January 18). Expert ties ex-player's suicide to brain damage. *The New York Times.* https://www.nytimes.com/2007/01/18/sports/football/18waters.html.

Siegel, B. (2019). Concussions and Capital: Tom Brady, CTE, and the NFL's Crisis of Identity. *Journal of Sport and Social Issues, 43*(6), 551–574. https://doi.org/10.1177/0193723519868192.

Skinner, J., & Smith, A. C. T. (2021). Introduction: Sport and COVID-19: Impacts and challenges for the future (volume 1). *European Sport Management, 21*(3), 323–332. https://doi.org/10.1080/16184742.2021.1925725.

Smith, L. R., & Sanderson, J. (2015). I'm going to Instagram! An analysis of athlete self-presentation on Instagram. *Journal of Broadcasting & Electronic Media, 59*(2), 342–358.

"Still our GOAT": Social media reacts to Simone Biles pulling out of team competition. (2021, July 27). *Los Angeles Times.* https://www.latimes.com/sports/story/2021-07-27/simone-biles-pulls-out-of-team-competition-social-media-reacts.

Swain, K. A. (2005). Approaching the quarter-century mark: AIDS coverage and research decline as infection spreads. *Critical Studies in Media Communication, 22*(3), 258–262.

Tallapragada, M., & Cranmer, G. A. (2020). Media narratives about concussions: Effects on parents' intention to inform their children about concussions.

Communication & Sport. Advance online publication. https://doi.org/10.117 /2167479520944549.

Turnock, B. J. (2015). *Public health: What it is and how it works* (6th ed.). Burlington, MA: Jones & Bartlett Learning.

Wachs, F. L., & Dworkin, S. L. (1997). "There's no such thing as a gay hero": Sexual identity and media framing of HIV-positive athletes. *Journal of Sport & Social Issues, 21*(4), 327–347. https://doi.org/10.1177/019372397021004002.

Waddington, I. (2000). *Sport, health and drugs: A critical sociological perspective*. London: E & FN Spon.

Walker, I., Brierley, E., Patel, T., Jaffer, R., Rajpara, M., Heslop, C., & Patel, R. (2021). Mental health among elite sportspeople: Lessons for medical education. *Medical Teacher*. Advance online publication. https://www.tandfonline.com/doi/ abs/10.1080/0142159X.2021.1994134.

Wallington, S. F., Blake, K., Taylor-Clark, K., & Vinswanth, K. (2010). Antecedents to agenda setting and framing in health news: An examination of priority, angle, source, and resource usage from a national survey of U.S. health reporters and editors. *Journal of Health Communication, 15*(1), 76–94.

Weeks, J. (1989). *AIDS: Social representation, social practices*. New York; London: Falmer Press.

Willis, J. (2017, May 17). Gisele just casually revealed that Tom Brady sustains concussions all the time. *GQ*. https://www.gq.com/story/tom-brady-concussions -gisele.

World Health Organization. (n.d.). *Constitution*. Retrieved from https://www.who.int /about/governance/constitution.

Yeo, A. (2021, June 1). French Open slammed for "hypocritical" response to Naomi Osaka's mental health concerns. Retrieved from https://mashable.com/article/ naomi-osaka-french-open-withdrawal-mental-health.

Chapter Three

Developing a Rhetoric of Mental Health from a Communication and Sport Perspective

Katherine L. Lavelle

When 2012 National Basketball Association (NBA) projected lottery pick Royce White's career functionally ended in 2013 because of an "impasse" with his team (the Houston Rockets) about the best way to accommodate his generalized anxiety and obsessive-compulsive disorders, sports law professor Michael McCann (2014) characterized this situation as an "employment dispute ... [with] ... no culprit and there was no one to blame" (p. 438). Despite White's openness about his experiences, which he chronicled on social media, he was unsuccessful playing in the NBA while managing his conditions (Cassilo, 2020). Since White's public disclosures in 2012–13, numerous elite athletes have revealed their mental health stressors and/or mental illness diagnoses. Retired Olympic gold medal swimmer Michael Phelps has discussed his experiences with depression and suicidal ideation in media appearances; he produced and starred in a documentary chronicling mental health stressors faced by elite athletes (Futterman, 2020). In the National Football League (NFL), Brandon Marshall disclosed throughout his career what it was like to be an active player living with borderline personality disorder (Gleeson & Brady, 2017). And in 2018, Kevin Love, DeMar DeRozan, and numerous active and retired NBA players, coaches, and referees described their various experiences with mental illness and/or mental health stressors (MacMullan, 2018). Even high-profile amateur and collegiate athletes have used their personal social media accounts to share the mental health stressors that they have faced in their lives (Cassilo & Kluch, 2021).

Eight years after Royce White's impasse with the NBA, in the summer of 2021, two of the most well-known female athletes in the world, gymnast Simone Biles and tennis player Naomi Osaka, stepped away from competition to address their mental health. Osaka (winner of four Grand Slam tournaments) pulled out of the French Open and Wimbledon tennis tournaments because of her anxiety, particularly around the mandatory post-match press conferences (North, 2021). Biles, winner of five Olympic gold medals in 2016, withdrew from several Tokyo Olympics gymnastics events after an error on the vault (Graves, 2021). Unlike White, who McCann (2014) recommended find "new treatments for his anxiety disorder and fear of flying so that they no longer impair his NBA career" (p. 438), Biles and Osaka were applauded for promoting open public dialogue about the effect of mental health stressors for elite athletes (North, 2021).

Increasingly, these mental health[1] and mental illness[2] revelations have occurred in mediated texts, such as interviews and social media posts. These disclosures have been an important new area to study to expand the study of athlete health. There is already a well-developed area of athlete physical health in communication and sport research, particularly on issues like concussions (Anderson & Kian, 2012; Cassilo & Sanderson, 2019) and managing potentially career-ending injuries (Sanderson et al., 2016). Studies conducted in our field have examined the various strategies used by elite athletes when publicly discussing their mental health (Elsey et al., 2020), how these revelations operate as individual acts of persuasion and advocacy shaped by hegemonic masculinity[3] (Lavelle, 2021), as well as examining traditionally understudied populations like college athletes (Cassilo & Kluch, 2021). Part of the reason that this area of research is relatively new is because male-identifying athletes in contact sports are expected to dominate opponents and suppress their emotions that might make them appear vulnerable (Foote et al., 2017). Mental health disclosures are often perceived as a "weakness" (Parrott et al., 2021). Mental health and/or illness is not just about the conditions or stressors themselves, but also the public dialogue surrounding these conditions.

Outside of the communication and sport discipline, interdisciplinary studies of the rhetoric of health and medicine have found that mental health research focuses on three major areas including: "stigma, institutional practices, and personal advocacy" (Molloy et al., 2020, p. vii). Stigmatization functions as "a rhetorical process" (Johnson, 2010, p. 462), an explicit link between persuasion, language, and larger contextual issues within society. Existing communication and sport scholarship should be extended by taking a more explicitly rhetorical approach. Using more direct rhetorical principles allows us as a discipline to better understand mental health and/or illness discourse as not just about the conditions and experiences of an individual athlete, but also how they function as persuasive acts within the context where they exist. In this chapter, I propose conceptualizing a rhetoric of mental health by using two connected rhetorical theories: Burke's notion of identification as persuasion (German, 2009) and the rhetorical ecology approach (Jenson, 2015).

This conceptualization is beneficial to analyzing the rhetoric of mental health in several ways. First, it provides a richer understanding of how disclosure, specifically the act of coming forward to share experiences or diagnosis, and discourse, how it operates as a condition for elite athletes, functions as persuasive arguments. Research examining media coverage of athlete physical health has emphasized how language is critical for creating meaning in health discourse, particularly since how mental health and/or illness is interpreted functions primarily through language (Cassilo & Sanderson, 2019; Sanderson et al., 2016). While the rhetoric of physical and mental health are critical topics to explore together, there is a gap in communication and sport research about how the rhetoric of mental health functions primarily through perception and language (Molloy et al., 2020). As noted by Elsey et al. (2020), revelations about mental health and/or illness come from an athlete starting the conversation, as opposed to a physical injury where the public might see it occur in-game. In this chapter, to develop a rhetoric of mental health, I will review relevant literature on mental health and elite athletes, discuss a rhetorical approach to mental health and/or illness discourse, provide specific directions for future research, and conclude with final thoughts on this research area.

MENTAL HEALTH AND ELITE ATHLETES

Playing Through Pain

Competitive success, especially in contact sports, emphasizes physically dominating opponents (Connell, 1995; Foote et al., 2017). Elite athletics is a site where hegemonic masculinity is upheld because sport includes the "worst aspects of 'masculine culture'" such as "aggressiveness [and] competitiveness" (Spandler & McKeown, 2012, p. 399). Athletes are encouraged to ignore physical pain and focus on winning (Cassilo & Sanderson, 2018; Jewett et al., 2019). This approach can be damaging to their health. To begin with, they might hide the presence or severity of physical injuries to keep their spot on the team (Brayton et al., 2019). As detailed by Anderson and Kian (2012), "phrases like 'man up,' 'no pain, no gain,' and 'pain is temporary, pride is forever,' encourage men to position their own bodies as an expendable weapon of athletic war" (p. 155). Second, athletes' physical bodies are seen as commodities to make money and entertain, as opposed to individual people who need protection to promote a better quality of life after sports (Brayton et al., 2019). Treating athletes as commodities can be detrimental when addressing their mental health and/or illness. Cassilo and Sanderson (2019), in their study of athlete online forums designated for those who have suffered concussions, found that participants disclosed experiencing severe depression connected to their physical injuries and social isolation during recovery. These responses make sense because, as explained by Poucher et al., (2021), "The endorsement of mental toughness and perseverance through injury or pain may lead to athletes developing beliefs that asking for help due to mental disorder reflects an inability to persevere (and is therefore mentally weak)" (pp. 65–66). Part of this minimization and criticism of athletes is linked to the fact that athlete mental health tends to be undermined and undervalued by encouraging them to continue to play.

Mental Health Propensity for Athletes

Even though elite athletes are just as likely to experience distressed mental health or mental illness as the general population, it is commonly assumed that they are resistant to these conditions because they are athletes (Reardon et al., 2021). Until recently, this misconception was so prevalent that there was less research in this area (Reardon & Factor, 2010). However, elite athletes are subject to more than 640 stressors, including stress on the body to be competitive, as well as certain mental illnesses (Souter et al., 2018). Being an elite athlete is risky. First, they encounter dangerous situations, especially if they participate in contact or action sports which carry increased risk of serious injury (Rice et al., 2016). Second, athletic conditioning can be extremely stressful (Rice et al., 2016). Elite athletes often train hours daily in order to maintain and reach peak physical shape, which can be hard on their bodies. Despite these risks, athletes do not always address their health. Valkonen and Hanninen (2012) found that depression can be exacerbated for an athlete if they fail to meet "masculinist standards" and consequently, they face "situational obstacles for performing their unique narrative of masculinity generated distress" (p. 177). It can be hard for them to make the connection about how their sport participation might reinforce or contribute to symptoms of depression (Valkonen & Hanninen, 2012).

If elite athletes do not seek out needed treatment, consequently, they may have difficulty managing their individual experiences with depression or suicidal ideation (Mocarski & Butler, 2016). Moreover, especially for professional athletes who might earn millions of dollars from endorsements and contracts, they can hesitate to seek specific psychiatric treatment or publicly admit a mental illness diagnosis because of the stigma associated with it

(Merz et al., 2020). Merz et al. (2020) found that athletes who came forward were the "least likely to be signed and offered less financial compensation when compared to healthy counterparts" (p. 448). Even though NBA player Kevin Love signed a $120 million contract extension after disclosing his experiences with depression and anxiety, he was uniquely positioned to be protected because he was an established athlete prior to coming forward (Lavelle, 2021).

MENTAL HEALTH AND ILLNESS IN COMMUNICATION AND SPORT RESEARCH

Communication and sport scholars have examined individual disclosures of athletes' mental health experiences and specific mental illness diagnoses in several studies. Elsey et al. (2020) conducted a conversation analysis of seven professional athletes' revelations functioning as an "absence from competition" (p. 14). In their study, they found that timing and conditions for revelations varied, especially when they were not linked to a specific physical injury. Fedorocsko and Bishop (2019) analyzed 2017 obituaries and tributes to former Major League Baseball (MLB) player and broadcaster Jimmy Piersall, who played in the 1950s. They found that Piersall's use of humor to describe his experiences was groundbreaking, but there was little examination of how he lived as a professional athlete with a mental illness, particularly at a time when that was not commonly accepted. Schuck's (2019) examination of MLB player Pete Harnisch's placement on the disabled list argued that MLB mental health support was reactive, not proactive. Players came forward to discuss their experiences, but MLB did not provide institutional responses and support which addressed the unique stressors faced by baseball players (Schuck, 2019).

Recent studies have examined individual disclosures by collegiate and professional basketball players. Using a framing analysis, Cassilo and Kluch (2021) found that coverage of collegiate men's player D.J. Carton was generally well received when he came forward, helping make these types of disclosures more typical. They stressed the importance of collegiate athletes openly discussing their conditions because of the frequency of mental illness among college students and the barriers they face getting needed support. In 2018, both Kevin Love (Cleveland Cavaliers) and DeMar DeRozan (Toronto Raptors) revealed their mental health experiences. DeRozan tweeted about having depression and participated in a follow-up interview in the *Toronto Star* (Cassilo, 2020). Love wrote a *Players' Tribune* essay in March about his November 2017 in-game panic attack, which he followed up with an extensive interview as part of a five-part ESPN.com series about mental health in the NBA (Lavelle, 2021).

Parrott et al. (2020) examined fan responses to Love's and DeRozan's disclosures, observing that fans were supportive and appreciative of their transparency. In 2021, Parrott et al. analyzed media frames used in coverage of DeRozan and Love, which they found encouraged mental health openness. Lavelle (2021) studied the intersection of Love's public discourse, hegemonic masculinity, and whiteness. While Love was able to maintain his status as a White NBA champion who signed a contract extension, it is unclear if a Black player would have the same latitude coming forward. Despite Love's privilege, he was still questioned about his ability to manage his career and mental health (Lavelle, 2021). Finally, Cassilo (2020) compared coverage of Royce White and DeMar DeRozan after they came forward. DeRozan was a veteran player when he revealed his experiences, while White came forward before he was drafted in the NBA. In studying this coverage together, Cassilo (2020) found that perception is important to how public mental health disclosures are received. This study identified conditions "such as context, time frames, tenure of athletes, and communication strategies" as crucial to understanding the success of coming forward (Cassilo, 2020, p. 20). While he played limited NBA minutes as a member of the Houston Rockets, White's candor and public discourse about the accommodations needed to manage his conditions in some ways signaled the future trajectory for elite sports, specifically the emphasis on providing accommodations for players who manage mental health stressors and/or conditions while playing.

A RHETORICAL APPROACH TO ATHLETE MENTAL HEALTH AND/OR ILLNESS DISCOURSE

Contemporary communication and sports studies have focused on three primary areas regarding athlete mental health and wellness: how athletes initially come forward, what conditions or perceptions they must deal with when they go public, and the role that legacy and social media have in framing this discourse. In order to expand and connect existing athlete mental health disclosure scholarship, an additional theoretical approach our discipline should take is articulating a rhetoric of mental health based on existing rhetorical elements: identification as persuasion and rhetorical ecology.

Identification

One way that a speaker can be persuasive is by emphasizing commonalities they share with their audience. As noted by Molloy et al. (2020) in their review of nearly 40 years of rhetorical scholarship, this research "distinguishes itself through a focus on discursive and symbolic communication—especially acts of persuasion and identification" (p. ix). Elite athletes who have publicly revealed their mental health stressors and/or illness were well received because they are well-liked and these disclosures make them more relatable to the public (Cassilo, 2020; Parrott et al., 2020). Identification and persuasion, as theorized by Kenneth Burke in 1945, occurs when a speaker directly or indirectly expresses commonality with their audiences, creating the conditions for persuasion to occur (as cited in Milford, 2019). For Burke, identification works through consubstantiality, which is a collaborative process where humans can transcend their differences to reach identification (German, 2009). Athletes are effective messengers disclosing their mental health and illness because they can create consubstantiality with the public. Professional athletes are often aspirational figures and by positioning them as both successful athletes and people who live with mental illness and/or manage mental health stressors, it increases their connection to their community. As scholars, we can more explicitly examine identity characteristics beyond mental health experiences and specific mental health diagnosis to explore how these issues relate together to better understand how discourse about these conditions and stressors function as persuasion.

Rhetorical Ecology

Using a rhetorical ecology approach (Jenson, 2015) allows us to examine how mental health and illness discourse functions not just as individual disclosures, but as something that reflects and is representative of the security where it exists. By using a circulation model, which operates "by tracing the communication of ideas, assumptions, and arguments along a largely chronological timeline" (Jenson, 2015, p. 523), we can study how this discourse reflects the culture and community where it originates. It is not just about the reaction to the disclosure or the individual athlete who comes forward, but the contextual factors that help illuminate how mental illness and/or health revelations fits into larger public conversations, and how it works in larger society. By adopting the rhetorical ecology approach, we are better equipped to examine the types of concerns that Royce White raised in 2012–13. If mental health stressors and/or illness is more typically part of athlete mental health disclosure, what happens after the initial disclosure? How does a sports team or league accommodate a player who lives with a specific mental illness or ongoing mental health stressors? From a communication and sport perspective, we need to study their management about how these connections function for athletes outside of their individual identity.

By adopting a rhetorical ecology model to examine the rhetoric of mental health, "rhetorical scholars investigate why certain arguments are persuasive to particular people at discrete points in time, how persuasiveness might continue across historical periods, and how discourses circulate and change as they are applied to new circumstances" (Hausman et al., 2014, p. 406). In the case of mental health and/or illness discourse in communication and sport, there are several places where existing research could be expanded using these rhetorical tools.

WHAT ARE THE SPECIFIC DIRECTIONS OF FUTURE RESEARCH?

Rhetoric as identification and rhetorical ecology are ways to analyze various ways that mental health discourse and/or mental illness arise in communication and sport situations. First, hegemonic masculinity is not just a feature of contact sports, but also an identity characteristic where there are opportunities for athletes who reveal their mental health experiences and/or illness to create consubstantiality. As noted by Lavelle (2021), part of the reason why Kevin Love's admission of his experiences with depression and anxiety was well received in Cleveland is because despite his multimillion-dollar salary, he was perceived to be like the fan base, especially because he was white and modeled for Banana Republic. Masculinity as a type of identification is an additional layer to understand how athletes are successful in disclosing their experiences.

Second, another area that would be amplified by studying the rhetoric of mental health as identification would be how Black female athletes manage multiple expectations on their identity including mental health and/or illness, as well as their social location. To begin with, as argued by Ferguson and Satterfield (2017), these athletes frequently engage in "hyper-femininity" to respond to expectations of how they should perform their identity. Hyper-femininity is "the over accentuation of one's physical characteristics or behaviors through the use of make-up, hair and/or nail extensions, to be perceived as more feminine" (Ferguson & Satterfield, 2017, p. 116). Also, unlike their white counterparts, who can more easily be positioned as conventionally feminine, Black female athletes "continuously face negative stereotypes related to race and gender" (Ferguson & Satterfield, 2017, p. 117). For example, tennis superstars Serena and Venus Williams have faced backlash throughout their professional careers for their independence from the tennis circuit, even facing criticism for taking a break from competition after the murder of their older sister (Douglas, 2012). They have been the target of racism from fans because they were often the highest-profile Black women in tennis, and frankly, in professional sports, during the height of their careers (Douglas, 2005).

This topic is not only of interest from an identification standpoint, but also could be studied as a rhetorical approach, specifically how intersectional pressures constituted by race and gender contribute to mental health stressors and/or illness. While Elsey et al. (2020) did examine Imani McGee-Stafford's 2015 mental health disclosure, the unique conditions faced by Black female athletes can be complicated by the intersection of their race and gender. Particularly considering the discourse generated by Biles, Osaka, and WNBA players Liz Cambage, A'ja Wilson, and Imani McGee-Stafford, there are athletes whose public discourse about their unique mental health experiences provides opportunities to move beyond just studying mental health discourse, but the role of stressors athletes face because of their race and gender. These connections are important to consider because Black women have less latitude to express their mental health stressors and illness as compared to their White counterparts (Beauboeuf-LaFontant, 2007; Norris & Mitchell, 2014; Stanton et al., 2017). Instead, they are expected to suppress a range of emotions, which can magnify specific mental health pressures. As Beauboeuf-LaFontant (2007) concluded in her qualitative study examining specific stressors and historical exclusions faced by Black women, "the eventual cost of being a strong Black woman may be depression, characterized as a silencing of a range of her human needs" (p. 47). More directly exploring these issues is key to understanding how racism and misogyny affect these athletes.

A second way to use the rhetorical ecology approach could be examining the role of mental health stressors that are prevalent within specific sports. As Schuck (2019) observed, focusing on individual disclosures, as opposed to the overall conditions that promote mental health stressors and/or illness in sports, prevents leagues and teams from addressing underlying issues promoted within their sport. In recent athlete disclosures, the conditions and expectations athletes have identified as mental health stressors are not experienced equally in all sports. For instance, Naomi Osaka cited post-match press conferences as a source of stress and anxiety for her (North, 2021). After Simone Biles' disclosure in July 2021, there were numerous explanatory pieces by retired gymnasts about the physical dangers to athletes when they have mental health lapses in competition (Lanese, 2021). Relatedly, athletes who suffer specific physical injuries, such as concussions, might experience a variety of mental health stressors because of their injuries and the isolation faced during recovery (Cassilo & Sanderson, 2019). This approach provides an opportunity to extend existing research linking retirement and depression (Jewett et al., 2019), particularly as athletes move in and out of active participation in sports while they recover from injury.

Another area to study is how athletes manage mental health stressors and/or illnesses throughout their careers. As noted by sports legal scholar Michael McCann (2014), when the Houston Rockets reached an impasse with Royce White in 2013, the focus was on legalistic language of his contractual obligations, as opposed to investigating how to accommodate a player living with a mental illness diagnosis and/or mental health stressors. Disclosure and affirmation of illness and/or experiences is an important step, but what does management of these conditions look like? Especially for an athlete with a diagnosed mental illness, they may experience it their entire careers. Relatedly, there has been increased recognition of mental health stressors in youth and collegiate athletes, especially since their schools have more resources for mental health counseling and support (Cassilo & Kluch, 2021). As these athletes move into the professional ranks, they might be expecting to be more open about their mental health because of the support they received when they were young. Not only might they feel more open, but just as celebrities in the entertainment industry have been more comfortable disclosing their own mental health and/or illness (Hoffner & Cohen, 2018), athletes might feel this way as well because it is accepted and encouraged within U.S. culture.

Finally, another area to explore from a rhetorical ecology perspective is how mental health stressors and mental illnesses function as a response to and/or an effect of larger societal oppression. This topic is particularly relevant in professional leagues where most players self-identify as Black or African American, such as the Women's National Basketball Association (WNBA) (Lapchick, 2021a) and NBA (Lapchick, 2021b). For instance, the 2021 ESPN film *144* documented how WNBA players experienced added stress in response to being separated from their families and communities during the restrictive COVID-19 protocols and were unable to directly participate in Black Lives Matter protests (Stowell & Contreras, 2021). The 2020 NBA and WNBA bubble seasons took place during the largest modern civil rights protests in history, a response to the May 2020 murder of George Floyd in Minneapolis, MN (a Black man killed by a police officer on camera), and the continued lack of accountability for police officers accused of killing Black and Brown people at disproportionately higher rates than White people (Arango, 2021). In August 2020, after the police shooting of Jacob Blake in Kenosha, WI, both the WNBA and NBA struck during regular season games to draw attention to inaction against police brutality (Jeong Perry, 2020). This issue was extremely personal to players. Several NBA players have been subjected to police brutality, including Sterling Brown, who reached a $750,000 settlement with the city of Milwaukee after an excessive use of force claim (Atwell et al., 2021) and Thabo Sefolosha, whose leg was broken by police during a false arrest in New York City (McKinley, 2017). In *144*, WNBA players described how emotionally taxing it is to be a professional basketball player while participating in social justice activism, fighting for more equitable and anti-racist policing. Outside of a global pandemic, living in a society that upholds systemic racism functions as a rhetorical ecology approach that would be an appropriate framework to study how mental health stressors and/or mental illness magnifies and complicates these issues.

FINAL THOUGHTS

Public discourse about athlete mental health and/or illness is part of broader conversations in U.S. society as these conditions and experiences become more accepted as part of athlete health. By more explicitly applying rhetorical principles to the understanding and analysis of athlete public health, we can have a better understanding of how these disclosures and overall mental health discourse functions. Examining the rhetoric of mental health as an issue of identification helps explain why a person would come forward about their experiences and connect with fans and the larger public. Using the rhetorical ecology approach, we can extend existing research to evaluate how the connection between larger contextual issues that might inform and magnify mental health stressors and/or conditions, such as hegemonic masculinity, intersectional pressures faced by Black female athletes, and the stress of balancing being elite athlete and public advocate. As communication and sport scholars who engage in this type of research, we want to continue to develop and apply theoretical tools to analyze the rhetoric of mental health, as they continue to be critical topics for our discipline, and I would encourage others to make this application as well.

REFERENCES

Anderson, E. & Kian, E. M. (2012). Examining media contestation of masculinity and head trauma in the National Football League. *Men & Masculinities, 15,* 152–173. https://doi.org/10.1177/1097184X11430127

Arango, T. (2021, June 25). Derek Chauvin is sentenced to 22 and a half years for the murder of George Floyd. *The New York Times.* https://www.nytimes.com/2021/06/25/us/derek-chauvin-22-and-a-half-years-george-floyd.html

Atwell, B., Close, D., & Sanchez, R. (2021, May 4). NBA player Sterling Brown's $750,000 settlement approved after 2018 incident where he was tased by police.

CNN.com. https://www.cnn.com/2021/05/04/us/sterling-brown-milwaukee-police-settlement/index.html

Beauboeuf-LaFontant, T. (2007). "You have to show strength": An exploration of gender, race, and depression. *Gender & Society, 21,* 28–51. https://doi.org/10.1177/0891243206294108

Brayton, S., Helstein, M. T., Ramsey, M., & Rickards, N. (2019). Exploring the missing link between the concussion "crisis" and labor politics in professional sports. *Communication & Sport, 7,* 110–131. https://doi.org/10.1177/2167479517740342

Cassilo, D. (2020). Royce White, DeMar DeRozan and media framing of mental health in the NBA. *Communication & Sport.* Advance online publication. https//doi.org/10.1177/2167479520933548

Cassilo, D. & Kluch, Y. (2021). Mental health, college athletics, and the media framing of D. J. Carton's announcement to step away from his team. *Communication & Sport.* Advance online publication. https://doi.org/10.1177/21674795211041019

Cassilo, D. & Sanderson, J. (2018). "I don't think it's worth the risk": Media framing of the Chris Borland retirement in digital and print media. *Communication & Sport, 6,* 86–110. https://doi.org/10.1177/2167479516654513

Cassilo, D. & Sanderson, J. (2019). From social isolation to becoming an advocate: Exploring athletes' grief discourse about lived concussion experiences in online forums. *Communication & Sport, 7,* 678–696. https://doi.org/10.1177/2167479518790039

Connell, R. W. (1995). *Masculinities.* Berkeley: University of California Press.

Douglas, D. D. (2005). Venus, Serena, and the Women's Tennis Association: When and where "race" enters. *Sociology of Sport Journal, 22,* 256–282. https://doi.org/10.1123/ssj.22.3.255

Douglas, D. D. (2012). Venus, Serena, and the inconspicuous consumption of Blackness: A commentary on surveillance, race, talk, and new racism(s). *Journal of Black Studies, 43,* 127–145. https://doi.org/10.1177/0021934711410880.

Elsey, C., Winter, P., Litchfield, S. J., Ogweno, S., & Southwood, J. (2020). Professional sport and initial mental public disclosure narratives. *Communication & Sport.* Advance online publication. https://doi.org/10.1177/2167479520977312

Fedorocsko, M., & Bishop, R. (2019). Running the bases backward: Journalists mark the death of Jimmy Piersall. *Communication & Sport, 9,* 438–457. https://doi.org/10.1177/2167479519867084

Ferguson, T. & Satterfield, J. W. (2017). Black women athletes and the performance of hyper-femininity. In L. D. Patton & N. N. Croom (Eds.), *Critical perspectives on Black women and college success* (pp. 115–127). New York: Routledge.

Foote, J. G., Butterworth, M. L., & Sanderson, J. (2017) Adrian Peterson and the "wussification of America": Football and myths of masculinity. *Communication Quarterly, 65,* 268–284, https://doi.org/10.1080/01463373.2016.1227347

Futterman, M. (2020, July 29). Michael Phelps: "I can't see any more suicides." *The New York Times.* https://www.nytimes.com/2020/07/29/sports/olympics/michael-phelps-documentary-weight-of-gold.html

German, K. (2009). Identification. In S. W. Littlejohn & K. A. Foss (Eds.), *Encyclopedia of Communication Theory* (p. 492). Los Angeles: SAGE Publications.

Gleeson, S. & Brady, E. (2017, August 30). When athletes share their battles with mental illness. *USA Today.* https://www.usatoday.com/story/sports/2017/08/30/michael-phelps-brandon-marshall-mental-health-battles-royce-white-jerry-west/596857001/

Graves, W. (2021, August 3). Biles returns to Olympic competition, wins bronze on the beam. *APNews.com.* https://apnews.com/article/2020-tokyo-olympics-gymnastics-simone-biles-8d61f4de9ec021860cda002f4eac5804

Hausman, B. L., Ghebremichael, M., Hayek, P., & Mack, E. (2014). "Poisonous, filthy, loathsome, damnable stuff": The rhetorical ecology of vaccination concern. *Yale Journal of Biology and Medicine, 87,* 403–416. https://www.ncbi.nlm.nih.gov/pmc/articles/PMC4257028/

Hoffner, C. A. & Cohen, E. L. (2018) Mental health-related outcomes of Robin Williams' death: The role of parasocial relations and media exposure in stigma, help-seeking, and outreach. *Health Communication, 33,* 1573–1582. https://doi.org/10.1080/10410236.2017.1384348

Jenson, R. E. (2015). An ecological turn in rhetoric of health scholarship: Attending to the historical flow and percolation of ideas, assumptions, and arguments. *Communication Quarterly, 63,* 522–526. https://doi.org/10.1080/01463373.2015.1103600

Jeong Perry, A. (2020, September 4). How Black women paved the way for the NBA strike. *Code Switch.* https://www.npr.org/sections/codeswitch/2020/09/04/909638021/how-black-women-athletes-paved-the-way-for-the-nba-strike

Jewett, R., Kerr, G., & Tamminen, K. (2019). University sport retirement and athlete mental health: a narrative analysis. *Qualitative Research in Sport, Exercise and Health, 11*(3), 416–433. https://doi.org/10.1080/2159676X.2018.1506497

Johnson, J. (2010). The skeleton on the couch: The Eagleton affair, rhetorical disability, and the stigma of mental illness. *Rhetoric Society Quarterly, 40,* 459–478. https://www.jstor.org/stable/40997107

Lanese, N. (2021, July 31). *What's happening inside Simone Biles' brain when the "twisties" set in?* https://www.livescience.com/simone-biles-what-are-twisties.html

Lapchick, R. (2021a). The 2020 racial and gender report card: Women's National Basketball Association. *The Institute for Diversity and Ethics in Sport.* https://43530132-36e9-4f52-811a-182c7a91933b.filesusr.com/ugd/138a69_639f0723482e432d8e2dcd6829d9244c.pdf

Lapchick, R. (2021b). The 2020 racial and gender report card: National Basketball Association. *The Institute for Diversity and Ethics in Sport.* https://43530132-36e9-4f52-811a-182c7a91933b.filesusr.com/ugd/138a69_676bda2f2e6a412cb4afe10a518c14ae.pdf

Lavelle, K. L. (2021). The face of mental health: Kevin Love and hegemonic masculinity in the NBA. *Communication & Sport, 9*(6), 954–971. https://doi.org/10.1177/2167479520922182

MacMullan, J. (2018, August 20). The courageous fight to fix the NBA's mental health problem. *ESPN.com.* http://www.espn.com/nba/story/_/id/24382693/jackie-macmullan-kevin-love-paul-pierce-state-mental-health-nba

McCann, M. A. (2014). Do you believe he can fly? Royce White and reasonable accommodations under the Americans with Disabilities Act for NBA players with anxiety disorder and fear of flying. *Pepperdine Law Review, 41,* 397.

McKinley, J. C. (2017, April 5). New York City to pay N.B.A.'s Thabo Sefolosha $4 million to end false-arrest suit. *The New York Times.* https://www.nytimes.com/2017/04/05/nyregion/thabo-sefolosha-ny-atlanta-false-arrest-suit.html

Mental health: Strengthening our response. (2018, March 30). *World Health Organization.* https://www.who.int/news-room/fact-sheets/detail/mental-health-strengthening-our-response

Merz, Z. C., Perry, J. E., Brauer, A. H., Montgomery, T. L., Schulze, J., & Ross, M. L. (2020). The cost of mental illness: The public's derogation of athletes with psychological distress. *Stigma and Health, 5,* 442–450. https/doi.org/10.1037/sah0000213

Milford, M. (2019). Spirits in the material world: The rhetoric of the Iroquois Nationals. In D. A. Grano & M. L. Butterworth (Eds.), *Sport, rhetoric, and political struggle* (pp. 101–114). New York: Peter Lang.

Mocarski, R. & Butler, S. (2016). A critical, rhetorical analysis of man therapy: The use of humor to frame mental health as masculine. *Journal of Communication Inquiry, 40,* 128–144. https://doi.org/10.1177/0196859915606974

Molloy, C., Holladay, D., & Meloncon, L. (2020). The place of mental health rhetoric research (MHRR) in *Rhetoric of Health & Medicine* and beyond. *Rhetoric of Health & Medicine, 3,* iii–x. https://doi.org/10.5744/rhm.2020.1011

Norris, C. M. & Mitchell, F. D. (2014). Exploring the stress-support-distress process among Black women. *Journal of Black Studies, 45,* 3–18. https://doi.org/10.1177/0021934713517898

North, A. (2021, July 30). America's mental health moment is finally here. *Vox.com.* https://www.vox.com/22596341/simone-biles-withdrawal-osaka-olympics-mental-health

Parrott, S., Billings, A. C., Hakim, S. D., & Gentile, P. (2020). From #endthestigma to #realman: Stigma-challenging social media responses to NBA players' mental health disclosures. *Communication Reports, 33,* 148–160. https://doi.org/10.1080/08934215.2020.1811365

Parrott, S., Billings, A. C., Buzzelli, N., & Towery, N. (2021). "We All Go Through It": Media depictions of mental illness disclosures from star athletes DeMar DeRozan and Kevin Love. *Communication & Sport, 9,* 33–54. https://doi.org/10.1177/2167479519852605

Poucher, Z. A., Tamminen, K. A., Kerr, G., & Cairney, J. (2021). A commentary on mental health research in elite sport. *Journal of Applied Sport Psychology, 33,* 60–82. https://doi.org/ 10.1080/10413200.2019.1668496

Reardon, C. L., Bindra, A., Blauwet, C., Budgett, R., Campriani, N., Currie, A., Gouttebarge, V., McDuff, D., Mountjoy, M., Purcell, R., Putukian, M., Rice, S., & Hainline, B. (2021). Mental health management of elite athletes during COVID-19: a narrative review and recommendations. *British Journal of Sports Medicine.* Advance online publication. 1–10. https://doi.org/10.1136/bjsports-2020-102884

Reardon, C. L. & Factor, R. M. (2010). Sport psychiatry: A systematic review of diagnosis and medical treatment of mental illness in athletes. *Sports Med, 40,* 961–980. https://doi.org/10.2165/11536580-000000000-00000

Rice, S. M., Purcell, R., De Silva, S., Mawren, D., McGorry, P. D., & Parker, A. G. (2016). The mental health of elite athletes: A narrative systematic review. *Sports Medicine, 46,* 1333–1353. https://doi.org/10.1007/s40279-016-0492-2

Sanderson, J., Weathers, M., Grevisou, A., Tehan, M., & Warren, S. (2016). A hero or sissy? Exploring media framing of NFL quarterback injury decisions. *Communication & Sport, 4,* 3–22. https://doi.org/10.1177/2167479514536982

Schuck, R. I. (2019). "I'd just like to let everybody know": Pete Harnisch on the disabled list and the politics of mental health. In D. A. Grano & M. L. Butterworth (Eds.), *Sport, rhetoric, and political struggle* (pp. 175–189). New York: Peter Lang.

Souter, G., Lewis, R., & Serrant, L. (2018). Men, mental health, and elite sport: A narrative review. *Sports Medicine, 4*(57), 1–8. https://doi.org/10.1186/s40798-018-0175-7

Spandler, H. & McKeown, M. (2012). A critical exploration of using football in health and welfare programs: Gender, masculinities, and social relations. *Journal of Sport and Social Issues, 36,* 387–409. https://doi.org/10.1177/0193723512458930.

Stanton, A. G., Jerald, M. C., Ward, L. M., & Avery, L. R. (2017). Social media contributions to strong Black woman ideal endorsement and Black women's mental health. *Psychology of Women Quarterly, 41,* 465–478. https://doi.org/10.1177/0361684317732330

Stowell, L. & Contreras, J. (Directors). (2021). *144.* [Film]. ESPN Films.

Valkonen, J. & Hanninen, V. (2012). Narratives of masculinity and depression. *Men and Masculinities 16,* 160–180. https://doi.org/10.1177/1097184X12464377

What is mental illness? (2021). *American Psychiatry Association.* https://www.psychiatry.org/patients-families/what-is-mental-illness

NOTES

1. For the purposes of this chapter, I use the World Health Organization's definition of mental health: "a state of well-being in which an individual realizes his or her own abilities, can cope with the normal stresses of life, can work productively and is able to contribute to his or her community" (Mental health: Strengthening, 2018, para. 2).

2. As defined by the American Psychiatric Association: "Mental Illness refers collectively to all diagnosable mental disorders—health conditions involving significant changes in thinking, emotion and/or behavior; distress and/or problems functioning in social, work or family activities" (What is mental illness?, 2021, para. 5).

3. In this chapter, I define hegemonic masculinity as "the configuration of gender practice which embodies the currently accepted answer to the problem of the legitimacy of patriarchy" (Connell, 1995, p. 77).

Chapter Four

Corporate Social Responsibility and Health Promotion Campaigns among Major U.S. Professional Sporting Leagues

Adam Rugg

From youth health and fitness to cancer awareness to pandemic health and well-being, major U.S. professional sporting leagues frequently utilize health promotion campaigns to engage their fans and the broader public on health-related issues. These health promotion campaigns are part of a broader constellation of campaigns among the leagues and their associated teams that target specific social issues and are outgrowths of an increasingly important public relations and community outreach strategy known as corporate social responsibility, or CSR for short. CSR is premised on the idea that corporations and other organizations should consider the social good in their operations and work to enhance the well-being of the communities in which they operate. Over time, corporations have increasingly created segments of their organization specifically dedicated to CSR efforts and initiatives. Despite the rise of CSR as an increasingly visible part of corporate strategies in the 1960s and 1970s, CSR was not a significant aspect of sporting leagues until the 1990s. By the end of the 2000s, however, sporting organizations were "entering into various socially responsible initiatives at a rapid pace" (Babiak & Wolfe, 2013, p. 18).

Significant milestones in league initiatives during this period included the National Basketball Association's (NBA) establishment of its "NBA Cares" CSR platform in 2005 and the National Football League's (NFL) launch of its "Fuel Up to Play 60" and "Crucial Catch" campaigns in 2009. The "Crucial Catch" campaign in particular provided a model for campaign-centered CSR efforts that utilized gameday activities and events for fans during the campaign, promoted the campaign on field areas and uniforms, incorporated the use of players for public service announcements (PSAs) and other educational and promotional content, and produced and sold campaign-specific apparel and accessories (Rugg, 2019). The NFL now has five campaigns that are integrated into the gameday experience both in the stadium and on television and cover the majority of its season. Other major professional sports leagues in the U.S. such as the NBA, Women's National Basketball Association (WNBA), Major League Baseball (MLB), and the National Hockey League (NHL) have followed suit and all offer CSR campaigns centered around similar areas of cancer awareness, military support and celebration, environmental sustainability, racial inequality and injustice, diversity and inclusion, and health and fitness.

While the evolution of corporations and other organizations to actively engage in activities to positively effect social well-being seems a welcome and much needed development in corporate behavior, the benefits and motivations of CSR have been repeatedly challenged by researchers. While the tone and tenor of many CSR campaigns is one of altruistic service to the social good, most corporations and organizations utilize CSR campaigns as part of broader public relations strategies that ultimately aim to benefit the organization. At the most basic level CSR campaigns operate to generate goodwill among consumers and positive press from the media. More problematically, corporations may initiate or expand CSR efforts as an image repair tactic after facing scandals or criticisms for unethical or immoral practices (Waddington, Chelladurai, & Skirstad, 2013). Organizations may even engage in CSR efforts for problems in which they are seen to be complicit. Most commonly this is seen in the act of "greenwashing," where industrial polluters or other organizations doing damage to the environment launch CSR efforts around environmental sustainability and protection (Ahluwalia & Miller, 2014; Cherry & Sneirson, 2012).

Other researchers have linked the extraordinary growth of CSR within large organizations to the ascendance of neoliberal ideologies in public policy and governance that marginalize state intervention in identifying and solving social problems in favor of increased involvement from private interests (Ferguson, 2010; Miller & Rose 2008). As Giulianotti (2015) argues, the result is a "strongly voluntarist approach that is centered on private giving" that reinforces pro-business discourses that "advocate private philanthropy and the voluntary self-regulation of corporations in terms of their market and other activities" (p. 245). Additionally, the lack of a "democratic mandate" for private corporations reduces the levels of accountability for their CSR efforts as compared to state actors and lessens the need for consultation and engagement with the impacted communities (p. 245). The relationship between CSR efforts and larger public relations strategies further incentivizes prioritizing protecting the reputation of the organization. Organizations are less likely to take on controversial, but necessary social interventions and avoid critical evaluations of program outcomes for efforts that are undertaken (Armstrong et al., 2018).

HEALTH PROMOTION CAMPAIGNS IN CONTEMPORARY SETTINGS

Youth Health and Fitness

One significant area of health promotion by sports leagues is in the area of physical activity and health among children. As Paramio-Salcines et al. (2013) explain, sport is uniquely suited to deliver CSR programming around physical fitness and health and to target issues such as childhood obesity. Most prominently in this space is the NFL's "Play 60" campaign against childhood obesity. Initially started in conjunction with the American Heart Association in 2006 as a month-long physical activity, "Play 60" was eventually expanded into a year-round campaign aimed at "tackling childhood obesity." As the program expanded, the NFL began partnering with many governmental agencies, non-profit organizations, and the CSR platforms of for-profit corporations. With the launch of the adjoining "Fuel Up to Play 60" campaign (with a $250 million commitment from the National Dairy Council) in 2009 the NFL began entering into schools en masse. The league claims to currently operate in over 73,000 schools and to have engaged with over 38 million students. The program, and the league, now stand at the center of a bevy of governmental and private sector relationships and programs centered on physical fitness and are authoritative voices in understanding youth health and fitness and in shaping school curriculums (Rugg, 2019).

As Montez de Oca et al. (2016a) argue, the campaign serves to provide the NFL with unfettered, unregulated access to students. As the campaign is built around engagement with NFL football and its stars, it works to not just build the connection between exercise and football but to enlist the students as consumer citizens who are educated in NFL lore and encouraged to become "avid fans." Further, the program operates as a counter to ongoing medical revelations of the widespread risks of playing football that has caused parents to increasingly question the safety of football as a physical activity for their children. As I argue in my analysis of "Play 60," the league has increasingly incorporated Flag football and USA Football into its Play 60 activities to create a "naturalized trajectory to ease children into the structures of tackle football" (Rugg, 2019, p. 84). Thus, in producing "Play 60," the NFL is able to teach children about the league, incorporate them into the structures of fandom and spectatorship, and encourage them to participate in the sport itself, all under the auspices of altruistic social good. As Montez de Oca et al. (2016b) show, the "Play 60" campaign is one part of a broader suite of educational and entertainment resources that the NFL utilizes to reach and market to youth populations.

The size and scope of the program has also led the league to partner with the non-profit Cooper Institute and its FITNESSGRAM initiative to carry out long-term surveillance studies measuring "aerobic capacity, body composition, and muscular strength, endurance, and flexibility" (Welk et al., 2016). The resulting data from the large-scale project has been used by researchers from the Cooper Institute, the University of Utah, and Iowa State University, among others, to produce a number of scholarly analyses of youth fitness levels in health and medical journals (Bai et al., 2015; Bai et al., 2017; Saint-Maurice et al., 2017; Welk et al., 2015).

The "Play 60" campaign remains the most prominent example of leagues engaging in youth health- and exercise-related CSR activities, yet its success has spurred other sport entities to run similar programs. The NBA and WNBA launched Jr. NBA in 2015 which focuses on promoting the game of basketball alongside content about health, safety, and exercise to children aged 6–14. Also, in 2015 MLB launched its "Play Ball" campaign to encourage youth to play baseball through the teaching of baseball skills and associated exercises. In 2017, MLB began targeting educational programs, though in a non-health context. It partnered with educational technology company EVERFI to launch "Summer Slugger," an online interactive platform for children to work on reading and math skills over the summer. In 2019, it expanded deeper into education curriculum by partnering with Discovery Education on a multi-year initiative that includes the incorporation of MLB-themed content into Discovery science and STEM textbooks that reach 5.6 million students (Lemire, 2019). While the NHL does not have a dedicated CSR campaign targeting youth health, various NHL teams such as the Nashville Predators, Minnesota Wild, San Jose Sharks, and Chicago Blackhawks have adopted the Play 60 model and provide a variety of programs for schools that utilize hockey and team branding to instruct students in fitness and exercise activities as well as in non-health areas like reading and STEM (Chicago Blachawks, n.d.; Minnesota Wild, n.d.; Nashville Predators, n.d.; San Jose Sharks, n.d.).

The COVID-19 pandemic has only accelerated these efforts as remote schooling and social distancing guidelines provided opportunities for leagues and teams to reach children isolated from educational and social institutions. In addition to its "Play 60" campaign, the NFL added a "Huddle at Home" component that provided Play 60–style curriculum and activities for children isolated to home settings. The NBA/WNBA and MLS took similar actions, extending their existing CSR platforms with "Jr. NBA at Home" and "MLS Unites to Inspire Kids" platforms, respectively. MLB similarly expanded its "Play Ball" campaign to "Play Ball at Home" and reframed it as not just a promotional tool for youth baseball, but also as a platform for kids to safely engage in exercises and physical activity during the pandemic. As these examples show, sports leagues and teams are increasingly invested in engaging with children in areas of fitness, health, and education and have established CSR platforms that can be operationalized to respond to events such as the COVID-19 pandemic. The decreased funding for physical education (and education in general) in the U.S. has allowed these organizations to easily expand into educational spaces governed by the state and articulate themselves as authorities on youth health and fitness. The continued success of these programs and initiatives suggests they will only expand in the future. More critical research will be necessary to unpack and understand the consequences of this deepening relationship between sporting leagues, educational systems, and kids.

THE COVID-19 PANDEMIC AND VACCINE PROMOTION

Sports have often been a visible topic of discussion during the COVID-19 pandemic. In the U.S., the NBA shut down its season indefinitely after Utah Jazz player Rudy Gobert tested positive for COVID-19 on March 11, 2020. The moment has come to be popularly seen as the defining moment where the nation was awakened to the seriousness of COVID-19 and the impact it would have on American society (Bagley, 2020; Pederson & Williams, 2020). The coming days would see many of the U.S. sporting leagues and events shut down with no clear timetable for return and lingering questions as to how sports would and could come back (Blinder & Drape, 2021).

During the pandemic, major U.S. professional sporting leagues began shifting their CSR efforts toward pandemic-related issues. As Smith and Casper (2020) show, these leagues either integrated COVID-19-related programs into their existing CSR platforms (such as in the case of the NFL, MLB, and NHL) or created new "umbrella communication vehicles" that exclusively focused on the pandemic and its effects (NBA, MLS). The nature of these integrations primarily revolved around three themes: educating fans on COVID-19 health facts and providing educational resources and physical activity exercises for children during shelter-in-place regulations; compelling fans to assist in COVID-19 relief efforts such as food drives and blood donations; and inspiring fans through celebrations of frontline workers and stories of community togetherness. As Smith and Casper (2020) argue, researchers will need to closely monitor and investigate these programs as their current incarnation is reflective of the relationship between U.S. society and the COVID-19 pandemic at the current moment. As the pandemic, its impact on U.S. society, and societal/governmental response shift and change, how these programs address COVID-19 and health will necessarily change as well.

One of the largest developments in the COVID-19 pandemic following Smith and Casper's analysis was the approval of COVID-19 vaccines by the U.S. Food and Drug Administration (FDA) and the subsequent efforts to vaccinate the U.S. population. Following Smith and Casper's call for increased attention to the evolution of how league CSR campaigns address COVID-19, it is worth examining what role major U.S. sporting leagues have taken in efforts to vaccinate the U.S. population against COVID-19. So far, the engagement with vaccines among the major U.S. professional leagues has been inconsistent despite the centrality of vaccines in public discourses around COVID-19 and the immense benefits and protections that come from increasing the country's vaccination rate. Notably, the NFL, WNBA, NHL, and MLS have not incorporated vaccine awareness or outreach into their league-led CSR initiatives. The NBA has also not made vaccine outreach a central part of its CSR platforms, though it has recorded 5 PSAs supporting vaccines starring retired and active players. MLB ran the most robust campaign, with an associated PSA titled "Join the Team, Get the Vaccine," the hosting of vaccine clinics around the country, and its "Vaccinate at the Plate" initiative which saw each of the 30 MLB teams offer vaccination clinics with free tickets for fans who come to the stadium and get vaccinated (Snyder, 2021).

Despite little in the way of centralized campaigns from league offices, numerous teams did engage in their own vaccination efforts, often in partnership with city or state government agencies. Teams across leagues made their stadiums available as vaccination sites while athletes from teams such as MLB's Milwaukee Brewers, the NBA's Brooklyn Nets, and the NFL's New England Patriots participated in PSAs (Brooks, 2021; Moraitis, 2021; Naczek, 2021; Sturm & Income, 2021). Perhaps most visible is the NHL's Philadelphia Flyers' ongoing "Take Your Shot" campaign which combines a multi-pronged approach of releasing PSAs with Flyers players and coaches, providing vaccine resources for fans, staging vaccination clinics in partnership with Penn Medicine, and making donations to organizations such as the Black Doctors COVID-19 Consortium (Whelan, 2021). Other teams across the major U.S. men's sports leagues have staged vaccination clinics at various home games, with some, such as the NBA's Dallas Mavericks and MLS' Seattle Sounders, offering vaccinations at every home game (Schumaker, 2021; Sweat, 2021).

Additionally, NFL Alumni, the association for retired NFL players (with no affiliation to the NFL) partnered with the U.S. Centers for Disease Control and Prevention (CDC) to launch a national vaccine promotion campaign utilizing 40 current and retired NFL players (Stapleton, 2021). While the WNBA as a league has also not incorporated vaccine awareness into its CSR platforms, the WNBA players' union, in contrast, has been very aggressive in vaccine education and promotion. While the league received much positive attention for quickly achieving a 99% vaccination rate among its players, it was the union and players that led the internal campaign to educate the league on vaccination and encourage getting vaccinated (Baccellieri, 2021). Shortly after, the players' union announced the launch of a dedicated campaign titled "Take The Shot for the WIN." The campaign was launched in conjunction with the Black Women's Health Imperative (BWHI) and the National Council of Negro Women (NCNW) and targeted toward increasing vaccination rates in communities of color (Black Women's Health Imperative, 2021).

A critical approach to analyzing the branding and marketing of sports (including CSR campaigns) as well as the politics of health can help in assessing the tempered efforts by major U.S. sporting leagues in vaccine education and awareness despite urgent calls to action by medical authorities. As Butterworth (2020) argues, sport is often romanticized as a site that "brings people together" under a rhetoric of unity (p. 454). In examining the NFL's focus on unity in response to President Trump's attack on protesting NFL players in 2017, Butterworth argues for the limits of the league's deep adherence to this rhetoric, stating, "this collective discourse invoked ideals about American diversity but denied the actual pluralism that defines democratic culture. Perhaps most importantly, it attempted to make unity an end in and of itself, thereby foreclosing ongoing contestation" (p. 465). In Butterworth's analysis, the fetishism of unity—whether a strategic public relations strategy or a sincere articulation of engrained U.S. nationalism—restricts necessary confrontation between competing discourses and ideas that is the defining productive element of democratic culture. In my own analysis of the NFL's "Inspire Change" campaign that launched in 2019, I argued that the initial media presence of the campaign, represented in the documentary content and advertisements, repeatedly emphasized a vague sense of unity that served to "repackage the activism put forth by Colin Kaepernick and other players into an audience-friendly enterprise that trades the demands for justice (and the reflection it calls for) for the convenience of passive support that suits the commercial needs of the NFL" (Rugg, 2020b, p. 623).

The rhetoric of unity pervades the major sporting leagues' engagement with the COVID-19 pandemic. In the case of the NBA and MLS, this is done quite literally in the naming of their respective dedicated COVID-19 CSR platforms, "NBA Together" and "MLS Unites." Across both these platforms and the general CSR platforms and messaging of other major sporting leagues there has been an extensive focus on uplifting messages of support for those in need and highlighting "heroes" who helped in their community. As Sobande (2020) argues, this has been a common feature of the pandemic where "brands have been quick to invoke ambiguous yet arguably commodified notions of connectivity, care and community" (p. 1034). Crucially, by sticking to these positive, unifying messages of support and celebration, sporting leagues can engage their fan bases in broadly positive ways that link both league and consumer together as partners in service of the leagues' strategic aims.

Projecting unity around vaccines is a much more difficult proposition, however. Since the vaccines were approved for use by the FDA, conspiracy theories and misinformation surrounding the virus and the vaccines circulate heavily on social media and partisan media outlets, with research showing this misinformation having material impacts on people's intent to get vaccinated (Loomba et al., 2021). Significantly, this misinformation has operated alongside (and in service to) significant amounts of criticism and skepticism toward the vaccines from prominent conservative politicians, commentators, and outlets, leading the vaccine itself to become a key reflection of partisan divide. Surveys taken after the approval of the COVID-19 vaccines showed Republicans much less likely to be vaccinated than Democrats while 17 of the 20 states with the lowest vaccination rates in the summer of 2021 were won by Republican candidate Donald Trump in the 2020 presidential election (Bolsen & Palm, 2021).

As Sobande further argues, the adherence to rhetoric of unity and togetherness "can conveniently cloak the reality that due to intersecting structural oppressions and socio-economic disparities which precede COVID-19, even if 'we're' all impacted by this crisis, 'we're' not all experiencing it in the same way" (pp. 1034–1035). The differing impact of the COVID-19 pandemic on various communities and its exacerbation of existing structural inequities in U.S. society is the central tenet of the WNBA Players Union's "Take The Shot for the WIN" vaccine awareness campaign, which centers around educating black women on the vaccines that was announced in part to address the "stark" outcomes for black women during the pandemic. In spearheading an intersectionally-focused vaccine promotion campaign that recognizes the disproportionate impact of the COVID-19 pandemic on specific communities, WNBA players have continued their legacy of directly confronting issues of racial inequality and injustice well beyond the extent of their own league and further challenged the conventional structures of league-led social messaging on the pandemic (Cooky & Antunovic, 2020).

FUTURE CONSIDERATIONS

The last decade has seen health campaigns—and corporate social responsibility campaigns in general—grow to be a significant aspect of major U.S. sport. The arrival of the COVID-19 virus and its momentous impact on sport and communities across the globe suggest this growth will only continue. Further research into these areas will need to grapple with the expanding scope of sports leagues' CSR efforts related to health, their increasing integration into public/private structures that govern and promote health practices, and their involvement and influence on political decision-making regarding health-related issues.

Adding additional complexity is the increasing entrepreneurship of individual athletes in activism and advocating for social causes. As scholars have ably documented, athlete activism is in an ascendant, rejuvenated period with many high-profile athletes committed to addressing a wide variety of social issues (Cooper et al., 2019; Kaufman & Wolff, 2010; Williams, 2021). The commitment to activism extends to non-professional athletes in college and high school athletics as well (Armstrong & Butryn, 2021; Kluch, 2020). The star-centered structures of contemporary sports coverage combined with the easily accessible platforms of social media have further amplified the voices of individual athletes and enabled them to loudly advocate for causes outside the approved campaigns of their team or league (Schmittel & Sanderson, 2015). During the COVID-19 pandemic, for example, many athletes used social media to engage the public directly on health issues related to the virus or safe social practices. Some prominent athletes engaged in popular, collaborative social media campaigns such as the #StayAtHomeChallenge on Twitter. Others used their platforms to educate their followers, such as when the NBA's Steph Curry interviewed Dr. Anthony Fauci, the head of the U.S. National Institute of Allergy and Infectious Diseases, on his Instagram account to roughly 50,000 viewers (Sharpe et al., 2020).

As Cooper et al. (2019) argue in their analysis of African American sport activism, the rich history of athlete activism cannot be understood as a single, monolithic activity, but as a variety of tactics and strategies with varying levels of engagement from the athletes and differing intended outcomes. Today, many athletes are increasingly expansive with their activism and philanthropy as they incorporate their efforts into their long-term personal and professional goals and have adopted strategies similar to the campaign-centered model of major professional U.S. sporting leagues. The previously discussed WNBA Players Union's "Take The Shot for the WIN" campaign represents a recent league-wide example of this. Additionally, in the area of health, the Kevin Love Fund (founded by NBA player Kevin Love) states its aim to help 1 billion people over a 5-year period and in 2020 established a Kevin Love Fund Chair in UCLA's Psychology Department centered on studying and treating anxiety and depression (Kole, 2021). In a non-U.S. context, Marcus Rashford of the English Premier League team Manchester United famously took on the UK government over providing free meals for vulnerable children and spearheaded a campaign to end child food poverty (Olusoga & Olusoga, 2020).

Other prominent non-health examples include the voting rights advocacy group "More Than A Vote," which emerged after the murder of George Floyd and was founded by prominent athletes across a variety of leagues including Lebron James (NBA), Patrick Mahomes (NFL), and A'ja Wilson (WNBA). During March 2021, the group launched a "Protect Our Power" campaign that coincided with the NBA's All-Star Weekend and included an ad narrated by James that aired during the NBA All-Star game (Turman, 2021). Similar to the WNBA Players Union's "Take The Shot for the WIN" campaign and its relationship to the WNBA, the "Protect Our Power" campaign was not affiliated with the NBA, yet became intertwined with the league's media presence through the involvement of many of its most prominent stars.

While the distinction between player-led campaigns and league-approved campaigns may not be clear (or matter) to sports fans, researchers examining health promotion campaigns within major U.S. sporting leagues will need to navigate the overlapping, yet distinct layers of actors participating in the space. As Armstrong et al. (2018) detail in their conversations with sports industry professionals, leagues factor in player-led initiatives and causes when evaluating sites for potential CSR activities and generally avoid supporting or intersecting with player-led causes that may be "controversial" to significant segments of the fan base. Thus, to fully understand and contextualize any given health promotion campaign researchers will need to not only place it within the larger web of activities carried out by athletes, alumni groups, teams, and other sporting organizations, but to analyze it in relationship to those activities.

Additionally, researchers must account for the ways in which league framings and priorities may be contested and/or shaped by players, fans, and others. For example, one of the NFL's newest campaigns, "My Cleats, My Cause," emerged after repeated incidents of players willingly violating the league's uniform policy to advocate for causes not officially sanctioned by the NFL. More prominently, the NFL's "Inspire Change" campaign against police brutality and racial inequality represented a negotiated compromise between the NFL and the players where the marketing structures of the campaign reflected the league's desire to create a voluntary, "unifying" message that could be tolerated by segments of the fanbase ideologically opposed or merely indifferent to the calls for social justice among players. However, the decision-making and funding apparatus of the campaign reflected player desire for more agency in dictating the actions of the campaign in local communities (Rugg, 2020). As players continue to recognize and wield the power of their platforms and engage in high-profile activist projects of their own—such as the WNBA Players Union's "Take The Shot for the WIN" campaign—the tension between their activities and efforts and those of the leagues they play in may escalate. Further research into this complex and overlapping relationship between players and leagues as it relates to health campaigns is needed.

Finally, researchers must continue to critically interrogate health promotion campaigns from sporting organizations through the lenses of racial, gender, and sexual inequities and larger societal power dynamics. As the above discussions and analyses has shown, health promotion activities of major U.S. sporting leagues should not just be understood as positive gestures toward society, no matter the universalizing and unifying rhetoric that often accompany them. Rather, researchers need to recognize how the pretense of expertise afforded to private and corporate organizations in identifying social issues and leading the efforts to resolve them has been increasingly normalized in our contemporary structures of neoliberal governance (Giulianotti, 2015). This is especially true in areas of health policy and public health practices (Ayo, 2012; Rugg, 2020a). In analyzing health promotion campaigns, it is imperative, then, that researchers question the framing of health issues and solutions by sporting entities, connect those framings and solutions to larger ideological frameworks and existing power dynamics in society, and pursue how those framings and solutions advance the interests of the entity and reinforce the structures and values of contemporary professional sport.

REFERENCES

Ahluwalia, P., & Miller, T. (2014). Greenwashing social identity. *Social Identities*, *20*(1), 1–4.

Armstrong, C. G., & Butryn, T. (2021). Educated activism: A focus group study of high school athletes' perceptions of athlete activism. In Rory Magrath (Ed.), *Athlete Activism* (pp. 20–31). New York: Routledge.

Armstrong, C. G., Butryn, T. M., Andrews, V. L., & Masucci, M. A. (2018). Athlete activism and corporate social responsibility: Critical lessons from sport industry professionals. *Sport Management Education Journal*, *12*(2), 110–113.

Ayo, N. (2012). Understanding health promotion in a neoliberal climate and the making of health-conscious citizens. *Critical Public Health*, *22*(1), 99–105.

Babiak, K., & Wolfe, R. (2013). Perspectives on social responsibility in sport. In J. L. Paramio-Salcines, K. Babiak, & G. Walters (Eds.), *Routledge handbook of sport and corporate social responsibility* (pp. 41–58). New York: Routledge.

Baccellieri, E. (2021, September 20). What can we learn from the WNBA's vaccination success? *Sports Illustrated*. https://www.si.com/wnba/2021/09/20/wnba-vaccination-99-percent-daily-cover

Bagley, B. H. (2020). Patient zero: Covid-19 and Rudy Gobert's reputational crisis. In P. M. Pedersen, B. J. Ruihley, & B. Li (Eds.), *Sport and the Pandemic* (pp. 264–269). New York: Routledge.

Bai, Y., Saint-Maurice, P. F., Welk, G. J., Allums-Featherston, K., Candelaria, N., & Anderson, K. (2015). Prevalence of youth fitness in the United States: baseline results from the NFL PLAY 60 FITNESSGRAM partnership project. *The Journal of Pediatrics*, *167*(3), 662–668.

Bai, Y., Saint-Maurice, P. F., Welk, G. J., Russell, D. W., Allums-Featherston, K., & Candelaria, N. (2017). The longitudinal impact of NFL PLAY 60 programming on youth aerobic capacity and BMI. *American Journal of Preventive Medicine*, *52*(3), 311–323.

Black Women's Health Imperative. (2021, August 16). Black Women's Health Imperative launches "Take The Shot for the WIN" vaccination awareness campaign with the Women's National Basketball Players Association and National Council of Negro Women, Inc." *PRNewswire*. https://www.prnewswire.com/news-releases/black-womens-health-imperative-launches-take-the-shot-for-the-win-vaccination-awareness-campaign-with-the-womens-national-basketball-players-association-and-national-council-of-negro-women-inc-301356151.html

Blingder, A., & Drape, J. (2021, March 6). When the clock stopped: The three days last March that changed sports. *New York Times*. https://www.nytimes.com/interactive/2021/03/06/sports/coronavirus-canceled-sports.html

Bolsen, T., & Palm, R. (2021). Politicization and COVID-19 vaccine resistance in the US. *Progress in Molecular Biology and Translational Science*, *188*, 81–100.

Brooks, K. (2021, February 9). More sport stadiums set to be used as Covid-19 vaccination sites. *CBS News*. https://www.cbsnews.com/news/covid-vaccine-sites-stadiums-arenas/

Butterworth, M. L. (2020). Sport and the quest for unity: How the logic of consensus undermines democratic culture. *Communication & Sport*, *8*(4–5), 452–472.

Cherry, M. A., & Sneirson, J. F. (2012). Chevron, Greenwashing, and the Myth of "Green Oil Companies." *Journal of Energy, Climate, and the Environment*, *3*, 133–154.

Chicago Blackhawks. (n.d.). *School programs*. https://www.nhl.com/blackhawks/community/school-programs

Cooky, C., & Antunovic, D. (2020). "This isn't just about us": Articulations of feminism in media narratives of athlete activism. *Communication & Sport*, *8*(4–5), 692–711.

Cooper, J. N., Macaulay, C., & Rodriguez, S. H. (2019). Race and resistance: A typology of African American sport activism. *International Review for the Sociology of Sport*, *54*(2), 151–181.

Ferguson, J. (2010). The uses of neoliberalism. *Antipode*, *41*, 166–184.

Giulianotti, R. (2015). Corporate social responsibility in sport: critical issues and future possibilities. *Corporate Governance*, *15*(2), 243–248.

Kaufman, P., & Wolff, E. A. (2010). Playing and protesting: Sport as a vehicle for social change. *Journal of Sport and Social Issues*, *34*(2), 154–175.

Kluch, Y. (2020). "My story is my activism!":(Re-)definitions of social justice activism among collegiate athlete activists. *Communication & Sport*, *8*(4–5), 566–590.

Kole, W. J. (2021, December 2). NBA All-Star Kevin Love honored for mental health advocacy. *Associated Press*. https://apnews.com/article/nba-kevin-love-mental-health-award-b0a4b324224d31023efc0bea16de3f1a

Lemire, J. (2019, January 15). MLB partners with Discovery Education on baseball-themed STEM. *SportTechie*. https://www.sporttechie.com/mlb-partners-with-discovery-education-on-baseball-themed-stem/

Loomba, S., de Figueiredo, A., Piatek, S. J., de Graaf, K., & Larson, H. J. (2021). Measuring the impact of COVID-19 vaccine misinformation on vaccination intent in the UK and USA. *Nature Human Behaviour*, *5*(3), 337–348.

Minnesota Wild (n.d.). *Wild about education*. https://www.nhl.com/wild/community/wild-about-education

Montez de Oca, J., Mason, S., & Ahn, S. (2020). Consuming for the greater good: "Woke" commercials in sports media. *Communication & Sport*, https://doi.org/10.1177/2167479520949283.

Montez de Oca, J., Meyer, B., & Scholes, J. (2016a). The children are our future: The NFL, corporate social responsibility, and the production of "avid fans." In M. A. Messner & M. Musto (Eds.), *Child's play: Sport in kids' worlds* (pp. 102–122). New Brunswick, NJ: Rutgers University Press.

Montez de Oca, J., Meyer, B., & Scholes, J. (2016b). Reaching the kids: NFL youth marketing and media. *Popular Communication*, *14*(1), 3–11.

Moraitis, M. (2021, July 27). Watch: Titans' Kevin Byard levels unsuspecting man in vaccine PSA. *USA Today*. https://titanswire.usatoday.com/2021/07/27/tennessee-titans-kevin-byard-covid-19-vaccine-psa/

Naczek, M. (2021, April 5). Milwaukee Brewers encourage vaccines with PSA and by getting vaccinated. *Milwaukee Business Journal*. https://www.bizjournals.com/milwaukee/news/2021/04/05/milwaukee-brewers-work-with-city-of-milwaukee-to-e.html

Nashville Predators (n.d.). *Preds fitness challenge*. https://www.nhl.com/predators/community/youthhockey/preds-fitness-challenge

NBA Cares. (2021, April 29). *NBA Players COVID-19 Vaccine PSA* [Video]. https://www.youtube.com/watch?v=kpraCK-_8Pw

Olusoga, D., & Olusoga, P. (2020, December 22). What Marcus Rashford's campaign for hungry children tells us about the footballer—and Britain. *The Guardian*. https://www.theguardian.com/lifeandstyle/2020/dec/22/what-marcus-rashfords-campaign-for-hungry-children-tells-us-about-the-footballer-and-britain

Paramio-Salcines, J. L., Babiak, K., & Walters, G. (2013). CSR within the sport industry. In J. L. Paramio-Salcines, K. Babiak, & G. Walters (Eds.), *Routledge handbook of sport and corporate social responsibility* (pp. 1–15). New York: Routledge.

Pedersen, Z. P., & Williams, A. S. (2020). The influence of sport on the public's recognition of a global pandemic: Time to get real. In P. M. Pederson, B. J. Ruihley, & B. Li (Eds.), *Sport and the Pandemic* (pp. 247–252). New York: Routledge.

Rugg, A. (2019). Working out their future: The NFL's Play 60 campaign and the production of adolescent fans and players. *Journal of Sport and Social Issues, 43*(1), 69–88.

Rugg, A. (2020a). For the good of the game: diffusing the dangers of football through the National Football League's "A Crucial Catch" campaign. *Critical Public Health, 30*(1), 79–90.

Rugg, A. (2020b). Incorporating the protests: The NFL, social justice, and the constrained activism of the "Inspire Change" campaign. *Communication & Sport, 8*(4–5), 611–628.

Saint-Maurice, P. F., Bai, Y., Welk, G. J., Bandelli, L. N., Allums-Featherston, K., & Candelaria, N. (2017). Impact of NFL PLAY 60 programming on elementary school children's body mass index and aerobic capacity: the NFL PLAY 60 FitnessGram partnership project. *Journal of School Health, 87*(11), 873–881.

San Jose Sharks. (n.d.). *School programs.* https://www.nhl.com/sharks/community/school-programs

Schmittel, A., & Sanderson, J. (2015). Talking about Trayvon in 140 characters: Exploring NFL players' tweets about the George Zimmerman verdict. *Journal of Sport and Social Issues, 39*(4), 332–345.

Schumaker, E. (2021, May 3). Unexpected places now offering Covid-19 vaccines. *ABC News.* https://abcnews.go.com/Health/creative-places-vaccinated-popping-country/story?id=77461117

Sharpe, S., Mountifield, C., & Filo, K. (2020). The social media response from athletes and sport organizations to COVID-19: An altruistic tone. *International Journal of Sport Communication, 13*(3), 474–483.

Smith, D. K., & Casper, J. (2020). Making an impact: An initial review of US sport league corporate social responsibility responses during COVID-19. *International Journal of Sport Communication, 13*(3), 335–343.

Snyder, M. (2021, June 4). Major League Baseball offers free tickets for COVID-19 vaccinations in "MLB Vaccinate at the Plate" initiative. *CBS Sports.* https://www.cbssports.com/mlb/news/top-item-on-every-mlb-teams-holiday-wish-list-hot-stove-signings-blockbuster-trades-extensions-more/

Sobande, F. (2020). "We're all in this together": Commodified notions of connection, care and community in brand responses to COVID-19. *European Journal of Cultural Studies, 23*(6), 1033–1037.

Stapleton, A. (2021, August 2). NFL Alumni, CDC fight COVID-19 vaccination hesitancy. *Associated Press.* https://apnews.com/article/sports-nfl-football-health-coronavirus-pandemic-d3a78a82eee06a94b569a472a718dfe1

Sturm, A., & Income, N. (2021, November 2). Nets, Liberty, and Gov. Hochul partner on new Covid-19 vaccine initiative. *Nets Daily.* https://www.netsdaily.com/2021/11/2/22760170/nets-liberty-and-gov-hochul-partner-on-new-covid-19-vaccine-initiative

Sweat, C. (2021, December 21). Convenience a priority at Dallas Mavericks COVID-19 testing, vaccine center. *NBC 5 Dallas Ft. Worth.* https://www.nbcdfw.com/news/local/convenience-a-priority-at-dallas-mavericks-covid-19-testing-vaccine-center/2843958/

Turman, J. (2021, March 5). Lebron James' More Than a Vote launches new campaign to defend voting rights. *CBS News.* https://www.cbsnews.com/news/lebron-james-more-than-a-vote-voting-rights/

Waddington, I., Challadurai, P., & Skirstad, B. (2013). CSR in sport: Who benefits? In J. L. Paramio-Salcines, K. Babiak, & G. Walters (Eds.), *Routledge handbook of sport and social corporate responsibility* (pp. 35–51). New York, NY: Routledge.

Welk, G. J., Bai, Y., Saint-Maurice, P. F., Allums-Featherston, K., & Candelaria, N. (2016). Design and evaluation of the NFL PLAY 60 FITNESSGRAM® Partnership Project. *Research Quarterly for Exercise and Sport*, *87*(1), 1–13.

Whelan, A. (2021, April 20). Flyers launch a vaccine campaign encouraging fans to "Take Your Shot." *The Philadelphia Inquirer.* https://www.inquirer.com/news/flyers-vaccine-campaign-covid-19-gritty-20210420.html.

Williams, A. L. (2021). The Heritage Strikes Back: Athlete Activism, Black Lives Matter, and the Iconic Fifth Wave of Activism in the (W)NBA Bubble. *Cultural Studies ↔ Critical Methodologies*. Advance online publication. https://doi.org/10.1177/15327086211049718

Chapter Five

Parent and Child Communication and Health Risks in Sport

Joseph McGlynn

Sport is a distinct context in which to analyze parent and child communication (Dorsch et al., 2015). Youth sports represent one of the most common activities for children (Billings & Butterworth, 2022), making it an "omnipresent component of society" (Cranmer, 2021, p. 71). Sports and physical activity offer important developmental tools for children's health (Dunn et al., 2003), with more than 70 percent of children between the ages of 6 and 12 playing an individual or team sport (Solomon, 2019). The importance of family interactions in sport settings is an emergent research topic (Cranmer, 2021), as sport experiences affect family dynamics, parent-child communication satisfaction, and the quality of parent-child relationships.

Family communication shapes youth sport experiences. Children often mirror parents' sport attitudes (Dixon et al., 2008), particularly at young ages (Fredericks & Eccles, 2005). Parents affect children's sport participation decisions (Boneau et al., 2020) and act as gatekeepers for children's sport participation (Register-Mihalik et al., 2017). Examining parent-child communication, social influences, and key factors that affect parent decisions for sport participation provides insight to children's sport attitudes, socialization processes, and associated health outcomes.

Accentuating athlete health in youth sports is a priority aspiration for parents and children, but parents and youth athletes conceptualize health in varied ways. Some parents emphasize physical health development for their children, while other parents prioritize their child's health in terms of social and emotional development. Parents indicate sport participation provides opportunities for children to develop physically, cognitively, and emotionally (McGlynn et al., 2020). However, some parents and youth athletes may be focused more on obtaining a college scholarship (Ahlquist et al., 2020), indicating a prioritization of financial well-being, sometimes at the risk of the athlete's long-term health. While most research focuses on physical health outcomes for youth athletes, communication research has the potential to provide an "interactionalist perspective" to sport settings (Cranmer, 2021, p. 71), emphasizing how the dynamics and structure of family environments influence children's health outcomes in sport contexts.

PARENT MOTIVATIONS FOR YOUTH SPORT PARTICIPATION

Many parents view sport participation as an integral bridge from youth to adulthood. Sport teaches lessons and instills values, such as fairness, effort, toughness, and persistence (Kremer-Sadlik & Kim, 2007), and parents promote participation as an instrument for developing character, work ethic, and enjoyment of group activities (Starcher, 2015). Instilling cultural values remains a driver of parents' enrollment decisions, as parents associate sport activity with the development of self-esteem, teamwork, and shared commitment to a goal (Dunn et al., 2003). Cognitive and social benefits also motivate sport participation, including persistence, discipline, camaraderie, and being part of a group collective (McGlynn et al., 2020). Sports present opportunities for children to learn societal values and life skills (Turman, 2007). In these ways, sport participation acts as a conduit for socialization into a larger social world (Dailey et al., 2020).

Family dynamics and social influences affect parent motivations for sport decisions. Parental history of sport participation influences youth behavior, often functioning as a cue for the child wanting to play (Dixon et al., 2008). Similarly, family identity shapes parents' tolerance and encouragement for children to participate in risky sports, such as tackle football (Boneau et al., 2020). Social influences, including community norms and media narratives, inform parents' understanding of risk-benefit tradeoffs. Specifically, exposure to information from topic experts (e.g., doctors, coaches) or influential voices (e.g., media) affect parent perceptions of risk and benefit (Boneau et al., 2020). When community members and peers express support for participation in risky sports, parents may experience reduced control over their child's participation (McGlynn et al., 2020).

PARENT-CHILD COMMUNICATION AND THE DECISION TO PLAY RISKY SPORTS

Parent-child communication influences children's health and risk decisions (Riesch et al., 2006). Effective parent-child communication reduces children's risk exposure, affects their emotional reactions to risk (e.g., academic challenges, reduced self-esteem), and promotes family discussion about children's involvement in risky activities (Riesch et al., 2006). As children often mirror parents' attitudes toward sports (Dixon et al., 2008), examining parents' attitudes toward sport risks provides awareness of factors that affect youth athlete health.

Parents do not always illustrate rational approaches to sport risks. Social norms and community influences affect parent risk decisions (Fontana et al., 2021; Murphy et al., 2017), as do cultural norms and socioeconomic status (Cassilo & Sanderson, 2018). Social comparisons to other athletes can affect parental risk judgments (McGlynn et al., 2022), indicating the relative nature of parents' risk assessments. If their child seems less at-risk for injury than other children playing the game, parents may adopt an overly optimistic attitude toward the risks inherent to playing contact sports. Furthermore, imprecise factors affect athlete health outcomes, making injury risks for parents and youth athletes difficult to quantify. Factors that influence youth injury outcomes include the timing of the injury, injury severity, whether the injury is repetitive or acute, proper or improper management of the injury, and the length of recovery time required to heal. Concussions, in particular, may be difficult to diagnose and manage for parents or other non-medical professionals (Mannings et al., 2014).

THE INFLUENCE OF PARENT-CHILD COMMUNICATION ON YOUTH SPORT HEALTH OUTCOMES

Parent-child communication affects children's youth sport experience, satisfaction, and likelihood of continuing to play. Children's sport enjoyment and self-esteem can be altered by parents' involvement (Bowker, 2006), and parent feedback on sport performance affects athletes' self-esteem (Smith & Smoll, 2002). Parental interpretations of sport experiences are a leading influence on children's sport socialization experience (Dixon et al., 2008). Cultural conversations surrounding athlete health have begun to include broader social constructs of parental consent, socioeconomic status, and the prioritization of athlete health (Cassilo & Sanderson, 2018). As parent-child communication patterns are pliable (Riesch et al., 2006), they present a worthy focus of interventions designed to reduce children's risk.

In sport settings, a primary health concern for parents is the risk of concussions, or traumatic brain injuries that occur from hits to the head or brain area. Parents show general awareness of the possibility of sport-related concussion risks for youth athletes (Rieger et al., 2018). Attitudes toward the perceived benefit of sport participation predict parents' likelihood of talking with their children about concussion risks (Fontana et al., 2021). Narratives of injury risks from relevant sources (e.g., players, media, coaches) can induce negative emotions from parents and motivate intentions to seek additional information and to discuss sport risks with their children (Tallapragada & Cranmer, 2020). Understanding parent communication regarding concussions is important for reducing the likelihood of athletes' willingness to play through concussion symptoms, a high-risk health behavior (Kroshus et al., 2019).

Parent-child communication affects the likelihood of children reporting concussion symptoms (Kroshus et al., 2019). Communication factors that increase the odds of a child reporting concussion symptoms during sport play include parents placing less pressure on children's athletic achievements and spending more time discussing concussions as a family (Kroshus et al., 2019). Perceived behavioral control (i.e., self-efficacy) is not a predictor of parental intention to discuss concussions (Fontana et al., 2021), indicating most parents feel able to talk to their children about concussion risks, if they are motivated to do so. However, athletes are less likely to report a concussion when they do not recognize the symptoms as concussion related (Zanin et al., 2020), showing the importance of parents talking to children about concussions and injury risks, so that the child clearly identifies and recognizes the symptoms of concussions and other injury risks in sport settings.

CHALLENGES RELATED TO PARENT AND CHILD COMMUNICATION AND HEALTH RISKS IN SPORT

Parents encounter challenges when contemplating youth sport participation for their children, including barriers to effective communication, biases that affect parental decisions, double-bind risks of participation and safety, social pressures for children to play through injury, and the debate of whether children should specialize in a single sport.

Communication Barriers

Effective parent-child communication can deter children from engaging in risky behaviors (Riesch et al., 2006). However, parents face hurdles in discussing sport-related injury risks with their children. For example, the child could consider their parents to be overly concerned if they broach the subject of possible injuries, or the child may not trust their parents' medical opinion regarding injury management. Furthermore, not all parents and children have a cohesive relationship that facilitates constructive conversation. The existence of family conflict, or parent-child conflict, can diminish the effectiveness of parents' guidance on sport risks. Communication processes associated with reduced risk behavior by children include satisfaction with family dynamics, open expression of feelings, and the ability for parents and children to manage conflict constructively (Riesch et al., 2006).

Parent uncertainty regarding injury risks can negatively impact child health outcomes. Parents may be uncertain in their role toward managing sport injuries, instead leaving it to coaches and trainers to make judgment decisions on the athlete's suitability to continue playing. Some parents prefer to stay out of children's sport decisions, illustrating a laissez-faire parenting approach to their child's participation (Boneau et al., 2020). A hands-off approach may yield benefits across the landscape of childhood development but invites concern regarding the potential effects of injury on children's physical and social development. For example, in one study of youth football athletes (ages 10–14), nearly 25% of parents had never talked to their children about concussion risks, and more than 50% had not discussed concussion risks with their child within the past year (Kroshus et al., 2019). Consistent messages from parents are vital for improving child health outcomes and successful injury management.

Parental Biases

Parental biases affect sport risk decisions. Although many analyses assume that parents take a rational approach to risk and health decisions (Murphy et al., 2017), parents and families illustrate cognitive biases that can affect judgments of sport-injury likelihood (McGlynn et al., 2022). For example, parents may show unquestioned trust in technology advances, equipment upgrades, and updated tackling policies as adequate protection against head injuries. However, advances in helmet technology cannot eliminate brain injuries (Carman et al., 2015) and improved return-to-play guidelines cannot fully protect players from head injuries (Johnson, 2012). In addition, parents' concern for concussion risks tends to focus on the large hits sustained by children, such as when children are knocked out or feel dizzy immediately following an impact. However, many brain injuries stem from the result of repeated small hits over time (Tagge et al., 2018). Improving parent understanding of the techniques and strategies that effectively reduce risk, and not just the perception of risk, remains vital for improving youth athlete health outcomes.

PARENTAL DOUBLE-BIND OF YOUTH HEALTH AND DEVELOPMENT

Parents face a double-bind situation with regard to children's health and development. On one hand, children need experience to develop proper risk awareness. Children can benefit from risk exposure at an early age, as it helps them build desired qualities, such as resilience (Barry, 2018). However, sports include an inherent risk component, as activity can lead to injuries resulting in missed time at school or other events. Furthermore, if parents disallow sport participation, they may engage social risks via lack of social interactions and missed development opportunities for their child (McGlynn et al., 2020). Although sport participation introduces risk to children's health, choosing not to play sports also can impede development, as well as children's ability to adapt to risky situations in the future.

Parents must also satisfy competing demands with regard to their child's sport participation. They need to support and encourage children in an effort to promote continued sport participation (Turman, 2007), while concurrently guiding and managing risk (Merkel, 2013). If a child voices displeasure with continuing to play a sport, parents could feel obligated to instill values of commitment and stress the obligation the child has to the team (Turman, 2007). For more dangerous sports, such as tackle football, parents may need to adjust their own expectations of "sticking with it." If a child feels unsafe or uncomfortable in the physically demanding setting, that hesitancy may warrant the child opting out of the remainder of the game or season. Children must continue to participate to garner the benefits of sport activity, but parents retain the obligation to weigh the positive and negative health effects of inactivity versus sport engagement.

PRESSURE TO PLAY THROUGH INJURY

A prominent health risk that children face in sports is the pressure to continue playing through injury. Athletes frequently encounter pressure to play through pain (Register-Mihalik et al., 2017), due in part to societal norms of hegemonic masculinity and toughness (Sabo, 2004). Athletes may not report injuries or concussion symptoms for many reasons, including cultural norms, perceived lack of severity, and fear of letting their teammates down (Sanderson et al., 2017). Athletes experience pressure to play through head injuries from coaches, teammates, fans, and parents, with more than 25% of athletes reporting they received pressure to continue playing from at least one source (Kroshus et al., 2015). When an athlete reports receiving pressure from multiple sources (e.g., both coaches and parents), they are particularly likely to express their intention to play through a head injury in the future (Kroshus et al., 2015).

Parents' desire for their children to have athletic success can impair risk judgments and place increased pressure for the child to continue playing through injury. Parents' attitudes toward risk-taking and toughness are associated with children's increased likelihood of playing through concussion symptoms (Kroshus et al., 2018). Some parents express "serious concern" that their child will lose playing time due to concussion injuries (Rieger et al., 2018), indicating the multiple considerations that parents consider when making health judgments for their children in sport settings. This desire to play through injury may also stem from family members wanting to justify the financial investment put forth for sport activities, as many sport parents illustrate a return-on-investment mindset (Hyman, 2012).

The rising cost of youth sport participation can place increased pressure on athletes to play through injury (Hyman, 2012). Families spend an average of $693 annually per child for one sport (The Aspen Institute, 2019). Among sports, the least expensive investment is track and field ($191) and the most expensive is ice hockey ($2,583). When parents incur additional expenses, such as camps, private coaching, or upgraded equipment, costs can exceed tens of thousands of dollars per year devoted to their child's sport participation (Hyman, 2012). Parental investment in sports places an inherent pressure on children's continued participation (Kroshus et al., 2018).

THREADING THE NEEDLE ON PARENTAL INVOLVEMENT AND CONTINUED YOUTH SPORT PARTICIPATION

Parent involvement in youth sports can be a boon or a detriment to children's enjoyment, development, and satisfaction (Weiss & Fretwell, 2013). Supportive parent communication enhances children's likelihood of continuing to play, but destructive parent communication can lead to burnout. Children who were coached by their fathers identified praise, quality time, and insider information as benefits of active parental involvement. However, children coached by their fathers also noted negative effects, including increased pressure, expectations, conflict, and criticism (Weiss & Fretwell, 2013). Over-involvement from sport parents remains a concern (Turman, 2007), as parental participation as the coach or as the "soccer mom" or "soccer dad" for their child's team can detract from children's enjoyment of the sport.

Understanding communication behaviors that lead to child burnout remains integral for continued youth sport participation (Cranmer, 2021). Factors that impede youth athletes' continued participation include intrapersonal constraints (e.g., lack of enjoyment, low self-perceptions of physical ability, negative feelings toward the coach), interpersonal constraints (e.g., parental pressure, not enough time to pursue other interests), and structural constraints (e.g., inadequate facilities, equipment, injuries, or prohibitive costs) (Witt & Dangi, 2018). Reduced enjoyment and fun leads to youth athlete dropout, with lack of enjoyment the number one reason children halt sport participation (Gardner et al., 2017).

While parent-child bonding over sport accomplishments can be beneficial for their relationship, parasitic parental associations with children's sport achievements can cause harm by increasing stress or pressure on the child to continue. Parents may seek to associate themselves with their child's athletic achievements, a behavior described as "reflected glory" (Cialdini, 2009, p. 169). This dynamic can become problematic when parents indicate frustration with athletic failures, or if children feel burdened to succeed to deter negative emotional outbursts from family members. Parents also sometimes communicate conflicting messages to their children (Smoll et al., 2011). For example, in anticipation of an important game, parents may communicate the child's need to perform at a high level, superseding messages of sports as a vehicle for enjoyment or developing a strong work ethic. This effect may be heightened in communities that emphatically support youth athletes, such as small towns in Texas famous for promoting football participation (Conine, 2016).

Sport Specialization

Parents face a conundrum with regard to youth athletes' sport specialization. Specialization represents the focus of youth athletes on one particular sport. Sport specialization for youth athletes is on the rise (Ahlquist et al., 2020), but the effects of early sport specialization (i.e., prior to age 14) are mixed. Athletes who specialize in their eventual varsity sport prior to age 14 are more likely to be recruited by colleges (92.9% vs. 82.1%) and receive scholarship offers (82.8% vs. 67.9%). However, they also are more likely to report an injury history, multiple injuries incurred, and more time missed due to injury, factors which can affect the child's health and development.

The amount of time athletes spend training for their specialized sport influences injury likelihood. Sport specialization and year-round participation are associated with overuse injuries (Post et al., 2017). Athletes who spent more than 28 hours per week training were significantly more likely to report multiple injuries (90.0% vs. 56.3%), including sustaining injuries that required surgery (30.0% vs. 4.7%). Perhaps because of increased time missed due to injuries, athletes who spent more than 28 hours a week training were not significantly more likely to be recruited (90.0% vs. 89.8%) or receive a scholarship (80.0% vs. 74.5%) (Ahlquist et al., 2020), indicating a lack of reward for the increased injury potential associated with overtraining.

Despite the increased injury potential, parents and athletes may determine the benefits of specialization are worth the risk. Importantly, youth athletes themselves believe early specialization improves their chances of making high school varsity squads and receiving a college scholarship (Brooks et al., 2018). This belief may create a "disturbing cycle" for youth sports, increasing competition levels and the pressure for athletes to specialize and compete year-round (Brooks et al., p. 5). Male athletes show lower concerns for injuries compared to female athletes, while female athletes express higher belief that specialization can lead to overuse injuries (Post et al., 2017). Female high school athletes are also more likely to specialize and compete year-round compared to male athletes (Post et al., 2017). In one study, approximately half of female athletes noted concern for overuse injuries due to year-round training, but the vast majority regarded specialization as a positive influence on their sport performance (Brooks et al., 2018). Questions remain for youth athletes on the ideal mix between activity, rest, specialization, and diversity of training regimens.

DIRECTIONS FOR FUTURE RESEARCH EFFORTS

Despite a growing body of literature at the intersection of health, sport, and parent-child communication, many avenues remain for researchers to pursue. Productive possibilities for research include an emphasis on family dynamics and children's perspectives, parent-child interactions, the influence of parent-child communication on continued sport involvement, identifying strategies for improved sport risk health communication, and expanding the focus of parent-child sport research contexts to include more diverse perspectives.

Family Dynamics and Children's Perspectives

Future work would benefit from an increased emphasis on dyadic investigations, where both parent perspectives and child perspectives receive attention from researchers. For practical and logistic reasons, children's direct input is less common than parental perceptions of children's attitudes toward sport and risk. Although children's perspectives often emulate those of their parents (Dixon et al. 2008), current knowledge could be supplemented with a specific focus on child perspectives toward health risks. Scant work has focused on children's own dispositions, competitive mindset, and desires as factors that affect playing through injury. Future research should seek to actively consider children's attitudes, personalities, and temperament as factors that determine their likelihood to play through injury. Understanding the factors that influence youth athletes' perceptions of sport risks will be critical for shedding light on important athlete health considerations, including perspectives toward head injuries, concussion reporting, overuse injuries (e.g., shoulder injuries in volleyball, arm injuries in baseball), and the risks of potentially chronic issues that affect athletes later in life, such as tendinitis or arthritis that result from overuse or acute trauma.

Parent-Child Communication Interactions

A dearth of research focuses on parent-child communication interactions in relation to sport. Examination of the specific messages that influence child and parent perceptions of sport risk would assist health communication research efforts (Cranmer, 2021). Understanding the particular parent behaviors that affect youth athletes' desire and decision to continue playing sports is also of continued interest (Turman, 2007). Additional work is needed on specific parent disclosures and effective communication strategies for reducing child injuries (Kroshus et al., 2019). Furthermore, considering parent-child communication in relation to the values of the community where they live can help both researchers and families to identify local and macro forces that affect children's sport experience.

Parent Communication and Children's Continued Sport Involvement

Parents try to gain compliance from their child in a variety of settings, such as getting dressed for school, leaving on time for appointments, or eating their vegetables. Understanding the compliance-gaining techniques that parents employ that successfully influence child compliance in sport contexts is a needed research area. Common compliance-gaining techniques from sport parents include the activation of impersonal commitments ("The whole family will be disappointed if you quit the team"), the development of expertise ("If you continue to participate you will then learn the value of discipline for later life experiences"), the offer of rewards (e.g., increased allowance for continued participation), or the enactment of punishments (e.g., losing privileges, such as the opportunity to drive the family car) (Turman, 2007). The activation of these techniques is common, but research is needed to assess the relative effectiveness of these compliance-gaining techniques in sport settings, as well as their persuasive effects on children's sport enjoyment and likelihood of continued participation.

Differences in the use of compliance-gaining techniques between mothers and fathers is also ripe for examination. In one study (Turman, 2007), fathers were more likely to activate impersonal commitments and to offer rewards than female parents or guardians. Focusing on how mothers and fathers differ in their communication behaviors and compliance-gaining approaches will yield insights into the effects of specific techniques on children's continued sport enjoyment and participation. In addition, examining how mothers and fathers differ in their support or encouragement for risky sport behaviors, and their communication behaviors to achieve those goals, remains a topic of research interest.

Strategic Messaging for Sport Health Risks

Opportunities remain to improve the effectiveness of strategic messaging in the context of sport and health. Health messages designed to promote sport safety and encourage parents to take precautions for their children can augment youth safety and promote long-term health outcomes associated with youth sport participation. For example, brain health advocates have used social media to raise awareness of the dangers of head trauma in football (Hull & Schmittel, 2015). However, more research is needed to identify specific message features and message frames that affect parents' risk perceptions.

Prior studies identified factors that influence parent perceptions of sport safety, including elements such as perceived risk severity, social norms, and benefits of participation (McGlynn et al., 2020; Murphy et al., 2017). However, these studies do not delineate the relative influence of the identified factors on parent risk assessments. Future research should seek to examine the proportional influence of each element on parental perceptions of risky sports. For example, a quantitative model that tests the influence of trust in coaches, safe positions on the field, and advances in equipment technology on parents' willingness to endorse participation for youth tackle football. Building more precise models that examine the relative influence of factors that decrease perceptions of sport risk will enable more effective health messaging efforts designed to raise awareness of important sport health issues (e.g., concussions, sport specialization risks), as well as informing educational efforts and improving communication between health professionals and sport parents.

Expanding the Contexts of Parent-Child Communication and Health Risk Research

Within research examining parent-child communication in relation to sports and health, youth tackle football has been an area of primary focus, in part due to prominent media attention on football-related concussions and the negative effects of head injuries on athlete well-being. While this emphasis is reasonable, it creates a natural overfocus of research on male athletes, as football is a sport dominated by male participants. Future research on sport health, concussions, risks, and youth safety should expand its focus to include co-ed sports (e.g., soccer) and female-dominated sports, such as field hockey. The expansion of research to include more sport contexts and diverse participants will provide a nuanced understanding of the effects of gender expectations, hegemonic masculinity, and social norms on athlete health.

Research is needed to understand how the use of statistics to measure youth athlete performance (e.g., player data on batting, pitching, and fielding efficacy) affects not only injury risk management (Sanderson & Baerg, 2020) but also player enjoyment and social development. An overt focus on statistical analysis of player performance at a young age may discourage players with slower physical development from continuing to stay involved in the sport and to work on their game. Furthermore, quantified performance indicators contain bias in the way player statistics are measured. An overt focus on statistics at the youth level could cause players' coaches to fail to acknowledge relevant sport attitudes and mental attributes that contribute to success (e.g., competitive attitude, winning mindset) and are necessary for athletes to develop their full on-field and off-field potential.

The influence of parent and child demographics (e.g., ethnicity, socioeconomic factors, or family structure such as single-parent household, married, or divorced) may affect youth sport participation (Cranmer, 2021), child sport satisfaction, or parents' ability to influence the child to consider health risks associated with sport involvement. Although research has identified individual-level factors that affect athletes' reporting of injuries, it is important to go beyond individual characteristics to recognize system-level factors that affect athlete injury reporting and sport experience, such as the influence of parents, coaches, and teammates (Kroshus et al., 2015).

The field of sport, health, and risk communication has garnered increased attention in recent years, yet ample opportunities remain for future research to investigate critical issues related to parent-child communication and health risks in sport.

REFERENCES

Ahlquist, S., Cash, B. M., & Hame, S. L. (2020). Associations of early sport specialization and high training volume with injury rates in National Collegiate Athletic Association Division I athletes. *Orthopedic Journal of Sports Medicine, 8*(3), 1–10. https://doi.org/10.1177/2325967120906825

Barry, E. (2018, March 10). In Britain's playgrounds, "bringing in risk" to build resilience. *The New York Times.* https://www.nytimes.com/2018/03/10/world/europe/britain-playgrounds-risk.html

Billings, A. C., & Butterworth, M. L. (2022). *Communication and sport: Surveying the field* (4th ed.). Thousands Oaks, CA: SAGE.

Boneau, R. D., Richardson, B. K., & McGlynn, J. (2020). "We are a football family": Making sense of parents' decisions to allow their children to play tackle football. *Communication and Sport, 8*(1), 26–49. https://doi.org/10.1177/2167479518816104

Bowker, S. E. (2006). The relationship between sports participation and self-esteem during early adolescence. *Canadian Journal of Behavioural Science, 38*, 214–229. https://psycnet.apa.org/doi/10.1037/cjbs2006009

Brooks, A., Post, E. G., Trigsted, S. M., Schaefer, D. A., Wichman, D. M., Watson, A. M., McGuine, T. A., & Bell, D. R. (2018). Knowledge, attitudes, and beliefs of youth club athletes toward specialization and sport participation. *The Orthopaedic Journal of Sports Medicine, 6*(5), 1–8. https://doi.org/10.1177/2325967118769836

Carman, A. J., Ferguson, R., Cantu, R., Comstock, R. D., Dacks, P. A., DeKosky, S. T., . . . Fillit, H. M. (2015). Mind the gaps: Advancing research into short-term and long-term neuropsychological outcomes of youth sports-related concussions. *Nature Reviews Neurology, 11*, 230–244. https://doi.org/10.1038/nrneurol.2015.30

Cassilo, D., & Sanderson, J. (2018). "I don't think it's worth the risk": Media framing of the Chris Borland retirement in digital and print media. *Communication & Sport, 6*(1), 86–110. https://doi.org/10.1177/2167479516654513

Cialdini, R. (2009). *Influence: Science and practice*. Boston: Pearson.

Conine, C. S. (2016). *The republic of football: Legends of the Texas high school game*. Austin: University of Texas Press.

Cranmer, G. A. (2021). Setting the agenda: A playbook for tackling family communication in sport. *Journal of Family Communication, 21*(1), 70–75. https://doi.org/10.1080/15267431.2020.1856852

Dailey, S. L., Alabere, R. O., Michalski, J. E., & Brown, C. I. (2020). Sports experiences as anticipatory socialization: How does communication in sports help individuals with intellectual disabilities learn about and adapt to work? *Communication Quarterly, 68*(5), 499–519. https://doi.org/10.1080/01463373.2020.1821737

Dixon, M. A., Warner, S. M., & Bruening, J. E. (2008). More than just letting them play: Parental influence on women's lifetime sport involvement. *Sociology of Sport Journal, 25*(4), 538–559. http://dx.doi.org/10.1123/ssj.25.4.538

Dorsch, T. E., Smith, A. L., Wilson, S. R., & McDonough, M. H. (2015). Parent goals and verbal sideline behavior in organized youth sport. *Sport, Exercise, and Performance Psychology, 4*(1), 19–35. https://doi.org/10.1037/spy0000025

Dunn, J. S., Kinney, D. A., & Hofferth, S. L. (2003). Parental ideologies and children's after-school activities. *American Behavioral Scientist, 46*(10), 1359–1386. https://doi.org/10.1177/0002764203046010006

Fontana, J., Cranmer, G. A., Ash, E., Mazer, J. P., & Denham, B. E. (2021). Parent-child communication regarding sport-related concussion: An application of the theory of planned behavior. *Health Communication.* Advance online publication. https://doi.org/10.1080/10410236.2021.1876326

Fredericks, J. A., & Eccles, J. S. (2005). Family socialization, gender, and sport motivation and involvement. *Journal of Sport & Exercise Psychology, 27*(1), 3–31. https://doi.org/10.1123/JSEP.27.1.3

Hull, K., & Schmittel, A. (2015). A fumbled opportunity? A case study of Twitter's role in concussion awareness opportunities during the Super Bowl. *Journal of Sport and Social Issues, 39*(1), 78–94. https://doi.org/10.1177/0193723514558928

Hyman, M. (2012). *The most expensive game in town: The rising cost of youth sports and the toll on today's families.* Boston: Beacon Press.

Gardner, L. A., Magee, C. A., & Vella, S. A. (2017). Enjoyment and behavioral intention predict organized youth sport participation and dropout. *Journal of Physical Activity and Health, 14*(11), 861–865. https://doi.org/10.1123/jpah.2016-0572

Johnson, L. S. M. (2012). Return to play guidelines cannot solve the football-related concussion problem. *Journal of School Health, 82*(4), 180–185. https://doi.org/10.1111/j.1746-1561.2011.00684.x

Kremer-Sadlik, T., & Kim, J. L. (2007). Lessons from sports: Children's socialization to values through family interaction during sports activities. *Discourse & Society, 18*, 35–52.

Kroshus, E., Babkes Stellino, M., Chrisman, S. P. D., & Rivara, F. P. (2018). Threat, pressure, and communication about concussion safety: Implications for parent concussion education. *Health Education and Behavior, 45*(2), 254–261. https://doi.org/10.1177/1090198117715669

Kroshus, E, Garnett, B., Hawrilenko, M., Baugh, C. M., & Calzo, J. P. (2015). Concussion under-reporting and pressure from coaches, teammates, fans, and parents. *Social Science & Medicine, 134,* 66–75. https://dx.doi.org/10.1016%2Fj.socscimed.2015.04.011

Kroshus, E., Hoopes, T., Bernstein, E., Chrisman, S. P. D., & Rivara, F. P. (2019). Direct verbal communication by parents, pressure related to sport achievement, and concussion safety in youth football. *Journal of Health Communication, 24*(10), 770–779. https://doi.org/10.1080/10810730.2019.1668512

Mannings, C., Kalynych, C., Joseph, M. M., Smotherman, C., & Kraemer, D. F. (2014). Knowledge assessment of sports-related concussion among parents of children aged 5 years to 15 years enrolled in recreational tackle football. *The Journal of Trauma and Acute Care Surgery, 77,* S18–S22. https://doi.org/10.1097/TA.0000000000000371

McGlynn, J., Boneau, R. D., & Richardson, B. K. (2020). "It might also be good for your brain": Cognitive and social benefits that motivate parents to permit youth tackle football. *Journal of Sport and Social Issues, 44*(3), 261–282. https://doi.org/10.1177/0193723520903226

McGlynn, J., Richardson, B. K., & Boneau, R. D. (2022). Factors that reduce parental concern for concussion risks in youth tackle football. Manuscript submitted for publication.

Merkel, D. L. (2013). Youth sport: Positive and negative impact on young athletes. *Open Access Journal of Sports Medicine, 4*, 151–160. https://dx.doi.org/10.2147%2FOAJSM.S33556

Murphy, A. M., Askew, K. L., & Sumner, K. E. (2017). Parents' intentions to allow youth football participation: Perceived concussion risk and the theory of planned behavior. *Sport, Exercise, & Performance Psychology, 6*(3), 230–242. https://psycnet.apa.org/doi/10.1037/spy0000102

Post, E. G., Trigsted, S. M., Riekena, J. W., Hetzel, S., McGuine, T. A., Brooks, M. A., & Bell, D. R. (2017). The association of sport specialization and training volume with injury history in youth athletes. *American Journal of Sports Medicine, 45*(6), 1405–1412. https://doi.org/10.1177/0363546517690848

Register-Mihalik, J. K., Volovich McLeod, T. C., Linnan, L. A., Guskiewicz, K. M., & Marshall, S. W. (2017). Relationship between concussion history and concussion knowledge, attitudes, and disclosure behavior in high school athletes. *Clinical Journal of Sport Medicine, 27*(3), 321–324. https://doi.org/10.1097/JSM.0000000000000349

Rieger, B., Lewandowski, L., Potts, H., Potter, K., & Chin, L. S. (2018). Parent knowledge and perceptions of concussion related to football. *Cureus, 10*(3), e2268. https://doi.org/10.7759/cureus.2268

Riesch, S. K., Anderson, L. S., & Krueger, H. A. (2006). Parent-child communication processes: Preventing children's health-risk behavior. *Journal for Specialists in Pediatric Nursing, 11*(1), 41–56. https://doi.org/10.1111/j.1744-6155.2006.00042.x

Sabo, D. (2004). The politics of sports injury: Hierarchy, power, and the pain principle. In K. Young (Ed.), *Sporting bodies, damaged selves: Sociological studies of sports-related injuries* (pp. 59–79). Amsterdam: Elsevier.

Sanderson, J., & Baerg. A. (2020). Youth baseball and data analytics: Quantifying risk management and producing neoliberal responsible citizenship through the GameChanger app. *Communication and Sport, 8*(1), 72–91. https://doi.org/10.1177/2167479518818185

Sanderson, J., Weathers, M., Snedaker, K., & Gramlich, K. (2017). "I was able to still do my job on the field and keep playing": An investigation of female and male athletes' experiences with (not) reporting concussions. *Communication & Sport, 5*(3), 267–287. https://doi.org/10.1177%2F2167479515623455

Smith, R. E., & Smoll, F. L. (2002). Youth sports as a behavior setting for psychosocial interventions. In J. L. Van Raalte & B. W. Brewer (Eds.), *Exploring sport and exercise psychology* (pp. 341–371). Washington, DC: American Psychological Association.

Smoll, F. L., Cumming, S. P., & Smith, R. E. (2011). Enhancing coach-parent relationships in youth sports: Increasing harmony and minimizing hassle. *International Journal of Sports Science and Coaching, 6*(1), 13–26. https://doi.org/10.1260/1747-9541.6.1.13

Solomon, J. (2019, September 4). Staying in the game: Challenges in youth sports. *Aspen Institute*. https://www.aspeninstitute.org/blog-posts/staying-in-the-game-progress-and-challenges-in-youth-sports/.

Starcher, S. C. (2015). Memorable messages from fathers to children through sports: Perspectives from sons and daughters. *Communication Quarterly, 63*(2), 204–220. https://doi.org/10.1080/01463373.2015.1012221

Tagge, C. A., Fisher, A. M., Manaeva, O. V., Gaudreau-Balderrama, A., Moncaster, J. A., Zhang, X., . . . Goldstein, L. E. (2018). Concussion, microvascular injury, and early tauopathy in young athletes after impact head injury and an impact concussion mouse model. *Brain, 141*(2), 422–458. https://doi.org/10.1093/brain/awx350

Tallapragada, M., & Cranmer, G. A. (2020). Media narratives about concussions: Effects on parents' intention to inform their children about concussions. *Communication & Sport*. Advance online publication. https://doi.org/10.1177/2167479520944549

The Aspen Institute. (2019). State of play: Trends and developments in youth sports. https://www.aspeninstitute.org/wp-content/uploads/2019/10/2019_SOP_National_Final.pdf

Turman, P. D. (2007). Parental sport involvement: Parental influence to encourage young athlete continued sport participation. *Journal of Family Communication, 7*(3), 151–175. https://doi.org/10.1080/15267430701221602

Weiss, M., & Fretwell, S. D. (2013). The parent-coach/child-athlete relationship in youth sport. *Research Quarterly for Exercise and Sport, 76*(3), 286–305. https://doi.org/10.1080/02701367.2005.10599300

Witt, A. P., & Dangi, B. T. (2018). Why children/youth drop out of sports. *Journal of Park and Recreation Administration, 36*(3), 191–199. https://doi.org/10.18666/JPRA-2018-V36-I3-8618

Zanin, A. C., Kamrath, J. K., Ruston, S. W., Posteher, K. A., & Corman, S. R. (2020). Labeling avoidance in healthcare decision-making: How stakeholders make sense of concussion events through sport narratives. *Health Communication, 35*(8), 935–945. https://doi.org/10.1080/10410236.2019.1598742

Chapter Six

Coach-Athlete Communication and Implications for Health

Gregory A. Cranmer, Rikishi T. Rey, and Sai Datta Mikkilineni

Sport participation is a significant context of health communication, as it is both a means of maintaining health (e.g., weight management, mental and social well-being) and a source of potential health risks (e.g., injury). The physical nature of sport (Guttman, 1978) ensures that health-related issues will always be present within the context of sport, as it requires physical strain and effort, often against the efforts of others, to accomplish tasks and objectives. Additionally, the competitive and technical aspects of sport participation can be cognitively taxing, and its cultural structures at elite levels have been associated with a host of detrimental health behaviors (e.g., substance use, risky sexual behavior, and violence) (Murray et al., 2021). Moreover, Hyman (2009) has highlighted numerous concerning trends in modern youth and adolescent sport, including the public health crisis of concussion, commonality of overuse injuries, and sporting climates that are psychologically damaging to athletes. Given that most athletes are youth or adolescents who are under the supervision of various adults in positions of authority (e.g., parents, coaches, administrators, or doctors), a proper understanding of health issues in sport requires a focus on how these stakeholders come to influence sporting environments.

Perhaps no stakeholder has as much influence on athletes' interactions within sport and their health-related experiences as coaches. Coaches facilitate the enactment of sport through their transmissions of sporting knowledge, organization of team environments, decisions regarding aspects of performance (e.g., strategies), and their role modeling of behaviors (Cranmer, 2019). As such, sporting experiences are largely the product of coaches' efforts. Unsurprisingly, our society often comes to revere successful coaches as mythical figures to whom we attribute the outcomes of games and development of athletes. For instance, we build statues of them, promote their philosophies as life guides (e.g., Pyramid of Success), and dedicate popular culture (e.g., films) to their accomplishments and experiences. Coaches also have great influence on the health and well-being of their athletes. For instance, the mode and amount of training they require of their athletes can invoke injury or slow recovery (Cranmer et al., 2018; Rey & Johnson, 2021). The way coaches communicate with their teams can also add or detract from the emotional distress or anxiety felt by athletes (Cranmer, 2019).

Unfortunately, youth and adolescent sport coaches are often untrained volunteers, with the most recent Project Play (2020) survey from the Aspen Institute revealing that roughly a third of them have never received training in basic first aid and CPR, with nearly half lacking education in concussion management and general safety and injury prevention. A central means of addressing such voids in knowledge is through the synthesis and dissemination of research in centralized accounts, such as literature reviews and book chapters. This chapter overviews communicative research that illustrates the health consequences of coach-athlete communication, as well as the applications and future directions for said scholarship.

COACH COMMUNICATION AND HEALTH RESEARCH

The intersections of coaching and athlete health is an underexplored but fertile area for research. Holistically, literature demonstrates coaches and their communicative strategies may have undue effects on their athletes, which extend well beyond the field of play. Thus, coaches must absorb and adopt pro-social discursive practices that will enable them to maintain beneficial relationships with athletes that enhance their on-and-off the field experiences (e.g., performance, esteem, and identity). The scope of extant research largely focuses on four aspects of athletes' health: (a) injury reporting, (b) injury recovery, (c) dietary/eating disorders, and (d) mental well-being.

Injury Reporting

Injury reporting, especially the lack of it, is an important and relevant issue within the scope of coach-athlete communication (Baugh et al., 2020; Sanderson et al., 2017). Inevitably, competitive athletes at some point in their career will experience an injury and will decide whether to report their condition to an athletic trainer or coach or to conceal it (Weinberg et al., 2013). The lack of reporting an injury is a major concern for coaches (Maurice et al.,

2021). Athletes may choose to hide an injury if they believe that reporting it will make them look weak, let their teammates down, or more importantly, anger or disappoint their coaches (Baugh et al., 2014; Kroshus et al., 2015; McAllister-Deitrick et al., 2022). Moreover, sports culture romanticizes narratives (e.g., the pain principle) that encourages playing through pain as indications of strength, toughness, and character (Cranmer & LaBelle, 2018; Kerr et al., 2014; Register-Mihalik et al., 2013). Unsurprisingly, athletes—from youth to collegiate athletics—struggle with injury reporting and often decide to play through pain (Deroche et al., 2011; Granquist et al., 2014).

Research with sport-related concussion (SRC) demonstrates that decisions not to report injuries are partially a consequence of coach-athlete relationships. SRC is one of the most prevalent injuries that athletes continue to conceal (Davies & Bird, 2015; Kroshus et al., 2015). DePadilla and colleagues (2018) reported that between 1.7–3-million athletes sustain a concussion every year while engaging in youth sports. These numbers only represent the athletes that choose to report their concussions; the true number of athletes who sustain a concussion each year due to sport-related activity is unknown. Specifically, an SRC is often caused by a jolt or blow to the head or body that results in symptoms such as headaches, dizziness, sensitivity to light and noise, behavioral changes, and trouble sleeping (Register-Mihalik et al., 2013; Sarmiento et al., 2017, 2019). These symptoms may be short- or long-term and can permanently change the way individuals learn, act, think, and feel (McCrea et al., 2013; Sarmiento et al., 2019).

Coaches have a large role in shaping the culture of their athletic programs (Becker, 2009; Cranmer & Buckner, 2017) and as such, hold vital roles in encouraging concussion and injury reporting from their athletes (Weinberg et al., 2013). Due to the invisible nature of some injuries, practitioners and health staff are largely dependent on athletes' self-reporting to coaches or athletic trainers (Cranmer & LaBelle, 2018). Despite considerable efforts to educate athletes about SRC, many choose to play through their symptoms or return before fully healing (Chrisman et al., 2013; Kurowski et al., 2015; Register-Mihalik et al., 2013). The hesitancy in reporting is largely attributed to stigmatization that is rooted in sporting cultural norms (Cranmer & LaBelle, 2018; Sanderson et al., 2017). However, coach-athlete relationships that support and encourage athletes to report symptoms and take time to recover offset such concerns (Baugh et al., 2014; Cranmer & LaBelle, 2018). Overall, coaches serve multifaceted roles in relation to injury prevention, as sources of knowledge and support.

Rehabilitation

A central health issue within sport is athletes' rehabilitation from injuries, as competitive athletes inevitably become injured at some point in their careers. While rehabilitation may largely be defined by medical access and treatments, coaches' communication serves a major role in the rates and efficiencies of athletes' recovery. The process of recovering from an injury is often isolating, as it accompanies surgeries, treatments, physical therapy, or rest that removes athletes from the team environment or marks them as deficient (e.g., a distinct color jersey in football often denotes an injured player who cannot practice with full contact). Additionally, rehabilitation requires adjustment to new roles that are usually of secondary importance (e.g., assisting with sporting equipment during practices) (de Groot et al., 2018). These detrimental experiences potentially foster loneliness, loss of identity, and depression within athletes (Christakou & Lavallee, 2009) and increase the need for additional social resources during rehabilitation. Although coaches often take a secondary role to medical staff and athletic trainers in the handling of injuries (Clement & Shannon, 2011; Robbins & Rosenfeld, 2001), their communication with athletes can offer emotional, psychological, and social resources that help athletes persevere and recover (Corbillon et al., 2008). The primary resource that benefits athletes during rehabilitation is the provision of social support.

Social support broadly includes the things that coaches say and do to help athletes and is a concept that links social relationships with individuals' well-being (Cranmer & Sollitto, 2015). In regard to injured athletes, coaches may share expressions of concern for athletes' well-being (e.g., *emotional support*), seek to reduce doubts about athletes' abilities to recover and return to proficient performance (i.e., *esteem support*), share knowledge about their injury or rehabilitation (i.e., *informational support*), or assist them in accessing or engaging in rehabilitation (i.e., *tangible support*). Additionally, coaches may offer support by listening to athletes' concerns and stressors (Robbins & Rosenfeld, 2001). Through the provision of social support coaches are able to foster better relationships with athletes, which leads to continued engagement and satisfaction with sport (Cranmer & Sollitto, 2015).

Such efforts become increasingly important after injury, as athletes seek additional support from coaches and others to assist in coping and managing the physical and psychological difficulties of rehabilitation (Yang et al., 2010). Failure to properly support athletes during this time can result in disinterest in sports participation, depression, and loss of identity (Clement & Shannon, 2011). Unfortunately, research indicates that coaches' provision of social support lags that of athletic trainers in its abundance and efficacy (Clement & Shannon, 2011; Yang et al., 2010). Such realities are especially concerning for youth and scholastic athletes, who may be enrolled in sporting programs that do not feature athletic trainers or medical staff.

Dietary/Eating Disorders

An additional health concern influenced by coach-athlete relationships is eating disorders. Eating disorders are behavioral conditions that drive athletes to restrict food intake, disrupt regular eating patterns, and adopt unhealthy weight management practices (Bonci et al., 2008). Despite this behavior prevailing among the general population, athletes are more likely to succumb to this dangerous behavior as physiology is central to athletic performance and sometimes even eligibility (e.g., wrestling weight class) (Martinsen & Sundgot-Borgen, 2013). With increased recognition and emphasis on their physiology, sports participation and culture may contribute toward athletes' eating disorders (Mosewich et al., 2009; Thompson & Sherman, 2010). Interactions with coaches are one means through which athletes gain a sense of their physical abilities and identity, as well as determine approaches toward their physical health (Heffner et al., 2003; Jones et al., 2005).

As such, the communication practices established between a coach and their athletes can stimulate eating disorder behaviors. For instance, Jones et al. (2005) observed how coaches' comments, like asking swimmers to remain "lighter and slimmer" (p. 384), disrupted their regular food consumption. Similar suggestions are common in other sports, such as gymnastics, cheerleading, figure skating, track or distance running, and sports highly associated with participants' weight (e.g., judo, wrestling, or boxing). Unsurprisingly, Engel et al. (2003) confirmed a positive relationship between coaches' strictness over weight management and athletes' drive for thinness or food restriction across nearly a dozen men's and women's sports. Yet, such communication patterns, especially with female athletes, can result in humiliation and diminished self-worth, with eating disorders being viewed as desirable (Engel et al., 2003). Therefore, the traditional practice of coaches advocating for an ideal body type (e.g., lean figure) with the goal of enhanced performance can risk athletes' health, effectuate eating disorders (Coker-Cranney & Reel, 2015), and lead to mental trauma (e.g., depression) (Beals, 2004).

Thus, while part of athletic coaching is assisting in the cultivation of athletes' bodies and physical abilities, the discursive practices toward addressing weight and body image, nevertheless, must be carefully established. Coaches should select words that prioritize empathy and demonstrate concern for their athletes (Selby & Reel, 2011). For instance, coaches should address weight management with athletes in private rather than among teammates, avoid judgmental statements and tones, and provide resources to professional care (e.g., physician). Such efforts leave athletes feeling equipped to refine their bodies without engaging in destructive health behaviors (Arthur-Cameselle & Baltzell, 2012). Additionally, coaches who demonstrate openness and create opportunities for the athletes to address their concerns mitigate the risk of succumbing to eating disorders. Experimental evidence also suggests that performance-centered approaches that focus on weight gain affecting game performance can lead to eating disorders, whereas person-centered approaches that address the long-term implications of excessive fat are more effective at preventing such issues (Biesecker & Martz, 1999). Therefore, coaches must carefully exercise their authority and be mindful of the power imbalances between themselves and athletes (Jones et al., 2005), which can eventually exacerbate an environment conducive to eating disorders (Coker-Cranney & Reel, 2015; Jones et al., 2005).

Mental Well-being

Recent sport communication scholarship has recognized the importance of athletes' mental well-being, with examinations of topics such as anxiety and depression that are increasing in commonality (Xanthopoulos et al., 2020). Coaching scholars have firmly established that coaches' selection of verbal strategies is directly associated with the mental well-being and self-concepts of athletes. Most consistently, these scholars have noted the detrimental outcomes associated with coaches' use of verbal aggression, which refers to their attacks on the self-concepts of athletes as a means of motivation (Infante & Wigley, 1986). Verbal aggression often takes the form of insults, threats, teasing, or excessive profanity, and its persistent use leads to a damaged self-concept, emotional distress, embarrassment, feelings of inadequacy, and depression (Infante, 1987). However, coaches' use of verbal aggression has been normalized, if not romanticized, within modern sporting culture, as many successful coaches (e.g., Bobby Knight) are viewed as excessively aggressive with their athletes (Kassing & Sanderson, 2010).

Therefore, communication scholars and sporting practitioners continue to draw attention to the detrimental effects of coaches' use of verbal aggression on athletes' well-being. Most scholars have inferred that the use of verbal aggression contributes to the social isolation of athletes from their teammates (Turman, 2003), coaches (Kassing & Infante, 1999; Martin et al., 2009; Mazer et al., 2013), and other sporting stakeholders (Kassing & Infante, 1999). Its use also role models antisocial behaviors that constitute poor sportsmanship, which are internalized and replicated by athletes toward opponents and officials (Kassing & Infante, 1999). Thus, hostile coach-athlete communication creates social climates in which even observers feel disconnected and uncomfortable, as well as promotes antisocial behaviors that violate cultural norms and risk the safety of others. Unsurprisingly, coaches' use of verbal aggression is associated with athletes' disinterest in continued sport participation (Martin et al., 2009; Mazer et al., 2013) likely because athletes desire to avoid interactions that are emotionally and psychologically destructive. Thus, coaches should attempt to integrate pro-social means of communication that affect motivation and effort, but do not risk a compromised self-concept. Such behaviors as *immediacy* (i.e., the use of verbal and nonverbal behaviors to reduce the physical or psychological distance with athletes; Turman, 2008), *confirmation* (i.e., a means of meeting the needs of athletes to be recognized, endorsed, and acknowledged; Cranmer & Brann, 2015), and *social support* (Cranmer & Sollitto, 2015). These behaviors can be demonstrated through relational communication during practice, film review, and informal periods of interaction (e.g., before practices).

APPLYING COACH-ATHLETE COMMUNICATION

The modern sporting landscape offers numerous opportunities for the exploration and application of health communication research within coaching. There are three specific issues that are increasing in their importance in contemporary settings. First, overuse injuries are occurring with greater frequency with the rapid onset of specialization and professionalization of youth sports—trends that are expected to continue. Young athletes are spending greater amounts of time training and playing one sport—often in highly competitive settings—and the subsequent effects of the repetitive movements on their bodies leads to overuse injury (e.g., stress fractions, deteriorated cartilage in joints, and strained or torn ligaments) (Hyman, 2009). For example, the commonality with which young baseball players are receiving Tommy John surgery (i.e., reconstructive surgery to repair ligaments in the elbow) has increased, with more than 50% of the surgeries being performed on 15–19-year-olds (Smith, 2019). As authorities within sport, coaches have a central role in addressing this issue. Coaches must create athlete-centered environments through their communication, relationships, and policies. For instance, there is a need to monitor athletes' output (e.g., pitch counts in Little League baseball or softball) to reduce the opportunities for excessive strain; many of these injuries are at least in part the result of such lapses in oversight. Coaches are also important sources of addressing the misinformation and warped perceptions that parents hold regarding the importance of specialization and likelihood of their child's professional or collegiate opportunities—contributing factors to the social climates that result in overuse injury (Hyman, 2013).

Second, the issue of SRC and associated traumatic brain injuries (TBI) appears to be increasing in their importance to modern sports leagues and the public at large. It has been nearly a decade since SRC have been identified as a public health crisis (Weibe et al., 2011), but research on SRC and TBI is still in its infancy, as the causes of such injuries are increasingly identified and the long-term, social and emotional effects are just being learned (Stein et al., 2015). The concerns about these injuries have resulted in attempts to create equipment, implement safety protocols, and change the rules of sports to enhance athlete safety (McCrory et al., 2013). Coaches are important stakeholders in addressing SRC and TBI, but unfortunately nearly two-thirds lack recent training in a host of crucial skills, including in general safety and injury prevention, CPR and basic first aid, and concussion management (Project Play, 2019). This is a cause for concern as coaches may assist in the identification of observed symptoms, are conduits for self-reporting, and may exert influence on medical staff's evaluation of athletes' health.

Third, there has also been increased attention on the risks posed to athletes' mental health and well-being stemming from coaching abuse. In 2013, Mike Rice Jr.—the men's basketball coach of Rutgers University—garnered extensive media attention as the result of a viral video depicting him verbally and physically abusing his players, including calling them slang terms for homosexuals and female genitalia, using personal insults (e.g., sissies, soft-ass bitches, and idiots), and striking players with objects. Rice was ultimately fired, which started a national trend termed the "Rice Effect" across collegiate and high school campuses that focused on investigating and removing abusive coaches. For example, the Rice Effect has been associated with the termination of several high-profile collegiate coaches, including Rutgers University's swimming coach, Petra Martin; Maryland University's strength and conditioning coach for football, Rick Court; and Utah University's swimming coach, Greg Winslow. More recently, several elite athletes (e.g., Simone Biles) publicly attributed withdrawals from competition to mental ailments, which in part stemmed from coaching abuse.

Together, these issues are at the forefront of conversations about the importance of coaching on athletes' health. Issues like concussion and overuse injuries coincide with established branches of athlete-coach communication such as injury reporting and rehabilitation, whereas the focus on coach abuse is consistent with athlete mental health. These parallels are encouraging and demonstrate that communication scholars are attempting to address the key issues of our time. Each of these issues may be communicatively managed through interactions that promote honesty, concern for athletes, and reduce stigma around states of unwellness.

FUTURE RESEARCH

Given the relevance and implications of athlete-coach communication within health contexts, this intersection of research is fertile ground for future scholars to explore. Unfortunately, much of athlete-coach research adopts instructional, organizational, group, or interpersonal perspectives—as opposed to health—and considers primarily relational and effective outcomes (Cranmer, 2019). Given the rigor of health scholarship at large, there are numerous opportunities for advancing athlete-coach research, including (a) implementing more diverse and rigorous methodologies, (b) building and refining theory, and (c) engaging in topics of interdisciplinary value.

Methodological Considerations

First, scholars should look to incorporate more methodologically diverse and rigorous research. This can be in the form of scale development or one's approach to conducting research. For example, Cranmer (2019) advocates for the creation of coaching-specific measures, as the current literature is largely dependent on borrowing scales from alternative contexts. Although using scales from other disciplines is warranted, specific to the nexus of athlete-coach relationship and health, the athlete-coach relationship, and sport, are distinct from patient-doctor relationships, and health. Therefore, it would be beneficial for scholars to create specific scales that measure athlete-coach communication and health.

More specifically, scholars should look to answer the call posed by Wenner (2021) that asks for researchers to take a more phenomenological and/or socio-psychological approach when researching to create empirical measurements. Indeed, methodological diversity—such as experimental designs and in-depth interviews—will strengthen health and sport communication (Cranmer, 2019). Incorporating more work from these traditions will assist in being able to further explain and predict the phenomenon in hopes of preventing and assisting future health issues. This information and knowledge can be further used to create interventions to assist in proper health education in sport via interventions and campaigns. For example, scholars can adopt empirical investigations that look at how stakeholders perceive athletes who fake injuries, fail to declare their injuries to the team management (e.g., physical trainers), or conceal the true nature of their injury from non-team members (e.g., media). Thus, future research should explore patterns and similarities in athletes' health decisions and conversations to be able to effectively assist in creating positive health environments; doing so may mitigate athletic dissent (Cranmer et al., 2018; Rey & Johnson, 2021).

Other methodological considerations may be longitudinal approaches that provide insight into the socialization function of sport (i.e., sense making of health, memorable messages about health) or effects/alteration in interaction over the cyclical/seasonal nature of sport (Turman, 2001). Understanding influences that dictate athlete health decisions may also illuminate and help address health issues beyond the field of play. Lastly, scholars should look to consider their samples. This is an important facet to consider as the health issues that arise in athletes, and the way they manage them (Cranmer et al., 2018; Rey & Johnson, 2021) are often distinctly different at various levels of athletics (e.g., high school, club, college, professional). The implementation of differing methodological approaches, homegrown scales, and differing samples will strengthen the field and lead to theoretical development specific to sport.

Theoretical Considerations

Next, thus far, broad calls have been made to create theory specific to sport (Martens, 1987; Sanderson, 2013). Therefore, if scholars look to develop the athlete-coach research further, attention should be focused on theoretical development. One reason for this is that, to date, the athlete-coach research is largely atheoretical (Cranmer, 2019). Although health contexts offer multiple frameworks and theories (e.g., Health Disclosure Decision Making Model) (Greene, 2009) from which the athlete-coach relationship can be understood, to continue moving the field of sport forward, sport communication would benefit from creating theory that is unique to sport and the athlete-coach relationship (Sanderson, 2013). Creating theory would progress the field by identifying a set of principles that explain the athlete-coach phenomenon in sport.

In addition to theory that explores the athlete-coach relationship, the field needs theory(ies) to explain and predict athlete development, success, and well-being. Specifically, the theory should address how varying stakeholders' communication impacts an athlete. As Berg and Warner (2019) argue, it is timely and imperative to empirically examine athlete development as stakeholders (e.g., coaches, athletic department, staff) look for ways to support the all-around development of athletes. To date, we do not know how these relationships and contexts come together, nor the degree to which they predict and account for an athlete's experiences in sport. By addressing this field of study, knowledge on this topic would assist in being able to support athletes through their careers from a holistic perspective. Moreover, building theory in sport communication would assist and support more interdisciplinary research.

Interdisciplinary Directions

The topics of inquiry that coaching scholars are best positioned to address hold immense interdisciplinary value. Emphasizing research areas that maximize the contributions of communication research to practitioners and those in other disciplines is one means of facilitating the spread and application of communication scholarship. Three interdisciplinary topics that especially warrant attention are athlete mental health, athlete socialization after sport, and the scope of health communication in sport.

Although growing, research concerning athletes' mental health, both in and outside of sport, is still in its infancy. Mental health encompasses an athlete's emotional, psychological, and social well-being. Perhaps, pro-social communicative practices may encourage athletes to prioritize their mental well-being, while antisocial approaches can hamper such discussions; only future research can explore so. From an emotional lens, research should look to identify and understand conversations that assist athletes to manage their emotions. These emotions can either be stimulated through sport participation (e.g., playing well, missing a shot), or those that stem from outside influence (e.g., relationship issues, family problems, school stress). Growing this line of research may help gain a deeper understanding of the coach-athlete relationship as well as an athlete's passion for the game. From a communicative lens, it is important to identify the conversations that positively and negatively influence an athlete's mental health mental state. Moreover, this may lead to a greater understanding of the line of research regarding eating disorders in athletes and assist in preventing negative psychological outcomes as athletes develop through sports.

Next, equally important is being able to effectively manage athletes' socialization out of sport due to health issues. An athlete's health may lead one to choose or even be forced to end their career. However, there are limited resources that address the ways in which athletes can successfully assimilate into their nonsporting life. This socialization may look different at varying levels, but athletes who must give up their athletic identity to pursue other avenues in life may be met with difficulties assimilating to a life post athletics. Therefore, research should focus on a line of inquiry addressing the most effective ways to socialize athletes post career-ending injuries. Research should look to identify valuable practices to socialize athletes after sport, to create platforms for athletes to receive information regarding socialization, and to design a platform for athletes to receive this information. By exploring and understanding ways to assist athletes into the next chapter of their lives, this line of research will provide and demonstrate care and understanding for the mental and physical hardship athletes go through when they simultaneously lose their identity, health, and sport all at once.

Lastly, future research should look to extend the scope of health communication in sport to other stakeholders. While coaches play a prime role in facilitating environments that influence athletes' health behaviors (Becker, 2009), other associates are equally critical. For instance, team members provide opportunities to influence their decision-making process as well as their overall health (i.e., physical, mental, emotional). As such, sport communication researchers should identify the communicative patterns found in stakeholders that trigger both positive and negative health environments for athletes. Doing so will create the opportunity to elicit change in stakeholders' negative approaches and support positive approaches.

REFERENCES

Arthur-Cameselle, J. N., & Baltzell, A. (2012). Learning from collegiate athletes who have recovered from eating disorders: Advice to coaches, parents, and other athletes with eating disorders. *Journal of Applied Sport Psychology, 24*(1), 1–9.

Baugh, C. M., Kroshus, E., Daneshvar, D. H., & Stern, R. A. (2014). Perceived coach support and concussion symptom-reporting: differences between freshmen and non-freshmen college football players. *The Journal of Law, Medicine & Ethics, 42*(3), 314–322. https://doi.org/10.1111/jlme.12148.

Baugh, C. M., Kroshus, E., Meehan, W. P., & Campbell, E. G. (2020). Trust, conflicts of interest, and concussion reporting in college football players. *Journal of Law, Medicine & Ethics, 48*(2), 307–314.

Beals, K. A. (2004). *Disordered eating among athletes: A comprehensive guide for health professionals*. Champaign, IL: Human Kinetics.

Becker, A. J. (2009). It's not what they do, it's how they do it: Athlete experiences of great coaching. *International Journal of Sports Science & Coaching, 4*(1), 93–119.

Berg, B. K., & Warner, S. (2019). Advancing college athlete development via social support. *Journal of Issues in Intercollegiate Athletics, 12*, 87–113.

Biesecker, A. C., & Martz, D. M. (1999). Impact of coaching style on vulnerability for eating disorders: An analog study. *Eating Disorders, 7*(3), 235–244.

Bonci, C. M., Bonci, L. J., Granger, L. R., Johnson, C. L., Malina, R. M., Milne, L. W., Ryan, R. R., & Vanderbunt, E. M. (2008). National Athletic Trainers' Association position statement: Preventing, detecting, and managing disordered eating in athletes. *Journal of Athletic Training, 43*(1), 80–108.

Chrisman, S. P., Quitiquit, C., & Rivara, F. P. (2013). Qualitative study of barriers to concussive symptom reporting in high school athletics. *Journal of Adolescent Health, 52*(3), 330–335.

Christakou, A., & Lavallee, D. (2009). Rehabilitation from sports injuries: From theory to practice. *Perspectives in Public Health, 129*(3) 120–126.

Clement, D., & Shannon, V. R. (2011). Injured athletes' perceptions about social support. *Journal of Sport Rehabilitation, 20*(4), 457–470.

Coker-Cranney, A., & Reel, J. J. (2015). Coach pressure and disordered eating in female collegiate athletes: Is the coach-athlete relationship a mediating factor? *Journal of Clinical Sport Psychology, 9*(3), 213–231.

Corbillon, F., Crossman, J., & Jamieson, J. (2008). Injured athletes' perceptions about social support provided by their coaches and teammates during rehabilitation. *Journal of Sport Behavior, 31*(2), 93–107.

Cranmer, G. A. (2019). *Athletic coaching: A communication perspective*. New York, NY: Peter Lang.

Cranmer, G. A., & Brann, M. (2015). "It makes me feel like I am an important part of this team": An exploratory study of coach confirmation. *International Journal of Sport Communication, 8*(2), 193–211.

Cranmer, G. A., & Buckner, M. M. (2017). High school athletes' relationships with head coaches and teammates as predictors of their expressions of upward and lateral dissent. *Communication Studies, 68*(1), 37–55.

Cranmer, G. A., Buckner, M. M., Pham, N., & Jordan, B. (2018). "I Disagree": An exploration of triggering events, messages, and effectiveness of athletes' dissent. *Communication & Sport, 6*(5), 523–546.

Cranmer, G. A., & LaBelle, S. (2018). Using the disclosure decision-making model to understand high school football players' disclosures of concussion symptoms. *International Journal of Sport Communication, 11*(2), 241–260.

Cranmer, G. A., & Sollitto, M. (2015). Sport support: Received social support as a predictor of athlete satisfaction. *Communication Research Reports, 32*(3), 253–264.

Davies, S. C., & Bird, B. M. (2015). Motivations for underreporting suspected concussion in college athletics. *Journal of Clinical Sport Psychology, 9*(2), 101–115.

de Groot, A. L., Weaver, A. G., Brown, S. N., & Hall, E. E. (2018). Social support provided to injured student-athletes. *Journal of Issues in Intercollegiate Athletics, 11*, 168–188.

DePadilla, L., Miller, G. F., Jones, S. E., Peterson, A. B., & Breiding, M. J. (2018). Self-reported concussions from playing a sport or being physically active among high school students—United States, 2017. *Morbidity and Mortality Weekly Report, 67*(24), 682–685.

Deroche, T., Woodman, T., Stephan, Y., Brewer, B. W., & Le Scanff, C. (2011). Athletes' inclination to play through pain: A coping perspective. *Anxiety, Stress & Coping, 24*(5), 579–587.

Engel, S. G., Johnson, C., Powers, P. S., Crosby, R. D., Wonderlich, S. A., Wittrock, D. A., & Mitchell, J. E. (2003). Predictors of disordered eating in a sample of elite Division I college athletes. *Eating Behaviors, 4*(4), 333–343.

Granquist, M. D., Podlog, L., Engel, J. R., & Newland, A. (2014). Certified athletic trainers' perspectives on rehabilitation adherence in collegiate athletic training settings. *Journal of Sport Rehabilitation, 23,* 123–133.

Greene, K. (2009). An integrated model of health disclosure decision making. In T. D. Afifi & W. A. Afifi (Eds.), *Uncertainty and information regulation in interpersonal contexts: Theories and applications* (pp. 226–253). New York, NY: Routledge.

Guttmann, A. (1978). *From ritual to record.* New York, NY: Columbia University.

Heffner, J. L., Ogles, B. M., Gold, E., Marsden, K., & Johnson, M. (2003). Nutrition and eating in female college athletes: A survey of coaches. *Eating Disorders*, *11*(3), 209–220.

Hyman, M. (2009). *Until it hurts: America's obsession with youth sports and how it harms our kids*. Boston, MA: Beacon Press.

Hyman, M. (2013). *The most expensive game in town: the rising cost of youth sports and the toll on today's families*. Boston, MA: Beacon Press.

Infante, D. A. (1987). Aggressiveness. In J. C. McCroskey & J. A. Daly (Eds.), *Personality and interpersonal communication* (pp. 157–197). Newbury Park, CA: Sage.

Infante, D. A., & Wigley, C. J. (1986). Verbal aggressiveness: An interpersonal model and measure. *Communication Monographs*, *53*, 61–69.

Jones, R. L., Glintmeyer, N., & McKenzie, A. (2005). Slim bodies, eating disorders and the coach-athlete relationship. *International Review for the Sociology of Sport*, *40*(3), 377–391.

Kassing, J. W., & Infante, D. A. (1999). Aggressive communication in the coach-athlete relationship. *Communication Research Reports*, *16*(2), 110–120.

Kassing, J. W., & Sanderson, J. (2010). Trash talk and beyond: Aggressive communication in the context of sport. In T. A. Avtgis & A. S. Rancer (Eds.), *Arguments, aggression, and conflict: New directions in theory and research* (pp. 253–266). New York, NY: Routledge.

Kerr, Z. Y., Register-Mihalik, J. K., Marshall, S. W., Evenson, K. R., Mihalik, J. P., & Guskiewicz, K. M. (2014). Disclosure and non-disclosure of concussion and concussion symptoms in athletes: review and application of the socio-ecological framework. *Brain Injury*, *28*(8), 1009–1021.

Kroshus, E., Baugh, C. M., Daneshvar, D. H., Nowinski, C. J., & Cantu, R. C. (2015). Concussion reporting intention: A valuable metric for predicting reporting behavior and evaluating concussion education. *Clinical Journal of Sport Medicine*, *25*(3), 243–247.

Kurowski, B. G., Pomerantz, W. J., Schaiper, C., Ho, M., & Gittelman, M. A. (2015). Impact of preseason concussion education on knowledge, attitudes, and behaviors of high school athletes. *The Journal of Trauma and Acute Care Surgery*, *79*(3). 21–28.

Martens, R. (1987). Science, knowledge, and sport psychology. *The Sport Psychologist*, *1*(1), 29–55.

Martin, M. M., Rocca, K. A., Cayanus, J. L., & Weber, K. (2009). Relationship between coaches' use of behavior alteration techniques and verbal aggression on athletes' motivation and affect. *Journal of Sport Behavior*, *32*, 227–241.

Martinsen, M., & Sundgot-Borgen, J. (2013). Higher prevalence of eating disorders among adolescent elite athletes than controls. *Medicine & Science in Sports & Exercise*, *45*(6), 1188–1197.

Maurice, S., Voelker, D. K., Kuklick, C., & Byrd, M. (2021). "We don't always get it right": Coaches' perspectives on supporting injured athletes. *Sports Coaching Review*. Advance online publication.

Mazer, J. P., Barnes, K., Grevious, A., & Boger, C. (2013). Coach verbal aggression: A case study examining effects on athlete motivation and perceptions of coach credibility. *International Journal of Sport Communication, 6*, 203–213.

McAllister-Deitrick, J., Beidler, E., Wallace, J., & Anderson, M. (2022). Concussion knowledge and reporting behaviors among collegiate athletes. *Clinical Journal of Sport Medicine, 32(1), 56–61.* https://doi.org/10.1097/JSM.0000000000000833.

McCrea, M., Guskiewicz, K., Randolph, C., Barr, W. B., Hammeke, T. A., Marshall, S. W., . . . & Kelly, J. P. (2013). Incidence, clinical course, and predictors of prolonged recovery time following sport-related concussion in high school and college athletes. *Journal of the International Neuropsychological Society, 19*(1), 22–33.

McCrory, P., Meeuwisse, W. H., Aubry, M., Cantu, B., Dvořák, J., Echemendia, R. J., . . . & Sills, A. (2013). Consensus statement on concussion in sport: the 4th International Conference on Concussion in Sport held in Zurich, November 2012. *British Journal of Sports Medicine, 47*, 250–258.

Mosewich, A. D., Vangool, A. B., Kowalski, K. C., & McHugh, T.-L. F. (2009). Exploring women track and field athletes' meanings of muscularity. *Journal of Applied Sport Psychology, 21*(1), 99–115.

Murray, R. M., Sabiston, C. M., Doré, I., Bélanger, M., & O'Loughlin, J. L. (2020). Longitudinal associations between team sport participation and substance use in adolescents and young adults. *Addictive Behaviors 116*(1), 106798.

Project Play. (2019). State of play: Trends and developments in youth sports. *AspenProjectPlay.org.* Retrieved from https://www.aspeninstitute.org/wp-content/uploads/2019/10/2019_SOP_National_Final.pdf.

Register-Mihalik, J. K., Linnan, L. A., Marshall, S. W., McLeod, T. C. V., Mueller, F. O., & Guskiewicz, K. M. (2013). Using theory to understand high school aged athletes' intentions to report sport-related concussion: Implications for concussion education initiatives. *Brain Injury, 27*(7–8), 878–886.

Rey, R. T., & Johnson, Z. D. (2021). "Detrimental to the Team Dynamic": Exploring College Student-Athlete Dissent. *Communication & Sport.* Advance online publication.

Robbins, J. E., & Rosenfeld, L. B. (2001). Athletes' perceptions of social support provided by their head coach, assistant coach, and athletic trainer, pre-injury and during rehabilitation. *Journal of Sport Behavior, 24*(3), 277–294.

Sanderson, J. (2013). Social media and sport communication: Abundant theoretical opportunities. In P. M. Pedersen (Ed.), *Routledge Handbook of Sport Communication* (pp. 70–79). New York, NY: Routledge.

Sanderson, J., Weathers, M., Snedaker, K., & Gramlich, K. (2017). "I was able to still do my job on the field and keep playing": An investigation of female and male athletes' experiences with (not) reporting concussions. *Communication & Sport, 5*(3), 267–287.

Sarmiento, K., Donnell, Z., & Hoffman, R. (2017). A scoping review to address the culture of concussion in youth and high school sports. *Journal of School Health, 87*(10), 790–804.

Sarmiento, K., Daugherty, J., & DePadilla, L. (2019). Youth and high school sports coaches' experience with and attitudes about concussion and access to athletic trainers by sport type and age of athlete coached. *Journal of Safety Research, 69,* 217–225.

Selby, C. L. B., & Reel, J. J. (2011). A coach's guide to identifying and helping athletes with eating disorders. *Journal of Sport Psychology in Action, 2*(2), 100–112.

Smith, M. (2019, April 12). Foul ball: More kids having Tommy John surgery. *Wedmd.com*. Retrieved from https://www.webmd.com/children/news/20190412/foul-ball-more-kids-having-tommy-john-surgery.

Stein, T. D., Alvarez, V. E., & McKee, A. C. (2015). Concussion in chronic traumatic encephalopathy. *Current Pain and Headache Reports, 19,* 47–58.

Thompson, R. A., & Sherman, R. T. (2010). *Eating disorders in sport.* New York, NY: Routledge.

Turman, P. D. (2001). Situational coaching styles. *Small Group Research, 32*(5), 576–594.

Turman, P. D. (2003). Coaches and cohesion: The impact of coaching techniques on team cohesion in the small group sport setting. *Journal of Sport Behavior, 26,* 86–104.

Turman, P. (2008). Coaches' immediacy behaviors as predictors of athletes' perceptions of satisfaction and team cohesion. *Western Journal of Communication, 72*(2), 162–179.

Weibe, D. J., Comstock, R. D., & Nance, M. L. (2011). Concussion research: A public health priority. *Injury Prevention, 17,* 69–70. doi:10.1136/ip.2010.031211.

Weinberg, R., Vernau, D., & Horn, T. (2013). Playing through pain and injury: Psychosocial considerations. *Journal of Clinical Sport Psychology, 7*(1), 41–59. https://doi.org/10.1123/jcsp.7.1.41.

Wenner, L. (2021). Media, sports, and society. In E. Pike (Ed.), *Handbook of research on sports and society.* Northampton, MA: Edward Elgar Publishing.

Xanthopoulos, M. S., Benton, T., Lewis, J., Case, J. A., & Master, C. L. (2020). Mental Health in the Young Athlete. *Current Psychiatry Reports, 22*(11), 1–15.

Yang, J., Peek-Asa, C., Lowe, J. B., Heiden, E., & Foster, D. T. (2010). Social support patterns of collegiate athletes before and after injury. *Journal of Athletic Training, 45*(4), 372–379.

Chapter Seven

Why Kinesiology and Athletics Departments Should Collaborate to Advance Health Equity

Larry D. Proctor, Sarah Stokowski, Danielle H. McArdle, and C. Keith Harrison

Health equity is defined as the attainment of the highest level of health for all people. Achieving health equity requires valuing everyone equally with focused and ongoing societal efforts designed to address avoidable inequities, contemporary injustices, and lowering health disparities. On the other hand, health inequities are differences in health that are avoidable, systematic, measurable, and unjust.

Health inequities are most visible in epidemiological indicators, such as life expectancy, infant mortality, and other measures of population health. Yet as health services research shows, inequities are also evident within the health care system itself—through bias, prejudice, and stereotyping on the part of health care providers, racial bias in the tools used to make clinical decisions, and through policies and systems that limit access to quality treatment.

Health inequities are also directly related to and reinforced by inequities within other parts of society, including the workplace, sports, education, and youth sport systems. These inequities have not only been produced by individual and collective historical decisions, but they are also maintained by contemporary—both individual and collective—decisions as well. The decisions were made by people in various leadership roles, in each of the previous industries mentioned; thereby, inequities are not natural or inevitable.

Understanding diversity, oppression, and social inequity brings us to the concept of social justice. Lee Anne Bell (2013) answers the question, "What is Social Justice?" by suggesting that it is both a process and a goal. The goal of social justice is full and equal participation of all groups in a society that is mutually shaped to meet their needs. Bell (2013) further establishes that social justice involves individuals, with a sense of their own agency and their own social responsibility towards and with others, their society, and the broader world.

No one wants to accept that they hold prejudices or even support inequalities by avoidance or being complicit. However, being open to the idea that a portion of what we were taught during our lifetime was incomplete or inaccurate is essential. We all have experienced microaggressions by students or colleagues in our institutions. However, have we thought about how we handled them? Did we ignore the situation or effectively address it? For many, it takes us by surprise, and we freeze, not knowing what to do. Learning can be maximized in diverse settings but just exposure to diversity does nothing to insure what Dr. Terrell Strayhorn calls "interactional diversity" in his 2017 keynote address.

Culp (2016) explains that while social justice has become part of institutional mission statements, these statements fail to address how social justice is interconnected on a larger scale. Culp (2016) also stated that institutions are a microcosm of the society in which they exist, and therefore have many of the same ills that exist in our society, like passive aversion to discussing social justice. It is critical to address all areas of marginalization and inequity due to sexism, class oppression, homophobia, xenophobia, and ableism.

Yet, conversations about race and racism tend to be some of the most difficult for people in this country to participate in for numerous reasons. Among the many reasons are a lack of knowledge or shared analysis of its historical and current underpinnings and outright resistance and denial that racism exists. Given the deep divides that exist between groups in the United States, understanding and empathy can be extremely challenging for many.

Collectively, we have an opportunity and obligation to overcome these fissures and create spaces for understanding and healing. However, when discussing this phenomenon, we can also understand and recognize the choice of passive aversion as this stuff is messy. It gets personal. It is political. It forces reflection that can result in feelings of guilt or anger. In many ways, it exists at a level of uncomfortableness due to feeling so uninformed about something that is painfully obvious to us; however, it is in this discomfort that we are motivated to change.

ADVICE GIVEN BY PREVIOUS AGENTS OF CHANGE

Before we present specifics in the various subject areas, we must first acknowledge that this endeavor has been pursued in times past and is not entirely new. In fact, there are many in both Kinesiology and Athletics who have worked tirelessly to inform the rest of us about diversity and social justice, through numerous presentations, ongoing research, and publications to whoever would accept our work. Consequently, the next step is to learn from those who have taken up the mantle of inclusivity.

In his 2014 Sargent Lecture, Dr. Sam Hodge (2014), after bringing our attention to and reviewing the choice made by Coach John Wooden to boycott the 1947 National Association of Intercollegiate Basketball National Tournament, after the tournament forbade the participation of Black players, emphasized the importance of standing up for social justice. We must look for opportunities to stand for social justice. So, if an opportunity arises that calls for you to speak to a practice that is not inclusive, take a stand and work to change that circumstance.

In his 2016 Hanna Lecture, Dr. Brian Culp suggested that complicating this endeavor are those who believe in the "intent of equity" but fail to administer penalties commensurate with the failures to uphold social justice, regardless of race, religion, or socio-economic status. Culp (2016) contends that once policies were commensurate, they would make equity for all a reality. He concluded his presentation by stating:

> As much as we might want to wish issues of inequity and injustice away, there is no progress that can be made without vigilance. Higher education is one of the few platforms where knowledge, values and learning can be incorporated to assist the public in meaningful and transformative ways. Therefore, involving approaches from kinesiology to solve inequities in our society is not only a notable effort but a necessary one for which we have the capacity to respond.

Stated differently, we must look for opportunities to ensure that the policies we enact do not continue the exclusive status quo, but rather foster an inclusive future. To do so, collaborate with a colleague, versed in inclusive practices, to ensure that your proposed practices are clear and truly inclusive when integrating into them into departments.

Dr. Martha James Hassan, in her (2016) NAKHE Hally Beth Poindexter Young Scholars Award presentation, echoed this by sharing that education and the process of schooling are always political and, therefore, if professors, administrators, concentrations, and/or departments are not working to teach students about institutional injustices, then they are unconsciously supporting the hegemonic maintenance of oppression. Simply, we must look for opportunities to bring others along on our journey to create a more inclusive future. Take a stand in your classrooms by infusing content and concepts related to diversity issues and social justice into your courses. Then, be sure to partner with a colleague to ensure that your understanding of the concepts is clear and in alignment with inclusionary practices when integrating them into your classroom.

Following in their footsteps, it is imperative that we begin to commit ourselves to collaborating with professionals from various specializations so that we can effectively infuse cultural diversity and social justice issues into professional practices.

OPPORTUNITIES TO TAKE FUTURE ACTION IN THE CLASSROOM

This new model acknowledges the fact that kinesiology is the discipline where many of the allied health professionals recruit from to address the diversity needs of the industry. Therefore, the purpose of this commentary is to propose credentialing changes across the various kinesiology concentrations within degree programs, levels of youth sport, and college sport as well as health and allied health systems that can most effectively cultivate the sport development, health, and well-being of youth across the United States.

COURSES TAUGHT

Among the proposed changes we suggest ask colleges to improve upon the actual courses that are provided for upcoming kinesiologists and health professionals to take. Two courses that are taught to students, but could be improved upon, are motor learning and development and data analytics. In this section, both classes will be discussed, in terms of how they could be improved.

Motor Learning and Development

Motor learning and development is an extremely important area of the kinesiology concentration and therefore it is taught in some form in each of our programs. Given this, courses on motor learning and development should explore how the environmental or socio-economic influences, that a student experiences, interact with a student's motor learning and motor development. Topics covered, in the course, should include a discussion of issues related to the effects of stressors, anxiety, hunger, oral health, obesity, and family trauma on the ability to learn and perform motor skills. More specifically, a discussion of Head Start and the Women, Infants and Children (WIC) programs can be used to frame such discussions related to addressing and other social interventions necessary to address the inequalities in our society.

Measurement and Data Analytics

Measurement and data analytics classes are two essential courses taught within health, physical education, and exercise physiology programs. More and more, developing and implementing a systematic analytics strategy can result in creating a sustainable competitive advantage within the allied health and sport business industry. As such, these timely and relevant courses carry the capacity to provide practical strategies. Courses should encourage students to collect data and then convert that data into meaningful, value-added information and actionable insights, including insights that are tied to diversity and inclusion initiatives. Particularly, we, who teach such courses, should aim to include discussions, in these courses, on school funding, in terms of the varying types of facilities and equipment available to them and/or technological differences.

Curriculum and Instruction Used

In every course, choosing the most valuable resources to be provided through instructional content is essential and can be an extremely challenging decision to make. This is especially true in Physical Education Teacher Education (PETE), Health Education Teacher Education (HETE), and Curriculum and Instruction (C&I) or clinical courses pertaining to licensure exams. As an example, *Elementary Physical Education: Curriculum and Instruction*, authored by Rovegno and Bandhauer (2013), includes an 18-page chapter on diversity. The chapter centers on the six characteristics crucial for creating inclusive, equitable classrooms that work against discrimination and prejudice. In contrast, a very popular text used for secondary schools' physical education curriculum and instruction includes a three-page section entitled "Consider the Personal Needs of Students" in a chapter on "Improving Instructional Effectiveness."

Using a textbook that provides content related to diversity and social justice is a great start, but collaboration will allow you to further increase your ability to more effectively address these issues as you decide the school or site to use for your clinical work and then to address the content of that context of that particular setting. Collaboration, with reputable colleagues, also can increase your awareness of the best resources available to support and infuse cultural diversity and social justice into your courses.

To truly bring about change, physicians and other health care workers, who are first responders for student-athletes and their medical needs, must develop a critical consciousness of the root causes and structural drivers of health inequities in their communities as well.

THE NEED FOR A NEW MODEL

In 2007, the Association for Supervision and Curriculum Development (ASCD) called for an acknowledgment of the interdependent nature of youth sports systems, Kinesiology, Sport programs, and Allied Health industries. We call on communities—educators, parents, businesses, health and social service providers, arts professionals, recreation leaders, and policymakers at all levels—to forge a new compact with our young people to ensure their whole and healthy development. We ask communities to redefine learning to focus on the whole person. We ask schools and parents to lay aside minor battles and instead align those resources in support of the whole child. Policy, practices, and resources must be realigned to support not only academic learning and health status for each child, but also the experiences that encourage development of the whole child—one which is socioeconomically supported, motivated, and engaged.

Health and well-being have, for too long, been put into silos-separated both logistically and philosophically from sport and health/lifelong learning. The traditional approach to youth sports systems, collegiate athletics, or kinesiology students has been to address the individual's medical-injury-related needs by physicians or athletic trainers. However, this model only partially addresses the health-and-wellness needs that are leading causes of morbidity and mortality among youth and young adults. Many of these needs can be seen in conditions and behaviors such as substance use, high-risk sexual behaviors, mental health problems, and police brutality (Eaton et al., 2008). Since most of the youth and college students only receive healthcare within the sports or medical system, comprehensive care that includes social determinants of health and health-related fitness behavioral factors must be included and nurtured in the new model of sport/kinesiology/adaptive care delivery system.

Indeed, in his meta-analysis, "Healthier Students Are Better Learners," Charles Basch called for a renewed focus on health-related fitness as the missing link in school reforms to close the achievement gap. Basch (2014) asserts that regardless of how well teachers are prepared to teach, how effectual the accountability measures put in place are, and how effective governing structures established for schools are, educational programs will be profoundly limited if students/athletes are not motivated to reach their potential and supported along the way. Though rhetorical support has increased in recent years, health is currently not a central part of the fundamental mission of youth sport systems, school systems, kinesiology, and athletic departments in America nor has it been well integrated into the broader national strategies to reduce the disparities in education, health, or sport industries.

Studies demonstrate that when the basic nutritional and health-related fitness needs of children are met, they attain higher achievement levels. Similarly, the use of school-based health centers and school-linked social services ensures that access to needed mental, oral, social, and emotional care improves attendance, behavior, and achievement. This development of wrap-around services creates a safety net of connected and supportive services which benefits teachers, enhances learning outcomes of students, and improves capitalization rates within each of the fields/industries (Kinesiology, Sport, and Allied Health industries) impacted by this improved collaborative use of available resources and expertise.

In turn, overall academic achievement and optimal health are an excellent indicator for the optimal well-being of youth and a primary predictor and determinant of adult health outcomes. Individuals with more education are likely to live longer; experience better health outcomes; and practice health-promoting behaviors such as exercising regularly, refraining from smoking, and obtaining timely health screenings.

Moreover, health-related fitness status affects individual educational achievement, society, the economy, and as such, must work in concert together whenever possible with other essential aspects of human development. Youth sports systems and school systems are perfect settings for this collaborative partnership to thrive. Schools are places and spaces for reaching youth and young adults to provide not only sport training, health-related fitness, and health services, but also social services, with such large percentages of all U.S. children attending schools. Integrating additional health services and social programs more deeply into the day-to-day lives of schools and students represents an uncaptured resource for raising academic achievement and lowering multiple disparities. In short, health-related fitness and achievement are interrelated and therefore must become our focus.

THE EXISTING MODEL

The traditional coordinated school health (CSH) approach has been a mainstay of schools' health in the United States of America since 1987. Promulgated by the Centers for Disease Control (CDC), the CSH approach has provided a succinct and distinct framework for organizing a comprehensive approach to school health. In addition to the CDC, many national health and education organizations have supported the CSH approach. However, it has been viewed by educators as primarily a health initiative focused only on health outcomes and has consequently gained limited traction across the education sector at the school for other important aspects of well-being.

The ASCD's Whole Child Initiative is an effort to change the conversation about education from a focus on narrowly defined academic/health achievement to one that promotes the long-term development and success of the whole child. Through the initiative, ASCD helps educators, coaches, community affiliates, and policymakers move from a vision about educating the whole child to sustainable, collaborative engagement. However, this approach has been viewed primarily by many stakeholders as an educational initiative and therefore has gained little traction with the health community.

Following this model, the Association for Supervision and Curriculum Development (ASCD) and the Centers for Disease Control and Prevention (CDC) developed the Whole School, Whole Communities, Whole Child (WSCC) model. This model combines and builds upon elements of the traditional coordinated school health approach and the whole child framework. The ASCD and the CDC developed this new model—in collaboration with key leaders from the fields of health, public health, education, and school health—to strengthen a unified and collaborative approach to learning and health equity.

The WSCC model responded to the call for greater alignment, integration, and collaboration of resources between youth sports systems, education, and health that is needed to improve each child's cognitive, physical, social, and emotional development. It incorporated the components of a coordinated school health program around the tenets of a whole child approach that provides a framework to address other systemic inequities present in our society. The focus of the WSCC model is an ecological approach that is directed at the whole school, with the school in turn drawing its resources and influences from the whole community and serving to address the needs of the whole child. The ASCD and the CDC encourage the use of the model as a framework for improving students' learning and health equity in our nation's schools and youth sports systems.

THE NEW MODEL (HOLISTIC KINESIOLOGY-ATHLETIC MODEL)

The Holistic Kinesiology-Athletic Model builds upon the WSCC model. Whereas the traditional approach contained eight components, this new model contains ten components, expanding the original components to Healthy and Safe School Environment and Family and Community Involvement into four distinct components. The expanded model focuses additional attention on the effects of the Social and Emotional Components in addition to the Physical Environment. Family and community involvement is divided into two separate components to emphasize the role of community agencies, businesses, and organizations as well as the critical role of addressing the social determinants of health engagement to achieve health equity. This change marks the need for greater emphasis on both the psychosocial and the physical environments as well as the ever-expanding roles that community agencies and families must play. Finally, this new model also addresses the need to engage students as active participants in their learning and health.

The new model redirects attention onto the ultimate focus of the various sectors—the child/young adult. It emphasizes a schoolwide approach rather than one that is subject- or location-specific, and it acknowledges the position of learning, health, athletics, kinesiology, and health care/allied health and the school as all being a part and reflection of the local community. The efforts to address the educational, health, and athletic/health care industry needs of the youth/young adult should be seen as a schoolwide endeavor as opposed to being confined to a subject or sector. Rather than being an initiative owned by one teacher, one nurse, one coach or department/profession, this model outlines the whole school, child, community approach, with every adult and every student playing a role in the growth and development of the peers, school, and/or community.

Just as the whole school plays its part, the new model outlines how the school, staff, and students are placed within the local community. While the school may be a hub, it remains a focus of its community and requires community input, resources, and collaboration to support its students. As with any relationship this works both ways. Community strengths can boost the role and potential of the school, but areas of need in the community also become reflected in the school, and as such must be addressed. Each child, in each school, in each of our communities deserves to be healthy, safe, engaged, supported, and challenged. That's what a whole child approach to learning, teaching, and community engagement really is about. More than merely a way to boost achievement or academics, the WSCC approach views the collaboration between learning, health, and industry impact as fundamental. The development of the whole child is more than the acquisition of knowledge or skills, behavior, or character; it is all of these.

The new model calls for a greater collaboration across sectors to meet the needs and reach the potential of each child. Collaboration truly is the key to moving from model to action as collaborative development of local youth sports systems, school system policies, processes, and practices work synergistically together like an ecosystem. The day-to-day practices within each sector require examination and collaboration so that they work in tandem, with appropriate complementary processes guiding each decision and action. Developing joint and collaborative policy is half the challenge; putting it into action and making it routine completes the task. To develop joint or collaborative policies, processes, and practices, with all parties involved should start with the end in mind regarding a common understanding about the interrelatedness of learning, health, athletic/sport and health industry impact on achieving health equity. From this understanding, current and future systems and actions can be adjusted, adapted, or crafted to jointly achieve optimal learning, health, athletic/sport and health industry impact on achieving health equity.

Young people cannot fully benefit from each of the developmental spaces and levels of physical activity and sports if they do not have access to participate. Ensuring universal access to physical activity and sports which are safe, affordable, and fun are the focus of this effort and crucial if health equity is to be achieved. Though physical activity and sports are cornerstones of youth development, research also indicates that there are other times when life skills and behavior management skills may take priority (Pfeiffer & Wierenga, 2019). These other priorities are important to successful implementation of youth sports systems and schools alike; however, helping young people also meet the daily physical activity guidelines (i.e., at least 60 min. a day of moderate to vigorous physical activity and 3 days of muscular strength and endurance) will maximize the benefits of participation (DHHS, 2018). Designing and implementing high-quality training for coaches, Kinesiology professors, athletic administration, and healthcare professionals supporting youth sports are an incredible challenge (Newman, Santos, Cardoso, & Pereira, 2020), particularly when many of these people are volunteers. However, to the extent that sport participation produces benefits over detriments involves the preparation and engagement of adults throughout the youth sports system.

LIMITATIONS OF THE CONCEPTUAL FRAMEWORK

Some factors will limit the ability of institutions to adopt this Holistic Kinesiology-Athletic Model. Each of our institutions (youth sport systems, school systems, kinesiology, and athletic departments) vary greatly in size, resources, and institutional structures. Many institutions will have limited sports medicine staff and will depend on professionals from their community to meet the needs of their programs. Having providers who are contracted to provide care and not available daily on campus may limit the ability to develop well-performing individuals, departments, and teams of professionals to deliver the holistic care we propose.

In addition, the process of integrating multiple units or departments on a campus who have not previously worked together will have challenges in group dynamics and leadership to make the collaborative, holistic approach happen. Institutions will need to remain mindful of creating structures and processes that will foster these interactions. Such efforts are best adopted as new policies are connected to current institutional policy and leadership to increase the likelihood of sustainability beyond individual providers and relationships.

SUMMARY AND FUTURE DIRECTIONS

Engagement in sports has many benefits beyond winning in the game, and health is more than being injury-free. Collegiate athletes make up a special population that needs a holistic approach to achieve optimal health and wellness. A wide variety of athletic healthcare services exist across NCAA divisions and institutions. Still, a common thread involves consistent access to healthcare professionals. However, too often healthcare services for athletes focus on pre-participation physical examinations to assess and address medical issues and clearance for return to play after injury. This Holistic Kinesiology-Athletic Model framework may facilitate a greater investment by sports medicine professionals in preparing student-athletes to become physically, mentally, and socially healthy, and establish healthful behavioral patterns that persist throughout the lifecycle. We encourage individuals involved in the sports medicine system at the collegiate level to continue capitalizing on the physical wellness, promoted by sports involvement, yet extend beyond a focus on an individual athlete's physical well-being and consider the environmental factors that impact his/her overall health and wellness, while providing culturally competent care.

The innovative Holistic Kinesiology-Athletic Model recommends that clinicians use a framework for working with student-athletes that involves healthcare professionals collaborating with other campus, academic, social, health, and sports management professionals to create an athletic healthcare system that is more connected and efficient. Institutions can maximize their available resources by connecting and linking professionals from across disciplines, so everyone has a role in addressing a particular aspect of student-athlete wellness.

In the future, researchers and practitioners alike should test the application of this model in the various types of sports medicine settings (youth sport systems, school systems, kinesiology, and athletic departments) to determine the impact on student-athletes' health and well-being, as well as the effect on health disparities. Researchers and practitioners alike need to collaborate with multiple stakeholders to develop and test a training intervention for sports/kinesiology leaders that teaches them how to 1) use a strength-based approach, 2) address social determinants of health, and 3) demonstrate cultural competency during clinical interactions with student-athletes. In addition, institutions need to develop and test organizational models that create collaborative work environments for the multiple professionals who contribute to the well-being of student-athletes.

REFERENCES

Basch, C. E. (2011) Healthier students are better learners: A missing link in school reforms to close the achievement gap. Columbia University; 2010. http://www.equitycampaign.org/i/a/document/12557_EquityMattersVol6_Web03082010.pdf. Accessed April 29, 2014.

Bell, L. A. (2013). Theoretical foundations. In M. Adams, W. J. Blumenfield, C. Casteneda, H. W. Hackman, M. L., Peters, & X. Zuniga (Eds.), *Readings for diversity and social justice*. New York: Routledge Publishing.

Centers for Disease Control and Prevention. (2013). *A Guide for Developing Comprehensive School Physical Activity Programs*. https://www.cdc.gov/healthyschools/professional_development/e-learning/CSPAP/index.html

Culp, B. (2016). Social justice and the future of higher education kinesiology. Quest, 68, 271–283.

Eaton, D. K., Kann, L., Kinchen, S., Shanklin, S., Ross, J., Hawkins, J., . . . & Lim, C. (2008). Youth risk behavior surveillance—United States, 2007. *Morbidity and Mortality Weekly Report, 57*(4), 1–131.

Hodge, S. (2014). Ideological repositioning: Race, social justice, and promise. Quest, 68, 169–180.

James-Hassan, M. (2016). Cultivating culturally fluent leaders for future of kinesiology. *Quest, 68*(2), 159–169.

"Jane Goodall." (n.d.) Retrieved from https://www.goodreads.com/author/quotes/18163.Jane_Goodall.

Newman, T. J., Santos, F., Cardoso, A., & Pereira, P. (2020). The experiential nature of coach education within a positive youth development perspective: Implications for practice and research. *International Sport Coaching Journal, 7*(3), 398–406. http://doi.org/10.1123/iscj.2019-0106

Pfeiffer, K. A., & Wierenga, M. J. (2019). Promoting physical activity through youth sport. *Kinesiology Review, 8*(3), 204–210. http://doi.org/10.1123/kr.2019-0033.

Rovegno, I. & Bandhauer, D. (2017). *Elementary Physical Education*. Burlington, MA: Jones & Bartlett Learning.

Strayhorn, T. (2017, October 20). Interactional Diversity. *Fall Forum on Teaching and Learning*. Keynote address given at Fall Forum on Teaching and Learning, DePaul University, Chicago, IL.

Chapter Eight

Health Policymaking in Organizations

Nicole Butterbaugh and Blair W. Browning

Organizational policy should be designed for the betterment of the organization and its stakeholders. The goal of policymaking in organizations should be to implement policies with the intent of capturing the collective interests of individuals within the organization, as well as creating a shared common interest (Jongsma et al., 2018). Organizations are characterized as being goal-oriented social entities, and policies in organizations should be designed to either constrain or promote certain behaviors, provide resources to allow for desired behaviors, or to specify or assign authority (Canary et al., 2015). In other words, policies are intended to provide clarity and to socialize constituents into what is normative in organizational life. When considering deviating from these established norms, policymakers should keep in mind the importance of creating a shared vision and purpose when creating or changing organizational policy (Lewis et al., 2006). The co-creation of policy, or at least keeping potential change in front of organizational members, can lead to smoother transition. Recently, in light of the global COVID-19 pandemic, there has obviously been greatly heightened and pointed attention toward health policies in organizations.

Health policymaking in organizations should follow the goals and concepts of general policymaking in organizations with the health and safety of the organization and its stakeholders at the forefront. In order for health policymaking to be effective, organizations should consider "the magnitude of the problem, the size of benefits and adverse effects, feasibility and acceptability, as well as resource and equity implications" (Vogel et al., 2013, p. 8). The use of research evidence is especially important in health policymaking. Policymakers should identify research evidence and implement the findings from the evidence accordingly in order to support health policymaking (Lavis et al., 2009; Sarkies et al., 2017). One interesting and unique area of health policymaking is sport organizations.

HEALTH POLICYMAKING IN SPORT ORGANIZATIONS

Organizational policy within sport, especially in regard to health policy, plays an important role in public policy and even in the functioning of society as a whole (Stenling & Sam, 2019). Sport organizations must create policy based on the environments they find themselves in, and the world must react to this with an equal or opposite reaction. In fact, much of the world failed to grasp the significance and impact of COVID-19 until the National Basketball Association (NBA) canceled the remainder of its regular season (although completing the playoffs in a bubble in Orlando), and the National Collegiate Athletic Association (NCAA) basketball tournament was canceled as well. The domino effect of cancellations (discussed more below as "interlinked chains") that followed due to these impactful decisions brought about an awareness of the severity of the global health crisis. Thus, at times, it is the reaction within a global environment, but sport organizations have always had to be mindful of reactions, such as who they are receiving their funding from and ensuring alignment with those funding opportunities (Stenling & Sam, 2019).

Strittmatter et al. (2018) defines the sport policy process as an "interlinked chain of legitimating acts," asserting that one action influences a subsequent action, and so forth. The cancellation of and changes in date to the 2021 Summer Olympics in Tokyo is a great example of this interlinked chain of legitimating acts at work, since the dates of other and future Olympic Games had the potential to be impacted, as well as the schedule for professional sports competition around the world during said time (Rowe, 2020). Indeed, four potential reasons for advocacy in and of sport organizations are time horizons and policy churn, accountability, budget politics, and political environment (Stenling & Sam, 2019).

Some examples of policy within sport organizations include: illegal drug use, extreme weather policies, professional and college football "targeting" policy and other penalty policies, concussion policies, and policies regarding the participation of transgender athletes, to name a few (Baugh et al., 2015; Chalmers et al., 2020; Richardson & Chen, 2020; Smith & Stewart, 2008; Westermann et al., 2016). Rather than casting a wide net and still failing to address every interesting policy, for the purpose of this chapter, we will focus specifically on sport organizational policies during the COVID-19 pandemic.

COVID-19 AND SPORT ORGANIZATIONAL POLICY

The COVID-19 pandemic involves a viral disease that arose from China during the end of 2019 and beginning of 2020 (Rothan & Byrareddy, 2020). The intensely communicable nature of the COVID-19 virus caused governments and other organizations to adopt and essentially normalize policies such as social distancing, contact tracing, and quarantining (Anderson et al., 2020; Hellewell et al., 2020). Although these procedures were designed to abate or halt the spread of the COVID-19 virus and were put into place in swift fashion, as noted earlier, many sporting events were still forced to be canceled at the recreational, collegiate, and professional levels.

Countless sport organizations required the creation and implementation of organizational policies promoting health and safety of their constituents in reaction to the COVID-19 pandemic. However, in the face of unforeseen adversity, professional sports leagues did not all respond in unison. Various sport organizations reacted differently from one another and implemented their own unique policies. As the pandemic continued, there were some similarities in policy among the leagues, but sport organizational policy regarding COVID-19 still differed, and continues to vary considerably.

Both the National Football League (NFL) and its subsequent National Football League Players Association (NFLPA) designed and implemented a detailed and comprehensive evidence-based COVID-19 monitoring protocol in order to allow for the start of the 2020 season, entitled the COVID-19 Testing and Surveillance Program, otherwise referred to as "the Program" (National Football League & National Football League Players Association, 2020). Since the NFL and NFLPA's Program called for regular testing, specific behavioral protocols, contact tracing, and other safety precautions, players and staff were allowed to reside in their home environments and continue work at their home practice facilities, while traveling to games (Mack, 2021).

While the NFL had a detailed plan focusing on behavior and precise monitoring, other leagues such as the NBA and National Hockey League (NHL) adopted a "bubble" approach or similar "hub" structure of the "bubble" approach in order to restart and continue their respective seasons. Major League Baseball (MLB) postponed numerous games and practices for much longer than other professional leagues and surveyed the viral contagion from afar, arguably causing quite a rift between stakeholders both in and around the organization. Differing outcomes were made regarding participation at the collegiate level as well despite all leagues being under the NCAA banner. Many leagues returned to play in the fall of 2020 (with policies, of course) while others, such as the Ivy League, canceled their entire Fall season for all sports.

Mega-sporting events as we knew them began to shift before our eyes once play was able to continue. The Summer Olympics did not take place in 2020 in any form. The crowd at Super Bowl LV was supplemented with cardboard cutouts to resemble a live audience as they allowed less than half of a capacity crowd to attend. It wasn't just the games themselves that were impacted, as popular award ceremonies and other high-spectacle events such as the Heisman Trophy Ceremony and the NFL Draft were switched to a virtual format. When fans were once again allowed to enter stadiums and arenas to cheer on their favorite teams, they were at a reduced capacity whether it was one-quarter, one-third, or some other minimized allotment. The typical fan might have described the gameday experience to be "eerie" during this time. For example, student sections at collegiate sporting events, if present, were not able to produce loud chants due to their diminished capacity; tailgating was prohibited within a certain radius of many stadiums; and no marching bands or spirit squads filled the field. Understandably, COVID-19's impact on sport organizations became an interest to the general public and the media (Rowe, 2020).

Health policies of sport organizations during the COVID-19 pandemic took many forms. Safety procedures such as face coverings, social distancing, plexiglass dividers, virtual payment and ticketing systems, and temperature checks were some of the most prominently adopted protocols at the onset of the pandemic. The list of health policies in sport organizations surrounding COVID-19 continues to expand and mutate just as the virus does itself, so for the purposes of this chapter, we will focus on health policies in sport organizations spotlighting three specific areas: the bubble, contact tracing, and the COVID-19 vaccine.

The Bubble

The bubble approach was designed as a way to allow sport to continue while mitigating the spread of COVID-19 as much as possible. Rather than risking the players and necessary personnel traveling across the country for practices and games, increasing their probability of contracting the COVID-19 virus, all necessary personnel would live and resume competition within a socially isolated "bubble." Succinctly put, the concept meant "living and playing in a protective bubble to reduce the risk of [COVID-19] infection" (Goldman, 2020). Several leagues instigated the use of the bubble approach, and others followed completely or in part by adapting the bubble approach to include multiple "hub" cities which essentially acted as mini-bubbles.

The NBA bubble is arguably the most known and popular among the general public. News about the emergence of the bubble was first leaked to the public through ESPN, which announced the plan for the bubble to take place at the ESPN Wide World of Sports, located within Walt Disney World Resort in Orlando, Florida (*NBA Details Virus Testing, Amenities for Orlando*, 2020). The bubble, enacted by the NBA, operated strictly with a fixed population of players and essential personnel (Salazar & Katz, 2021). With the use of daily testing, social isolation, and other safety and behavioral protocols, the bubble allowed the players and personnel to participate regularly in unmasked, indoor, close-contact activities that were considered high-risk to transmission of the COVID-19 virus (Salazar & Katz, 2021).

After the NHL paused their season and missed a total of 189 games, teams qualifying for the playoffs were determined off of a points basis with the data from the portion of the season that had been played (*NHL Plans to Return with 24 Teams Competing for Stanley Cup*, n.d.). In order to facilitate the playoffs and eventually crown a 2020 Stanley Cup champion, the NHL chose to implement a similar bubble strategy to the NBA, but utilized two "hub" bubble locations in Canada; Toronto for the Eastern Conference qualifiers, and Edmonton for the Western Conference qualifiers and Stanley Cup Final (Goldman, 2020; *NHL Plans to Return with 24 Teams Competing for Stanley Cup*, n.d.). Rules regarding traveling personnel and an intricate COVID-19 testing system were used in tandem with the "hub" cities in order to make the playoff season possible (*NHL Plans to Return with 24 Teams Competing for Stanley Cup*, n.d.).

The MLB chose not to utilize the bubble strategy for gameplay during the regular season and continued to travel and play games in all thirty of the team's home cities, with the exception of the Toronto Blue Jays, who temporarily relocated their home base to Buffalo, New York in order to participate in the regular season (Goldman, 2020; *Timeline of How the COVID-19 Pandemic Has Impacted the 2020 Major League Baseball Season*, n.d.). The MLB did implement a "hub"-type bubble strategy for the 2021 playoffs; utilizing both Minute Maid Park in Houston, Texas and Globe Life Field in Arlington, Texas for the National League playoffs, and both Dodger Stadium in Los Angeles, California, and Petco Park in San Diego, California, for the American League playoffs (*MLB Playoffs At Petco Park SPORTS: "Bubble" Baseball Brings Benefits*, n.d.).

Clearly, the popularity and success of the bubble approach prompted imitations, and "more and more events are being staged in bio-bubbles as governments and sporting authorities look to limit the impact of COVID-19" (Cardinelli, 2021, p. 1) Both the National Women's Soccer League and the National Women's Hockey League adopted the use of bubbles in order to continue competition (Bustillos, 2021; *First League Into the Coronavirus Bubble: Women's Soccer*, n.d.). The COVID-19 pandemic supported and fundamentally changed the practicable concept of the sporting bubble, allowing room for conflicts between the physical and mental health safety and the delicacy of potential injury between those involved (Pavlidis & Rowe, 2021). While the success of the bubble benefited many stakeholders of sport organizations, the potential adverse effects of the bubble need to be examined.

The bubble approach can have a negative impact on the mental health of its members. Players have begun to voice their mental health struggles with the sport organizational policies that were implemented regarding COVID-19, such as the mental impact of the bio-bubbles (Cardinelli, 2021). The bubble essentially isolates its members from the outside world, causing them to have a limited social experience, which can ultimately lead to a disconnect from internal feelings of reality (Pavlidis & Rowe, 2021). The overarching question to be asked is whether the potential benefits of the bubble approach outweigh the potential consequences. Notably, this is a common ethical conflict with creation and implementation of organizational health policy.

Although the bubble's success in limiting the spread of COVID-19 is clear, it is important to note that the procedure did not go without a hitch. Rowe (2020) mentions the close relationship between sport and the media, especially during the pandemic, and how the media and the general public wanted to either watch, report, and/or talk about the members of the bubble's every move. This close relationship between sport and the media could have posed a disadvantage for athletes and other personnel in the bubble who were toeing the line of COVID-19 policy, as their "bubble breaches" were seemingly easy to identify and punish.

There were many breaches of the bubble protocol, ranging from athletes traveling for a night out on the town to romantic partners sneaking into the bubble for some one-on-one time (Pavlidis & Rowe, 2021). Breaches to the NBA's COVID-19 protocols (i.e., breaching the bubble) had the potential to result in monetary fines and other punishments from the league including dismissal from the bubble. This occurred during the Western Conference semifinals when Houston Rockets player Danuel House "breached the league's health and safety protocols by inviting an unauthorized guest to his hotel room" (Cacciola, 2020). The NBA added that House would not be participating with the Rockets in additional games that season. This was not an insignificant loss as House averaged playing about 25 minutes per game for the Rockets, who advanced to the Conference semifinals before losing to the eventual NBA champion the Los Angeles Lakers.

The bubble approach is widely considered to have been a successful approach to mitigating the spread of COVID-19. However, both the limitations and implications of the bubble need to be highlighted. The successful completion of the NBA and NHL seasons in bubble environments necessitate additional study. While the COVID-19 case numbers were either low (NBA) or non-existent (NHL), it remains unclear if it was specifically attributable to the bubble or simply due to having young, healthy, and non-immunocompromised athletes (Goldman, 2020; Salazar & Katz, 2021).

Proximity Tracking Devices

Contact tracing is an important protocol involved in stopping the spread of the COVID-19 virus (Hellewell et al., 2020). Contact tracing involves identifying individuals within a proximity of six feet who remained in what is considered that close-contact proximity either consecutively or cumulatively for a certain period of time—generally around fifteen minutes—and then notifying those individuals of their exposure. Typically, contact tracing results in the monitoring of symptoms, testing, and even quarantining.

Since manual contact tracing can be difficult to facilitate, many organizations adopted the use of proximity tracking devices to aid with the process of contact tracing. These proximity tracking devices were seen in many forms, from wearable devices to video analysis, and even phone applications. Sport organizations typically utilized a wearable proximity tracking device designed by KINEXON, and some leagues even had these KINEXON devices sewn into players' jerseys (Mack, 2021).

Proximity tracking devices were used in the NFL's program to aid in contact tracing. Mack (2021) noted that the NFL required players and personnel to wear KINEXON wearable proximity devices at all times when in club environments. The KINEXON wearable proximity devices eased the process of contact tracing by tracking the minutes and seconds of time in which individuals were within six feet from one another, whether that be during one interaction or over the course of multiple interactions. If and when a positive COVID-19 case were to arise, the officials consulted those who were deemed necessary by their proximity devices (Mack, 2021).

All Tier 1 participants for the 2021 NCAA Men's Basketball Tournament were required to wear KINEXON proximity tracking devices in order to aid in contact tracing at all times during the tournament, including during practices and games (*NCAA Announces Health and Safety Protocols for DI Men's Basketball Championship*, n.d.). These devices show time measurements of those who are within close contact of someone who tests positive for COVID-19, and when paired with video analysis, helped officials in determining necessary quarantines for individuals (*NCAA Announces Health and Safety Protocols for DI Men's Basketball Championship*, n.d.). If an interaction within six feet of an individual who had recently tested positive was less than fifteen minutes total over a twenty-four-hour period, then a quarantine may not have been required (*NCAA Announces Health and Safety Protocols for DI Men's Basketball Championship*, n.d.).

Limitations and implications of proximity tracking device use in sport organizations is something to be considered. Sport organizations should be cautioned about the pros and cons of investing in large quantities of wearable devices, as the devices are expensive and the cons may outweigh the benefits in certain circumstances (Smith, 2021). Additionally, sport organizations need to confirm the analyses and results of the proximity devices' contact tracing ability to make educated decisions about the protocols for those who are deemed "exposed." Wearable technology can be helpful, and it can be invasive; it can be informative, and we are still awaiting data concerning its reliability. Thus, proximity tracking devices and the policies surrounding them warrant continued study and will be intriguing to follow in the years ahead.

COVID-19 Vaccine

The creation and dispersion of the COVID-19 vaccine called for even more swift policy creations and adaptations. For many leagues, their COVID-19 policy changed to allow for more movement and freedom for those who had fully received the vaccine. For others, the COVID-19 vaccine was mandated to even attend an event in the respective arena or stadium. Thus, many leagues provided incentives and sought to achieve a high vaccination rate as quickly as possible for both players and fans, in hopes of limiting the spread of COVID-19 and hopefully allowing for some normalcy to return to sport. As of June 2021, the WNBA led the way among professional sports teams in regard to vaccination rate, with 99 percent of players fully vaccinated, constituting that all twelve teams were considered to have met the fully-vaccinated threshold (WNBA, 2021).

Sport organizations adapted their COVID-19 protocols as the vaccine became available and was administered. The Professional Golf Association (PGA) Tour announced in July of 2021 that they would stop their weekly COVID-19 testing for players even if a player was not vaccinated (*Changes Announced to PGA TOUR's COVID Protocols*, n.d.). Only players who were unvaccinated and had come into close contact with someone who has tested positive for COVID-19 would require testing (*Changes Announced to PGA TOUR's COVID Protocols*, n.d.). The PGA Tour Senior Vice President Tyler Dennis said that these policy changes were made possible because of the high vaccination rate among the PGA Tour constituents and the positively trending factors across the country (*Sports and COVID-19: The Impact on the Sports-Event Industry*, n.d.).

The Euro 2020 Group Stage soccer matches at Wembley Stadium in London, England were the first sporting events in the United Kingdom to require the usage of vaccine passports in order to enter the stadium (Ziegler, n.d.). The 2021 BNP Paribas Open, a popular professional tennis tournament, required all fans, players, volunteers, staff, sponsors, media, and vendors to show valid proof of vaccination in order to enter the Indian Wells Tennis Garden for the tournament (*Health and Safety*, n.d.). The list of venues and events requiring proof of vaccination for individuals to enter the venue continues to expand nationally and globally including events such as the 2021 US Open tennis tournament, 2021 home games for the NFL's Buffalo Bills, and the 2022 Fútbol World Cup.

Some leagues are employing incentives for their constituents to receive the vaccine. The NFL and the NFLPA have made it clear that individuals who are fully vaccinated do not have to participate in daily testing; do not have to wear masks; do not have to quarantine due to contact tracing; and do not have travel restrictions or weight room capacity limits (National Football League & National Football League Players Association, 2020). Individuals who are employed by any of the NFL's teams are required to be vaccinated if they want to maintain their Tier 1 status (National Football League & National Football League Players Association, 2020). The MLB is even targeting vaccination incentives at fans, as teams have offered vaccination events at their games where those who receive a vaccine also receive free tickets to an upcoming game, a movement called "vaccinate at the plate" (*MLB Vaccinate at the Plate*, n.d.).

As with the other policies discussed in this chapter, the limitations and implications regarding the numerous COVID-19 vaccination policies must be discussed. The creation and implementation of policy regarding the COVID-19 vaccine is particularly interesting because of the emergence of breakthrough cases. Breakthrough COVID-19 cases occur when an individual contracts the virus after receiving full vaccination doses. It is said that the severity and longevity of symptoms are lessened in breakthrough cases (O'Brien, 2021). It seems as though many of the COVID-19 vaccination policies put forth by sport organizations did not account for breakthrough cases, causing apprehension in reacting to positive COVID-19 results paired with proof of vaccination. The first popular example of this scenario occurred in May of 2021 with the New York Yankees (*Statement—Update on Yankees COVID-19 Positive Tests*, n.d.). Their press statement was strategically ambiguous, implying that the organization did not know how to effectively combat this nuanced breakthrough COVID-19 scenario. Strategic ambiguity (Eisenberg, 1984) can be an organizational strategy that leaves space for different and multiple interpretations. Breakthrough COVID-19 cases brought uncertainty and impacted additional sport organizations as well as the mega-sporting events. At the 2021 Summer Olympics in Tokyo, two members of Uganda's Olympic team tested positive for COVID-19 despite having received the vaccine and being quarantined the recommended fourteen days after vaccination (*Uganda Olympic Team Member Tests Positive for Coronavirus*, 2021).

Breakthrough COVID-19 cases are not the only obstacle with vaccination mandates in sport organizations. Additionally, the mandate of the COVID-19 vaccine could be framed as discriminatory toward those who cannot receive the vaccine due to medical reasons or to those who do not wish to receive the vaccine for religious or personal reasons. Some NFL players publicly voiced their concerns and hesitations about getting the COVID-19 vaccine (*Sports and COVID-19: The Impact on the Sports-Event Industry*, n.d.).

IMPACTS OF COVID-19 ON SPORT ORGANIZATIONS

Recruiting

The COVID-19 pandemic and its subsequent policies had a tremendous impact on college recruiting in sports that we may not ultimately see the effects of until at least 2023 (*How COVID-19 Has Changed College Football and Basketball Recruiting Landscapes*, 2020). Specific policies involving recruiting as well as eligibility waivers will have significant impact.

The "Dead Period," which is a time in which coaches are unable to communicate with prospective recruits, was extended for over a year, coupled with the fact that many high school juniors and seniors did not get to play. The fallout from these two significant events will mean that the recruiting classes, and therefore the overall team makeup over the next few years, will be heavily impacted by the pandemic.

Collegiate athletic coaches anticipated their recruiting budgets to suffer as a result of the pandemic (*College Coach Insights on Recruiting During Coronavirus*, n.d.). Coaches incorporated many mediated communication efforts into the recruiting process (*College Coach Insights on Recruiting During Coronavirus*, n.d.; *How COVID-19 Has Changed College Football and Basketball Recruiting Landscapes*, 2020). A favorite among these unique virtual recruiting efforts was an online Madden tournament including the Texas A&M football coaches and their recruits, where they battled tournament-style to crown a champion while building relationships with the athletes through virtual communication (*How COVID-19 Has Changed College Football and Basketball Recruiting Landscapes*, 2020).

Coaches also began to shift their focus to more of a value-centered approach rather than the typical "wow factor" that in-person visits and facility tours can provide and entice athletes. With this "no smoke" ideology guiding the conversations, some coaches feel that the athletes are able to make more educated and informed decisions (*How COVID-19 Has Changed College Football and Basketball Recruiting Landscapes*, 2020).

An important policy change and implementation to discuss is the extended year of NCAA eligibility for athletes whose athletic seasons were impacted by the pandemic. This provided a tension for some coaches in their recruiting efforts. Although the extra year of eligibility did not count toward the 85 scholarship limit for teams, the programs were expected to pay for any additional scholarships applied to incoming recruits. For some programs, this meant deciphering between a high school recruit or honoring a veteran member's scholarship (*How COVID-19 Has Changed College Football and Basketball Recruiting Landscapes*, 2020).

Mental Health

The COVID-19 pandemic has demonstrated both acute and lasting effects on individuals' mental health. As noted earlier, numerous players from the NBA bubble reported that social isolation was harmful to their mental health (Stein, 2021). Mental health issues in the NCAA increased by up to 250% in the spring of 2020 when college sporting events were canceled and postponed (National Collegiate Athletic Association, 2020). During this time, it has been proven that athletes were feeling helpless, had low motivation, and had high stress (Bullard, 2020).

Revenue

Professional sports faced an approximate $13 billion sales decrease as a result of the COVID-19 pandemic (Kochkodin, 2020). With this dramatic sum of money lost, there has been a surge of new motivations for creation and diversification of revenue streams (*Sports and COVID-19: The Impact on the Sports-Event Industry*, n.d.).

Many sports organizations sold cardboard cutouts of fans for placement in stadium seats, as an interactive way to increase the feeling of participation from fans and spectators while attempting to curb some of the devastating sales losses during the pandemic. One of the clearest examples of new revenue streams can be seen through the NHL's implementation of helmet advertisements. While these helmet advertisements began as a way to generate revenue amidst the pandemic, NHL Commissioner Gary Bettman states that the helmet ads are likely to stay in subsequent seasons (*Bettman: Helmet Ads "More Likely Than Not" to Stay in NHL*, n.d.).

The NFL has demonstrated this through discussion to expand their international exposure into potentially Germany and other Europe locations, in addition to their existing London reach, in hopes of generating more international revenue (*Sports and COVID-19: The Impact on the Sports-Event Industry,* n.d.). Similarly, the NHL should expect revenue generation from their expansions into Seattle with the Kraken and Las Vegas with the Golden Knights, and the NBA has even begun discussion about a potential expansion into one of these cities as well (*Sports and COVID-19: The Impact on the Sports-Event Industry,* n.d.).

FUTURE DIRECTIONS

Most of the research on sport policymaking and the organizational dynamic of sport is done at an international or national level, primarily studying professional sport (Stein, 2021). Research on the foundational, or "ordinary-people" level of sport organization and policymaking is absent (Skille, 2008). Future research needs to be done on the topic of policymaking within sport organizations.

As COVID-19 cases continued to increase and the pandemic continued to spread, the media shifted their focus to the topics of health, safety, and quality of life within the area of sports (Sadri et al., 2021). With the emergence of the COVID-19 pandemic, and its impact on society, it has pressured sport organizations into the role of high reliability organizations. Future research could be done in applying High Reliability Organizational Theory to sport organizations. For example, this theory could be applied to sport organizational policy in future research as it relates to policies such as concussions, return to play, and targeting policy. Again, with conversations about potentially lethal health and safety risks in sport such as CTE in the NFL, High Reliability Organizational Theory can be applied to sport organizational policy.

Future research needs to be done regarding the mental health impacts of COVID-19 on the athletes and personnel involved. As mentioned in this chapter, the mental health consequences of the bubble have surfaced. Some leagues did provide mental health services during the COVID-19 pandemic, and research could be done to see if this temporary, short-term model of mental health aid was effective during the COVID-19 pandemic.

In conclusion, organizational policies should be designed for the betterment of the organization and its stakeholders. Using the bubble or a hub-bubble environment, contact tracing, and vaccines, we have seen innovative policies implemented to enable sports to continue. The long-term results may not fully be known for some time but the immediate outcome was a return to the field, court, and ice for many athletes and a bit of normalcy during a time that could be described as anything but normal. These new health policies in sports organizations had to be decisively integrated while accomplishing the goal of providing clarity to their constituents as individuals were socialized into "the new normal."

REFERENCES

Anderson, R. M., Heesterbeek, H., Klinkenberg, D., & Hollingsworth, T. D. (2020). How will country-based mitigation measures influence the course of the COVID-19 epidemic? *The Lancet*, *395*(10228), 931–934. https://doi.org/10.1016/S0140-6736(20)30567-5.

Baugh, C. M., Kroshus, E., Daneshvar, D. H., Filali, N. A., Hiscox, M. J., & Glantz, L. H. (2015). Concussion management in United States college sports: Compliance with National Collegiate Athletic Association concussion policy and areas for improvement. *The American Journal of Sports Medicine*, *43*(1), 47–56. https://doi.org/10.1177/0363546514553090

Bettman: Helmet ads "more likely than not" to stay in NHL. (n. d.). *SportsLogos.Net News*. Retrieved October 3, 2021, from https://news.sportslogos.net/2021/03/12/bettman-helmet-ads-more-likely-than-not-to-stay-in-nhl/hockey-2/.

Bullard, J. B. (2020). The impact of COVID-19 on the well-being of Division III student-athletes. *The Sport Journal*, *22*. https://thesportjournal-org.ezproxy.baylor.edu/article/the-impact-of-covid-19-on-the-well-being-of-division-iii-student-athletes/.

Bustillos, B. (2021, January 28). Inside The National Women's Hockey League's Coronavirus Bubble. *All Things Considered (NPR)*. National Public Radio, Inc. http://ezproxy.baylor.edu/login?url=https://search.ebscohost.com/login.aspx?direct=true&db=n5h&AN=6XN2021012810&site=ehost-live&scope=site.

Cacciola. (2020, September 11). Rockets' Danuel House leaves N.B.A. bubble after violation. *The New York Times*. https://www.nytimes.com/2020/09/11/sports/basketball/nba-houston-rockets-danuel-house.html.

Canary, H. E., Blevins, M., & Ghorbani, S. S. (2015). Organizational policy communication research: Challenges, discoveries, and future directions. *Communication Reports*, *28*(1), 48–64. https://doi.org/10.1080/08934215.2013.865063.

Cardinelli, J. (2021, April 5). Rolling with the punches: To survive in a bio-bubble, sports teams will need to think outside the box. *Daily Maverick* [BLOG]. http://www.proquest.com/docview/2508687581/citation/7A108BBA2F46472EPQ/1.

Chalmers, S., Anderson, G., & Jay, O. (2020). Considerations for the development of extreme heat policies in sport and exercise. *BMJ Open Sport & Exercise Medicine*, *6*(1), e000774. https://doi.org/10.1136/bmjsem-2020-000774.

Changes announced to PGA TOUR's COVID protocols. (n.d.). PGATour. Retrieved September 18, 2021, from https://www.pgatour.com/news/2021/06/28/changes-announced-to-pga-tour-covid-19-coronavirus-protocols.html.

College Coach Insights on Recruiting During Coronavirus. (n.d.). Retrieved October 3, 2021, from https://www.ncsasports.org/coronavirus-sports/college-coach-insights-covid-19.

Eisenberg, E. (1984). Ambiguity as strategy in organizational communication. *Communication Monographs, 51*, 227–242.

First League Into the Coronavirus Bubble: Women's Soccer (n.d.). *WSJ.com*. Retrieved October 3, 2021, from https://www.wsj.com/articles/first-league-into-the-coronavirus-bubble-womens-soccer-11593000021.

Goldman, T. (2020, August 1). Saturday sports: Hockey and basketball follow MLB as athletes compete in "bubbles." *NPR*. https://www.npr.org/2020/08/01/898099587/saturday-sports-hockey-and-basketball-follow-mlb-as-athletes-compete-in-bubbles.

Health and Safety. (n.d.). BNP Paribas Open. Retrieved September 18, 2021, from https://bnpparibasopen.com/plan-your-visit/health-and-safety/.

Hellewell, J., Abbott, S., Gimma, A., Bosse, N. I., Jarvis, C. I., Russell, T. W., Munday, J. D., Kucharski, A. J., Edmunds, W. J., Sun, F., Flasche, S., Quilty, B. J., Davies, N., Liu, Y., Clifford, S., Klepac, P., Jit, M., Diamond, C., Gibbs, H., . . . Eggo, R. M. (2020). Feasibility of controlling COVID-19 outbreaks by isolation of cases and contacts. *The Lancet Global Health, 8*(4), e488–e496. https://doi.org/10.1016/S2214-109X(20)30074-7.

How COVID-19 has changed college football and basketball recruiting landscapes. (2020, November 10). *ESPN.com*. https://www.espn.com/college-football/insider/story/_/id/30250225/how-covid-19-changed-college-football-basketball-recruiting-landscapes.

Jongsma, K., Rimon-Zarfaty, N., Raz, A., & Schicktanz, S. (2018). One for all, all for one? Collective representation in healthcare policy. *Journal of Bioethical Inquiry, 15*(3), 337–340. https://doi.org/10.1007/s11673-018-9870-9.

Kochkodin, B. (2020, November 5). NBA, MLB, NFL Facing Nearly $13 Billion in Covid Losses. *Bloomberg*. https://www.bloomberg.com/news/articles/2020-11-05/u-s-sports-leagues-facing-nearly-13-billion-in-covid-losses.

Lavis, J. N., Oxman, A. D., Lewin, S., & Fretheim, A. (2009). SUPPORT Tools for evidence-informed health Policymaking (STP). *Health Research Policy and Systems, 7*(S1). https://doi.org/10.1186/1478-4505-7-S1-I1.

Lewis, L. K., Schmisseur, A. M., Stephens, K. K., & Weir, K. E. (2006). Advice on communicating during organizational change. *Journal of Business Communication, 43*(2), 113–137. https://doi.org/10.1177/0021943605285355.

Mack, C. D. (2021). Implementation and evolution of mitigation measures, testing, and contact tracing in the National Football League, August 9–November 21, 2020. *Morbidity and Mortality Weekly Report, 70*. https://doi.org/10.15585/mmwr.mm7004e2.

MLB Playoffs at Petco Park SPORTS: "Bubble" Baseball Brings Benefits. (n.d.). Retrieved September 16, 2021, from https://go-gale-com.ezproxy.baylor.edu/ps/i.do?p=GPS&u=txshracd2488&id=GALE|A639172349&v=2.1&it=r.

MLB Vaccinate at the Plate. (n.d.). *MLB.com*. Retrieved September 18, 2021, from https://www.mlb.com/tickets/vaccinate-ticket-offer.

National Collegiate Athletic Association. (2020). 2020RES_NCAASACOVID-19SurveyPPT.pdf. https://ncaaorg.s3.amazonaws.com/research/other/2020/2020RES_NCAASACOVID-19SurveyPPT.pdf.

National Football League, & National Football League Players Association. (2020, September 5). NFL-NFLPA COVID-19 Protocols for the 2020 regular season. NFL.com. https://www.nfl.com/playerhealthandsafety/health-and-wellness/covid-19/nfl-nflpa-covid-19-protocols-for-the-2020-regular-season.

NBA details virus testing, amenities for Orlando. (2020, June 17). *ESPN.com.* https://www.espn.com/nba/story/_/id/29321006/in-documents-nba-details-coronavirus-testing-process-orlando-campus-life.

NCAA Announces Health and Safety Protocols for DI Men's Basketball Championship. (n.d.). Retrieved September 7, 2021, from https://www.ncaa.org/about/resources/media-center/news/ncaa-announces-health-and-safety-protocols-di-men-s-basketball-championship.

NHL plans to return with 24 teams competing for Stanley Cup. (n.d.). *NHL.com.* Retrieved September 18, 2021, from https://www.nhl.com/news/nhl-plans-to-return-with-24-team-stanley-cup-playoffs/c-317031010.

O'Brien, K. (2021, August 13). Episode #49—Can I get infected after vaccination? World Health Organization. https://www.who.int/emergencies/diseases/novel-coronavirus-2019/media-resources/science-in-5/episode-49-can-i-get-infected-after-vaccination.

Pavlidis, A., & Rowe, D. (2021). The sporting bubble as gilded cage: Gendered professional sport in pandemic times and beyond. *M/C Journal*, *24*(1), https://doi.org/10.5204/mcj.2736.

Richardson, A., & Chen, M. A. (2020). Comment on: "Sport and Transgender People: A Systematic Review of the Literature Relating to Sport Participation and Competitive Sport Policies." *Sports Medicine*, *50*(10), 1857–1859. https://doi.org/10.1007/s40279-020-01323-7.

Rothan, H. A., & Byrareddy, S. N. (2020). The epidemiology and pathogenesis of coronavirus disease (COVID-19) outbreak. *Journal of Autoimmunity*, *109*, 102433. https://doi.org/10.1016/j.jaut.2020.102433.

Rowe, D. (2020). Subjecting pandemic sport to a sociological procedure. *Journal of Sociology*, *56*(4), 704–713. https://doi.org/10.1177/1440783320941284.

Sadri, S. R., Buzzelli, N. R., Gentile, P., & Billings, A. C. (2021). Sports journalism content when no sports occur: Framing athletes amidst the COVID-19 international pandemic. *Communication & Sport*, 21674795211001936. https://doi.org/10.1177/21674795211001937.

Salazar, J. W., & Katz, M. H. (2021). COVID-19 Lessons from the National Basketball Association bubble—can persistently SARS-CoV-2–positive individuals transmit infection to others? *JAMA Internal Medicine*, *181*(7), 967. https://doi.org/10.1001/jamainternmed.2021.2121.

Sarkies, M. N., Bowles, K.-A., Skinner, E. H., Haas, R., Lane, H., & Haines, T. P. (2017). The effectiveness of research implementation strategies for promoting evidence-informed policy and management decisions in healthcare: A systematic review. *Implementation Science*, *12*(1), 132. https://doi.org/10.1186/s13012-017-0662-0.

Skille, E. Å. (2008). Understanding sport clubs as sport policy implementers: A theoretical framework for the analysis of the implementation of central sport policy through local and voluntary sport organizations. *International Review for the Sociology of Sport*, *43*(2), 181–200. https://doi.org/10.1177/1012690208096035.

Smith, A. C. T., & Stewart, B. (2008). Drug policy in sport: Hidden assumptions and inherent contradictions. *Drug & Alcohol Review*, *27*(2), 123–129.

Smith, A. N. (2021). A review of the physical, societal and economic effects of wearable devices in sports. *The Sport Journal*. https://thesportjournal-org.ezproxy.baylor.edu/article/a-review-of-the-physical-societal-and-economic-effects-of-wearable-devices-in-sports/.

Sports and COVID-19: The Impact on the Sports-Event Industry. (n.d.). *SportsTravel*. Retrieved September 7, 2021, from https://www.sportstravelmagazine.com/sports-and-covid-19-what-happened-earlier-this-summer/.

Statement—Update on Yankees COVID-19 positive tests. (n.d.). *MLB.com*. Retrieved October 3, 2021, from https://www.mlb.com/press-release/press-release-statement-update-on-yankees-covid-19-positive-tests.

Stein, M. (2021, May 22). The N.B.A. vs. the coronavirus may be the toughest playoff matchup. *The New York Times*. https://www.nytimes.com/2021/05/22/sports/basketball/covid-nba.html.

Stenling, C., & Sam, M. (2019). From "passive custodian" to "active advocate": Tracing the emergence and sport-internal transformative effects of sport policy advocacy. *International Journal of Sport Policy and Politics*, *11*(3), 447–463. https://doi.org/10.1080/19406940.2019.1581648.

Strittmatter, A.-M., Stenling, C., Fahlén, J., & Skille, E. (2018). Sport policy analysis revisited: The sport policy process as an interlinked chain of legitimating acts. *International Journal of Sport Policy and Politics*, *10*(4), 621–635. https://doi.org/10.1080/19406940.2018.1522657.

Timeline of how the COVID-19 pandemic has impacted the 2020 Major League Baseball season. *CBSSports.com*. (n.d.). Retrieved September 7, 2021, from https://www.cbssports.com/mlb/news/timeline-of-how-the-covid-19-pandemic-has-impacted-the-2020-major-league-baseball-season/.

Uganda Olympic team member tests positive for coronavirus. (2021, June 20). *CBS17.com*. https://www.cbs17.com/news/uganda-olympic-team-member-tests-positive-for-coronavirus/.

Vogel, J. P., Oxman, A. D., Glenton, C., Rosenbaum, S., Lewin, S., Gülmezoglu, A. M., & Souza, J. P. (2013). Policymakers' and other stakeholders' perceptions of key considerations for health system decisions and the presentation of evidence to inform those considerations: An international survey. *Health Research Policy and Systems*, *11*(1), 19. https://doi.org/10.1186/1478-4505-11-19.

Westermann, R. W., Kerr, Z. Y., Wehr, P., & Amendola, A. (2016). Increasing lower extremity injury rates across the 2009–2010 to 2014–2015 seasons of National Collegiate Athletic Association football: An unintended consequence of the "targeting" rule used to prevent concussions? *The American Journal of Sports Medicine*, *44*(12), 3230–3236. https://doi.org/10.1177/0363546516659290.

WNBA. (2021, June 28). The following was released by the WNBA: https://t.co/ZrDR7lkXk5 [Tweet]. *@WNBA*. https://twitter.com/WNBA/status/1409527468864704515.

Ziegler, M. (n.d.). Vaccine "passports" to be used for Euro 2020 matches at Wembley. Retrieved September 18, 2021, from https://www.thetimes.co.uk/article/vaccine-passports-to-be-used-for-euro-2020-matches-at-wembley-2cmglqgbk.

Chapter Nine

Sport and Health Risk Culture

Jennifer McMahon, Kerry R. McGannon, and Chris Zehntner

Sport participation has long been recommended by organizations such as the World Health Organization (WHO) as a pursuit that enhances health, with the capacity to prevent non-communicable diseases worldwide (WHO, 2012). Sport is said to improve cardiorespiratory function, muscular strength, endurance, flexibility, and body composition (Garber et al., 2011; WHO, 2012). However, Baker et al. (2014) warn that there remains an uncritical assumption amongst the public, further reinforced by some athletes on social media (e.g., Olympic swimmer Stephanie Rice), politicians, and policy makers alike, that sport only positively influences health. While there is no disputing the potential for physiological health benefits, a growing body of research (i.e., Kavanagh, 2014; Kerr et al., 2019; McMahon et al., 2012) has found sport contexts to be environments where an exploitation of power and authority occurs, resulting in dehumanizing practices (Anderson, 2010; Brackenridge, 2006; David, 2005; Lang, 2010a, 2010b) and abuse (Kavanagh, 2014; Kerr et al., 2019; Stirling & Kerr, 2013) justified in the name of enhanced competitive performance (McMahon, 2018). Researchers in the International Olympic Committee (IOC) Consensus Statement on harassment and abuse have warned how athlete maltreatment (i.e., which includes psychological abuse, physical abuse, neglect, sexual abuse) can affect athletes' health negatively in both the short-term and long-term, as well as impacting their continued participation in sport as outlined (Mountjoy et al., 2016).

While there has been some research investigating the link between sport participation and long-term health issues resulting from concussion (e.g., Manley et al., 2017) as well as sports injury (e.g., Maffulli et al., 2010), a critical consideration of the relationship between abuse and athletes' (ill) health remains limited. This is concerning given the high rates of abuse, particularly non-sexualized types found to be occurring for athletes competing at different levels (e.g., children, adolescents, adults, elite), and across sporting contexts (e.g., gymnastics, swimming, athletics, football). For example, one study conducted by Stafford et al. (2015) showed that 75% of athletes experienced psychological abuse. With a similarly high statistic reported in their study, Kerr et al. (2019) found that 67% of athletes experienced neglect. Current research also reports that around 20% of athletes are experiencing sexual harm, while approximately 13% are experiencing physical harm (Kerr et al., 2019).

As such, there remains much more to be understood about how abuse impacts athletes' health not only during their time served in sport, but also post-sport. Indeed, in the same way that academic literature highlights the positive health benefits of participating in sport (e.g., Khan et al., 2012; Leblanc, 2010), a critical examination of how the sports-health nexus is impacted by abuse is urgently needed given the high rates to be occurring (Kerr et al., 2019; Stafford et al., 2015). Accordingly, in this chapter, we provide an overview of studies which have shown a link between abuse and negative health consequences, drawing on contemporary real-life examples of athletes which have experienced abuse and reported an ill-health link either in sport research or in the media. The chapter is then concluded with directions for future research.

There has been a large body of research conducted outside of sport which centers on child abuse, detailing a clear link between maltreatment experiences and subsequent health consequences. Indeed, this research points to the need to pursue this line of inquiry in sport as it has shown that childhood abuse victims suffer severe health effects into adulthood (e.g., Afifi et al., 2016; Fuller-Thomson et al., 2016; Widom et al., 2012). Health consequences were found to include physical injury, gynecological complications (for girls), headaches, depression, fear, low self-esteem, poor school performance, inability to trust, anger, sexual dysfunction, eating and sleeping disorders, fear of intimacy, post-traumatic stress disorder, self-harm (including risky sexual behavior), and suicide (see Bogar & Hulse-Killacky, 2006; Bonanno et al., 2003; Filipas & Ullman, 2006; Futa et al., 2003; Leitenberg et al., 2004; UNICEF, 2010). Specifically in a study conducted by Filipas and Ullman (2006), it was shown that adult childhood sexual abuse (CSA) victims had long-term mental health consequences (e.g., depression, anxiety, suicidal thoughts, anger issues, etc.) and were more likely to use drugs or alcohol, act out sexually, or withdraw from people as a way of managing their mental health, which in turn impacted their physical health (e.g., liver issues, etc.).

Subsequently, the type of abuse a child experiences can increase the risk for specific physical health conditions (Widom et al., 2012). For instance, the study of Yang et al. (2018) found that children who had experienced neglect were at increased risk of poor lung functioning and vision, and oral health problems. While children who had been physically abused were at higher risk for diabetes and malnutrition (Afifi et al., 2016). Moreover, children who were victims of sexual abuse were more likely to contract hepatitis C and HIV (Widom et al., 2012), while those who were subjected to neglect were more likely to experience psychological problems such as depression, anxiety, suicidal thoughts (Fuller-Thomson et al., 2016). A caveat outlined by researchers in the IOC consensus statement was that the "risk of non-suicidal self-injury/self-harm, suicide attempts, and completed suicide attempts increases with the number of harassment types that an adolescent experiences" (Mountjoy et al., 2016, p. 6), further confirming the need to explore the health of athletes who have experienced abuse both in the short-term and post-sport.

CONTEMPORARY SPORTS SETTINGS AND THE SPORT-HEALTH NEXUS

Given that current research has shown that athlete abuse occurs across diverse sports and levels (Kerr et al., 2019; Mountjoy et al., 2016), this next section includes a number of reports (i.e., media, research) from different contemporary sport settings (e.g., amateur swimming contexts, elite sport contexts in gymnastics, running, swimming) which exemplify non-sexualized types of abuse (e.g., psychological, non-contact physical abuse, neglect) and an (ill) health link.

A growing number of athletes are reporting to the media about how they are experiencing abuse (albeit different types) in their sports, with many also detailing the severe impacts to their health. One recent report which received widespread international coverage was that of elite American distance runner Mary Cain who revealed the systematic crisis in women's sports and at Nike's Oregon Project. Cain provided details of where she, along with other young female runners' bodies were subjected to emotionally and physically abusive systems which resulted in severe health consequences (Young, 2019). Cain reported that she was told by her coach (Alberto Salazar) to become "thinner and thinner and thinner in order to win races" (Hruby, 2019). Cain was weighed in front of teammates and publicly shamed if she weighed more than 114 pounds. She was also given birth-control pills and diuretics to assist with weight loss (Hruby, 2019). As a result of Salazar's abusive coaching, Cain missed her period for three years, broke five bones, and developed an eating disorder that prompted suicidal thoughts (Hruby, 2019).

The mental health effects of the foregoing led her to experience anxiety, depression, and eventually, self-harm (cutting herself) to manage the abuse

(The Associated Press, 2021), further revealing the systematic and insidious aspect of weight surveillance, body shaming, and mental health struggles. Cain recently announced a lawsuit against Nike who failed in their duty of care and turned a blind eye to athlete health issues for profit.

> Nike was letting Alberto weight-shame women, objectify their bodies, and ignore their health and well-being as part of its culture, said Kristen West McCall, a Portland lawyer representing Cain. This was a systemic and pervasive issue. And they did it for their own gratification and profit. (The Associated Press, 2021)

The health consequences that Cain experienced are no surprise. Sungot-Borgen et al. (2013) warns that a focus on low body weight and body fat content by coaches and other sporting stakeholders can carry severe long-term health consequences for athletes post-sport such as bone density issues, cardiac issues, and endocrine issues to name just a few.

Similarly, four-time Olympian Emily Seebohm also revealed her own personal experiences of the weight-focused culture in swimming in Australia and how she was weighed often and ridiculed by coaches for being perceived to be too fat which led her to develop a long-term eating disorder, severely affecting her mental health (Halloran, 2021). Seebohm revealed in a social media post in 2019 that a coach commented negatively on her body,

> which triggered a year-long spiral into an eating disorder. "They said the only way I was going to do better than I'd ever done was to be smaller than I was," Seebohm says. "That was the way that it was put to me, and those words became stuck in my brain." It was not just said once to Seebohm, but on "several" occasions that the "only way" she was going to perform better, was if she was thinner. It was harsh and brutal and at the time she didn't even question it. (Halloran, 2021)

As a result, Seebohm explained how she has constantly binged, purged, and taken laxatives. She also counted calories, skipped meals, and constantly weighed herself, judging her body every time she was in front of a mirror (Wondracz & Prentice, 2021). Laxative abuse is considered a dangerous practice that can result in severe medical and physical consequences such as damage to the gastrointestinal tract, weakening and softening of bones, as well as severe bowel tumors and kidney issues (Ekern, 2017).

The foregoing public acts of body shaming and associated abuse is not limited to only female athletes. Three-time Olympic swimmer Daniel Kowalski from Australia revealed that as a result of being body shamed and weighed daily by his coach, he developed an eating disorder which affected him in the long term (Byrne, 2005). Kowalski said:

> I had a coach at the Australian Institute of Sport who made us weigh in everyday and he would make comments. That did not sit comfortably with me. I would get up in the middle of the night, see a reflection of myself in a mirror and think I was fat. I would go for a walk around Lake Ginninderra at 3am to try and lose weight. It was a really hard time, but because of the stigma that guys aren't bulimic, I did not feel that I could talk to anyone about it. (Byrne, 2005)

Consequently, bulimia has been shown to be a serious medical condition that not only has significant short-term repercussions but can also have severe long-term effects on both physical and mental health (Smith, 2018). Some of these health consequences have been found to include diabetes, brittle bones, reproductive difficulties, dental problems, high cholesterol, and damage to the esophagus to name just a few (Smith, 2018).

Body shaming and associated health consequences are not limited to running and swimming and have been found to occur in other sports. For example, in the Women's Super League (football) it was recently reported as being the worst in years with players being forced to maintain a certain body aesthetic via restrictive eating. According to Tomas (2020),

> The footballers' weights were recorded and displayed on a chart which could be viewed by anyone, and for those who did not meet the perceived ideal weight number, they were put into the "fat club" by coaches.

Enforced restrictive eating as described by footballers in the Women's Super League is indeed physical maltreatment as outlined by Fortier et al. (2020) and has been linked to long-term health issues such as eating disorders (i.e., binge eating disorder, anorexia nervosa, and bulimia nervosa), disordered eating (i.e., not diagnosed as an "eating disorder" but occurs when there is abnormal behavior around food and eating), dehydration, mental health problems, and psychological disorders (Fortier et al., 2020; Mountjoy et al., 2016).

There has also been widespread media coverage of body shaming and associated abuse occurring in the sport of gymnastics where it has been reported that young girls were virtually starved, constantly body shamed, and forced to train with broken bones or other injuries (Weiss, 2018). For example, American gymnast Ashley Davis reported that in training one day, she tumbled, until a snap loud enough for the whole gym to hear occurred. The snap was the sound of her foot breaking. Davis explains how she fell to the ground as she could not stand on the limb. No one stopped when her injury occurred; the tumbling continued around her. Davis says her coach berated her, saying the broken foot occurred because of her weight. Specifically, the coach said, "this is what five extra pounds looks like." He then proceeded to tell her that she was "washed up and should go to college instead of university" (Green,

2021). Sundgot-Borgen et al. (2013) warns that very low body weight, low body fat percentages, and menstrual dysfunction in female athletes leads to insufficient bone density which can commonly cause fractures and long-term issues such as osteoporosis.

The acts of body shaming and weight control measures have been found to constitute many forms of abuse including psychological abuse (e.g., ridiculing athletes' bodies, yelling at them when they put on weight) as well as physical abuse (e.g., excessive exercise enforced on athletes to lose weight, enforced severe calorie restriction), often resulting in serious ongoing health consequences for athletes (McMahon et al., 2021). For example, McMahon et al. (2012) found that three swimmers across levels of sport (e.g., amateur, and elite contexts) retrospectively recalled the body practices they were exposed to as adolescents fit "psychological abuse" and "physical abuse" criteria. In this research, it was revealed that 11-year-old Carly was punished with excessive running in the middle of the night after being caught eating an ice cream by her coach. We draw on the conversation between 11-year-old Carly and her coach to exemplify how, consequently, she was subjected to physical abuse at training camp.

> Coach: "Get up Carly, you need to run off that ice cream you ate today! Get your running shoes on; you haven't burnt it off yet!"
>
> Carly: "What do you mean? It is 11pm?"
>
> Coach: "Get your running shoes on and get out here! You haven't burnt off that ice cream yet! You've got 11 kilometres! Need to burn off that ice cream you ate." (McMahon et al., 2012, p. 188)

The second phase of their research explored how body shaming and punishment (if at all) that the adolescent swimmers were exposed to affected them into adulthood, 10–30 years post-career (McMahon et al., 2012). For Carly, 30 years after that aforementioned experience, she consumed food in secrecy, rather than in front of others, for fear of being judged. She also constantly weighed herself throughout the day with an increase in weight numbers severely debilitating her (McMahon et al., 2012). The findings of this research further show that all three swimmers had some form of disordered eating in life post-sport, highlighting a link between the exposure to body shaming in their adolescence and the consequences of this abuse into their adulthood, long after they have left the sport (McMahon et al., 2012). Subsequently, another athlete in this study who was introduced to bulimia in her adolescence by a fellow swimmer as a way of controlling her weight and as a result of coaches' ridiculing and punishing her (e.g., coaches withheld food) was still using bulimia 30 years later as a weight control method and a form of self-harm, highlighting the longevity of abuse on athlete well-being. Sungot-Borgen et al. (2013) warns that there are serious gastrointestinal, cardiovascular, renal, and endocrine health complications that result from the bingeing and purging behaviors of athletes such as bradycardia, swollen parotid glands, hypotension, and edema, to just name a few.

These revelations are no surprise, given that sport contexts are sites where daily weigh-ins, calorie deprivation, and body classification is normalized and perceived necessary for enhanced competitive performance (Cosh et al., 2012; McMahon et al., 2012; Papathomas & Lavallee, 2014). Unfortunately for those athletes who fail to meet the culturally accepted and perceived ideal shape (e.g., slim and fatless bodies), abuse has ensued (McMahon et al., 2021; McMahon & Barker-Ruchti, 2017; McMahon et al., 2012; Stirling & Kerr, 2008) and has contributed to athletes' (ill)health.

Coaches and team managers are not the only perpetrators of body shaming and weight control practices. Female athletes in the University of Oregon's track and field program recently reported how nutritionists (i.e., also known as dietitians) were advising runners to drop their body fat percentages to dangerously low levels. One athlete explained that she was given her first DEXA scan at Oregon despite the nutritionists knowing that she had not had a menstrual period in a year and a half. She explained how a scan showed her body fat percentage at 16%, but she was told by the nutritionist that she should consider lowering it to about 13% (Goe, 2021). These revelations can be further exemplified in the research conducted by McMahon and McGannon (2020) where it was shown that doctors were complicit and/or accomplices in perpetuating dominant cultural ideologies such as "slim to win" (where a fatless body is perceived to enhance competitive performance). This was achieved through their surveillance, manipulation, and medical treatment of the athletes' bodies so they could conform to a perceived shape, weight, or body fat percentage which they thought would enhance their competitive performance (McMahon & McGannon, 2018). Indeed, through their medical treatment, the doctors co-contributed to the legitimization and normalization (Foucault, 1977) of "slim to win" and "performance" ideologies by prescribing weight-loss medications such as thyroxine. As exemplified through Jacki's voice,

> As I walk into his (sports doctor) office, I notice he has my blood work which he ordered me to have a couple of days ago. "I am going to prescribe you some thyroxine. Thyroxine is a medication, which alters your thyroid function. I realise your blood work says your thyroid function is normal, but an overactive thyroid function can assist in weight loss. Take the tablets and it will speed things up for you." (McMahon & McGannon, 2020, p. 62)

Sport literature has presented many overarching themes where the pressures to be thin for performance gains saturate sporting environments, placing athletes at increased risk of eating disorder development and other health-related issues (Papathomas & Lavallee, 2014). While the above contextual examples have focused on non-sexualized forms of abuse which can be normalized within sport contexts and may be perceived as necessary for enhanced competitive performance, the harrowing sexual abuse that American gymnasts were subjected to by Larry Nassar, an osteopathic doctor who has recently been criminally investigated and subsequently reported on internationally. Gymnast McKayla Maroney provided a testimony in court outlining her own harrowing experience of sexual abuse during her time as an athlete.

> Nassar gave me a sleeping pill for the plane ride to then work on me later that night. That evening, I was naked, completely alone with him on top of me molesting me for hours. I told them I thought I was going to die that night. Because there was no way that he would let me go. But he did. (FoxSports, 2021)

It was also reported during the criminal investigation that hundreds of young gymnasts were required to undergo "pelvic examinations" by Nassar unsupervised (Freeman, 2018) where he would put his fingers into their vaginas and anuses (Adams, 2018). Nasser admitted that as a doctor, he was in a position of authority over his victims, and that he used that position to coerce them to submit to the penetration (Adams, 2018). The psychological consequences of this sexual abuse was reported in the media by Simone Biles who said,

> I was so depressed that I slept all the time, and it's basically because sleeping was basically better than offing myself. It was like my way to escape reality. And sleeping was the closest thing to death for me at that point, so I just slept all the time. (Iervolino, 2021)

While there are serious psychological consequences of sexual abuse (e.g., suicide, anxiety, depression), there are also other ongoing health effects including self-harm, sexually transmitted infections, substance abuse, dissociation, panic attacks, eating disorders, sleep disorders, and suicide (RAINN, 2021).

The legacy of all types of abuse is serious and points to sporting organizations needing to urgently extend their duty of care post-sport for those athletes who have been abused while under their care. McMahon and McGannon (2021) investigated the legacy of abuse post-sport and how athlete abuse victims who were left to fend for themselves self-managed their trauma by engaging in self-injury. In this research, three athletes managed their abuse post-sport by engaging with self-injury practices as a way of reconfiguring the pain associated with their maltreatment. Consequently, the athletes were found to engage with [self-injurious] acts including bulimia, promiscuity with men, overuse of alcohol, and excessive use of a prescription medication. For instance, one of the athletes revealed the trouble she had at night and how she used excessive alcohol as a self-medication method.

> Night after night, I have trouble sleeping. It is in the darkness of the night where I go over and over the abuse that I experienced from a national coach years ago. As a way of managing the long-drawn-out nights, I drink red wine and a lot of it. (McMahon & McGannon, 2021)

Indeed, other self-injury behaviors were adopted as a way of transforming or reconfiguring (Hochschild, 1979) the ongoing effects of abuse post-sport (McMahon & McGannon, 2021) as exemplified by another swimmer in this study who used sex as a way of controlling men, a contrast to what she experienced as a swimmer when male coaches controlled and abused her.

> Before long, I have him doing exactly what I want him to be doing. We are in the toilet of my local pub. I am the one in control and he is at my mercy. I see him as a sexual object. I am no longer the victim at the hands of a controller [national coach], but instead, I am the one with the power, treating the man as an object or puppet that I can manipulate and control. (McMahon & McGannon, 2021, p. 8)

The ongoing daily struggles the athletes experienced as shown in this research (McMahon & McGannon, 2021) thus exemplify the sustained effect of abuse, which is not surprising given the caveat in the IOC consensus statement (Mountjoy et al., 2016) which highlights the long-term and harmful effects of abuse on athletes' health.

CONCLUSION AND DIRECTIONS FOR FUTURE RESEARCH

While sport participation has been long recommended as a pursuit that enhances health (WHO, 2012), this chapter has provided an overview of how the health of athlete abuse victims is affected both in the short- and long-term. Health consequences such as depression, eating disorders, alcohol and drug use, acting out sexually, and suicidal thoughts resulted for those athletes who were subjected to maltreatment. Indeed, this chapter shows that maltreatment in sport is complex and multifaceted and has the potential to pose a significant threat to athlete well-being, a contrast to what is proposed by WHO (2012). More research is desperately needed in relation to the health consequences for those athletes who are subjected to all types of abuse. Knowing this information may assist sporting organizations to support athletes in post-sport life, thus extending their duty of care.

Another recommendation for future research to understand how evidence-based education, specifically athletes' stories of (ill)health as a result of normalized forms of abuse may impact the decision making and practice of policy makers, coaches, parents, and/or athletes. Indeed, evidence-based abuse education was identified by IOC researchers as a primary way to prevent abuse (Mountjoy et al., 2016). Although the IOC (Mountjoy et al., 2016) has suggested that evidence-based education should be used to teach about abuse, we propose that it should also be used to teach about the health consequences of abuse. We also suggest that with additional research and consideration of this, that sporting organizations will move from a compliance (with minimum safeguarding standards) approach to coach education and elevate coach (re)training using evidence-based education so that members are better able to understand how historically normalized coaching practices can have immediate, medium, and long-term health effects on athletes. Coaches and high-performance teams (i.e., nutritionists, doctors) must be aware that their responsibility is not just to "get the most from an athlete" but ensure that high performance happens in an environment that is considerate of athlete well-being and health, both now and into the future.

REFERENCES

Adams, D. (2018, January 25). Victims share what Larry Nassar did to them under the guise of medical treatment, IndyStar. Retrieved from: https://www.indystar.com/story/news/2018/01/25/heres-what-larry-nassar-actually-did-his-patients/1065165001/.

Afifi, T. O., MacMillan, H. L., Boyle, M., Cheung, K., Taillieu, T., Turner, S., & Sareen, J. (2016). Child abuse and physical health in adulthood. *Health Reports*, 27, 10–18.

Anderson, E. (2010). *Sport, theory and social problems: A critical introduction.* London: Routledge.

Baker, J., Safai, P., & Fraser-Thomas, J. (2014). *Health and elite sport: Is high performance sport a healthy pursuit?* London: Routledge.

Bogar, C. B., & Hulse-Killacky, D. (2006). Resilience determinants and resiliency processes among female adult survivors of childhood sexual abuse. *Journal of Counselling and Development*, 84, 318–327. doi:10.1002/j.1556-6678.2006.tb00411.x.

Bonanno, G. A., Noil, J. G., Putnam, F. W., O'Neill, M., & Trickett, P. K. (2003). Predicting the willingness to disclose childhood sexual abuse from measures of repressive coping and dissociative tendencies. *Child Maltreatment*, 8, 302–318. doi:10.1177/1077559503257066.

Brackenridge, C. H. (2006). Youth sport re-focussed—a review essay on Paulo David's human rights in youth sport: A critical review of children's rights in competitive sports. *European Physical Education Review*, 12(1), 119–125.
Byrne, F. (2005, April 24). My battle with Bulimia. *The Sunday Mail*. Retrieved from: http://funkyswim3.tripod.com/dan/articles/article050425.ht.
Cosh, S., Crabb, S., LeCouteur, A., & Kettler, L. (2012). Accountability, monitoring and surveillance: Body regulation in elite sport. *Journal of Health Psychology*, 17(4), 610–622. doi:10.1177/1359105311417914.
David, P. (2005). *Human rights in youth sport*. London: Routledge.
Ekern, J. (2017). Laxative abuse: Side effects and long-term health risks. Retrieved from: https://www.eatingdisorderhope.com/blog/laxative-abuse-long-term-risks.
Filipas, H. H., & Ullman, S. E. (2006). Child sexual abuse, coping responses, self-blame, posttraumatic stress disorder, and adult sexual revictimization. *Journal of Interpersonal Violence*, 21, 652–672. doi:10.1177/0886260506286879.
Fortier, K., Parent, S., & Lessard, G. (2020). Child maltreatment in sport: Smashing the wall of silence: A narrative review of physical, sexual, psychological abuses and neglect. *British Journal of Sports Medicine*, 54(1), 4–7. doi:10.1136/bjsports-2018–100224.
Fox Sports. (2021, September 16). Simone Biles, American gymnasts give harrowing testimony over sexual abuse, Fox Sports Online. Retrieved from: https://www.foxsports.com.au/more-sports/simone-biles-american-gymnasts-give-harrowing-testimony-over-sexual-abuse/news-story/ecee913a1f505694dbe7abb90be4a1c1.
Freeman, H. (2018, January 27). How was Larry Nassar able to abuse gymnasts for so long? *The Guardian*. Retrieved from: https://www.theguardian.com/sport/2018/jan/26/larry-nassar-abuse-gymnasts-scandal-culture.
Fuller-Thomson, E., Baird, S. L., Dhrodia, R., Brennenstuhl, S. (2016). The association between adverse childhood experiences (ACEs) and suicide attempts in a population-based study. *Child: Care, Health and Development*, 42, 725–734. doi:10.1111/cch.12351.
Futa, K. T., Nash, C. L., Hansen, D. J., & Garbin, C. P. (2003). Adult survivors of childhood abuse: An analysis of coping mechanisms used for stressful childhood memories and current stressors. *Journal of Family Violence*, 18(4), 227–239. doi:10.1023/A:1024068314963.
Garber, C. E., Blissmer, B., Deschenes, M. R., Franklin, B. A., Lamonte, M. J., Lee, I. M., Nieman, D. C., & Swain, D. P. (2011). American College of Sports Medicine. American College of Sports Medicine position stand. Quantity and quality of exercise for developing and maintaining cardiorespiratory, musculoskeletal, and neuromotor fitness in apparently healthy adults: Guidance for prescribing exercise. *Med Sci Sports Exerc*, 43(7), 1334–59. doi:10.1249/MSS.0b013e318213fefb.
Goe, K. (2021, October 25). Women athletes allege body shaming within Oregon Ducks track and field program, *The Oregonian*. Retrieved from: https://www.oregonlive.com/trackandfield/2021/10/women-athletes-allege-body-shaming-within-oregon-ducks-track-and-field-program.html.

Green, L. (2021, July 30). The medals keep piling up. But, at what cost? Daily Cover. Retrieved from: https://www.si.com/olympics/2021/07/30/can-usa-gymnastics-be-saved-daily-cover.

Halloran, J. (August, 2021). "I was starving": Seebohm's harrowing health battle, *The Australian*. Retrieved from: https://www.theaustralian.com.au/sport/how-an-eating-disorder-nearly-ended-seebohms-swimming-career/news-story/2715dd0679644965018eb77ae343d10c.

Hochschild, A. R. (1979). Emotion work, feeling rules, and social structure. *American Journal of Sociology*, 85(3), 551–575.

Hruby, P. (November, 2019). Will Mary Cain's story of a broken running culture initiate change? Global Sport Matters. Retrieved from: https://globalsportmatters.com/culture/2019/11/19/the-broken-culture-that-broke-mary-cain/.

Iervolino, S. (2021, July 08). Simone Biles opens up about depression she suffered after being sexually abused. Good Morning America. Retrieved from: https://www.goodmorningamerica.com/culture/story/simone-biles-opens-depression-suffered-sexually-abused-78735393.

Kavanagh, E. J. (2014). The dark side of sport: Athletes' narratives of maltreatment in high performance environments. Thesis (Unpublished PhD). UK: Bournemouth University.

Leblanc, A. G. (2010). Systematic review of the health benefits of physical activity and fitness in school-aged children and youth. *International Journal of Behaviour*, Nutrition and Physical Activity, 7, 40–56.

Kerr, G., Willson, E., & Stirling, A. (2019). Prevalence of maltreatment among current and former national team athletes. University of Toronto/AthletesCAN.

Khan, K. M., Thomson, A. M., Blair, S. N. et al. (2012). Sport and exercise as contributors to the health of nations. *Lancet*, 3(80), 59–64.

Lang, M. (2010a). Intensive training in youth sport: A new abuse of power? In: K. Vanhoutte, & M. Lang (Eds.). *Bullying and the abuse of power: From the playground to international relations*. Inter-Disciplinary Press.

Lang, M. (2010b). Surveillance and conformity in competitive youth swimming. *Sport, Education and Society*, 15(1), 19–37.

Leitenberg, H., Gibson, L. E., & Novy, P. L. (2004). Individual differences among undergraduate women in methods of coping with stressful events: The impact of cumulative childhood stressors and abuse. *Child Abuse and Neglect*, 28, 181–192. doi:10.1016/j.chiabu.2003.08.005.

Maffulli, N., Longo, U G, Gougoulias, N., Loppini, M., & Denaro, V. (2010). Long-term health outcomes of youth sports injuries, *British Journal of Sports Medicine*, 44, 21–25. doi:10.1136/bjsm.2009.069526.

McMahon, J. (2018). Will to win: The darker side of elite sport. In J. Piggin, L. Mansfield, & M. Weed (Eds.). *Routledge handbook of physical activity policy and practice* (pp. 464–474). New York: Routledge.

McMahon, J., & Barker-Ruchti, N. (2017). Assimilating to a boy's body shape for the sake of performance: Three athletes' body experiences in a sporting culture. *Sport, Education and Society*, 22(2), 157–174. doi:10.1080/ 13573322.2015.1013463.

McMahon, J., & McGannon, K. R. (2020). The athlete–doctor relationship: power, complicity, resistance and accomplices in recycling dominant sporting ideologies. *Sport, Education and Society*, 25(1), 57–69. doi:10.1080/13573322.2018.1561434.

McMahon, J., & McGannon, K. R. (2021). I hurt myself because it sometimes helps: Former athletes' embodied emotion responses to abuse using self-injury. *Sport, Education and Society*, 26(2), 161–174. doi:10.1080/13573322. 2019.1702940.

McMahon, J., Penney, D., & Dinan-Thompson, M. (2012). Body practices—Exposure and effect of a sporting culture? Stories from three Australian swimmers. *Sport, Education and Society*, 17(2), 181–206. doi:10.1080/ 13573322.2011.607949.

McMahon, J., McGannon, K. R., & Palmer, C. (2021). Body shaming and associated practices as abuse: Athlete entourage as perpetrators of abuse. *Sport, Education and Society*, doi:10.1080/13573322.2021.1890571.

Manley, G., Gardner, A. J., Schneider, K.J., et al. (2017). A systematic review of potential long-term effects of sport-related concussion. *British Journal of Sports Medicine*, 51, 969–977.

Mountjoy, M., Brackenridge, C., Arrington, M., Blauwet, C., Carska-Sheppard, A., Fasting, K., . . . Budgett, R. (2016). International Olympic Committee consensus statement: Harassment and abuse (non-accidental violence) in sport. *British Journal of Sports Medicine*, 50, 1019–1029. doi:10.1136/bjsports-2016–096121.

Papathomas, A., & Lavallee, D. (2014). Self-starvation and the performance narrative in competitive sport. *Psychology of Sport and Exercise*, 15(6), 688–695. doi:10.1016/j.psychsport.2013.10.014.

RAINN. (2021). Effects of sexual violence. Retrieved from: https://www.rainn.org/effects sexual-violence.

Smith, K. (2018). The Aftermath of Eating Disorders: Long-Term Effects of Bulimia. Retrieved from: https://www.psycom.net/long-term-effects-of-bulimia/.

Stafford, A., Alexander, K., & Fry, D. (2015). "There was something that wasn't right because that was the only place, I ever got treated like that": Children and young people's experiences of emotional harm. *Childhood*, 22, 121–137. doi:10.1177/0907568213505625.

Stirling, A. E., & Kerr, G. A. (2008). Defining and categorizing emotional abuse in sport. *European Journal of Sport Science*, 8(4), 173–181. doi:10.1080/17461390802086281.

Stirling, A. E., & Kerr, G. A. (2013). The perceived effects of elite athletes' experiences of emotional abuse in the coach athlete relationship. *International Journal of Sport and Exercise Psychology*, 11(1), 87–100. doi:10.1080/ 1612197X.2013.752173.

Sundgot-Borgen, J., Meyer, N. L., Lohman, T. G., Ackland, T., Maughan, R., Stewart, A., & Muller, W. (2013). How to minimise the health risks to athletes who compete in weight-sensitive sports review and position statement on behalf of the Ad Hoc Research Working Group on Body Composition, Health and Performance, under the auspices of the IOC Medical Commission. *British Journal of Sports Medicine*, 47, 1012–1022.

The Associated Press. (2021, October 12). Distance runner Mary Cain sues ex-coach, Nike for millions over alleged abuse. CBC. Retrieved from: https://www.cbc

.ca/sports/olympics/summer/trackandfield/runner-abuse-lawsuit-cain-salazar-1.6208876.

Tomas, F. (2020, October 23). Weight charts, "fat clubs" and disordered eating: The hidden health crisis in women's football. *The Telegraph*. Retrieved from: https://www.telegraph.co.uk/football/2020/10/23/weight-charts-fat-clubs-disordered-eatingthe-hidden-health-crisis/.

UNICEF (2010). Protecting children from violence in sport: A review with focus on industrialized countries. Retrieved from: www.unicefirc.org/publications/pdf/violence_in_sport.pdf.

Weiss, M. (February, 2018). U.S. gymnasts speak of eating disorders, emotional abuse, training on broken bones. Global Sports. Retrieved from: https://globalnews.ca/news/4045312/usa-gymnastics-abuse-victims/.

Widom, C. S., Czaja, S. J., Bentley, T., & Johnson, M. S. (2012). A prospective investigation of physical health outcomes in abused and neglected children: New findings from a 30-year follow up. *American Journal of Public Health*, 102, 1135–1144. doi: 10.2105/AJPH.2011.300636.

Wondracz, A., & Prentice, A. (2021, January 29). Emily Seebohm announces her next move after opening up on her two-year eating disorder battle, *The Daily Mail*. Retrieved from: https://www.dailymail.co.uk/news/article-9199495/Emily-Seebohm-joins-EndED-revealing-struggle-eating-disorder.html.

World Health Organization. (2012). Ensuring sports for all. Retrieved from: https://www.who.int/activities/ensuring-sports-for-all.

Yang, M., Font, S. A., Ketchum, M., & Kim, Y. K. (2018). Intergenerational transmission of child abuse and neglect: Effects of maltreatment type and depressive symptoms. *Children and Youth Services Review*, 91, 364–371. doi:10.1016/j.childyouth.2018.06.036.

Young, S. (2019). Eight Nike Oregon Project athletes confirm Mary Cain's allegations of abuse to Sports Illustrated. https://ca.sports.yahoo.com/news/eight-nike-oregon-project-athletes-confirm-mary-cains-allegations-of-abuse-to-sportsillustrated-223642373.html?guccounter=1.

Chapter Ten

The U.S. Center for SafeSport

Preventing Abuse and Misconduct in Sport

Erin McConnell and Nicole Johnson

Taking part in sports is broadly recognized as a healthy activity with multiple personal and social benefits, particularly for youth and young adults. Unmistakably, sports participation has long been a widespread and endearing pastime for young people in the United States. Estimates suggest that nearly 60% of the approximately 50 million children in the United States between the ages of 6 and 17 years participate annually in either an individual or team sport (U.S. Department of Health & Human Services, 2019; Noble & Vermillion, 2014; U.S. Census Bureau, 2020). Decades of research suggests that youth sports participation is associated with numerous positive outcomes, both short- and long-term. A recent clinical report from the American Academy of Pediatrics highlights many benefits of sports for youth who participate, including within the areas of physical health, academic achievement, self-regulatory and life-skills development, and personal self-efficacy and self-esteem (Logan & Cuff, 2019). Many of these benefits appear to go beyond that which can be attributed to physical activity alone, suggesting that sports may offer a highly instrumental pathway to fostering positive youth development (Eime et al., 2013). Likewise, a smaller body of research suggests there are mental, physical, and social health benefits of sports participation in adulthood (Doré et al., 2018; Lastuka & Cottingham, 2015; Lechner, 2009).

However, it has become increasingly apparent that athletes at all levels are experiencing physical, emotional, and sexual maltreatment[1] within the context of sport, and at far higher rates than previously understood or acknowledged. In the mid- to late-2010s, an outpouring of reports of abuse shook the elite gymnastics community and beyond, drawing national attention to the need for greater protections for amateur athletes (Ford et al., 2020; Mountjoy, 2019). In answer to this call, the U.S. Center for SafeSport (the Center), an independent non-profit committed to ending all forms of abuse in sport, opened its doors in March of 2017. Less than a year later, Congress passed the Protecting Young Victims from Sexual Abuse and Safe Sport Authorization Act of 2017. Notably, this Act designated the U.S. Center for SafeSport as the congressionally authorized national safe sport organization, with the responsibility to develop and implement policies and procedures to prevent the abuse of amateur athletes within the Olympic and Paralympic Movement (the Movement). In 2020, another momentous federal law passed, the Empowering Olympic, Paralympic, and Amateur Athletes Act, which further delineated the Center's role in athlete safety across the Movement and secured a reliable annual funding stream from the U.S. Olympic and Paralympic Committee (USOPC) to sustain and strengthen the Center's operations.

This chapter focuses on the work of the Center when it comes to addressing physical, emotional, and sexual abuse and misconduct in amateur sports. We begin with an overview of the prevalence of maltreatment in sport environments, highlighting the significant need for more and better prevention efforts. We then discuss the Center's multi-tiered framework for responding to and preventing abuse and misconduct. We conclude with a discussion of next steps and future directions aimed at creating safer environments for all athletes and advancing the field of prevention in sports.

Types and Prevalence of Maltreatment in Sports

In order to effectively prevent abuse and misconduct in sports, it is crucial to have a clear understanding of the nature and scope of the problem. The SafeSport Code for the U.S. Olympic and Paralympic Movement (the SafeSport Code) applies to all participants in the Movement and defines prohibited conduct and related policies. Conduct that is prohibited under the SafeSport Code includes various forms of sexual, physical, and emotional abuse, bullying, harassment, hazing, and a number of other violations such as retaliation against individuals who report misconduct. As a form of sexual misconduct, the SafeSport Code also prohibits adults from engaging in any intimate or romantic relationship where a power imbalance exists, such as between a coach and an athlete over whom they have authority (U.S. Center for SafeSport, 2021a). Table 10.1 provides a high-level summary of the various types of misconduct that are detailed within the SafeSport Code.

Table 10.1 Types of Prohibited Conduct under the SafeSport Code*

Sexual	Emotional & Physical	Other Prohibited Conduct
Sexual or Gender-related Harassment	Bullying (including cyber bullying)	Child Abuse in any form
Nonconsensual Sexual Contact (including intercourse)	Contact or Non-Contact Violations	Failing to Report Abuse or Misconduct
Exposing a Minor to Sexual Content/Imagery	Exclusion	Retaliation
Sexual Exploitation	Stalking	Abuse of Process
Bullying, Hazing, or Other Inappropriate Conduct of a Sexual Nature	Acts that Deny Attention or Support	Filing False Allegations
Intentional Exposure of Private Body Parts	Verbal or Physical Violations	Aiding and Abetting
Sexual or Intimate Relations when a Power Imbalance exists	Hazing	Criminal Conduct, Charges, Dispositions, Warrants for Arrest, or being a Registered Sex Offender

*This is not a comprehensive list. Find the latest version of the Code at the Center's website (uscenterforsafesport.org).

In 2020, the Center conducted a large-scale survey to learn more about the experiences of athletes in regard to a host of issues, including abuse and misconduct in sports (U.S. Center for SafeSport, 2021b). Nearly 4,000 current and former athletes representing more than fifty sports responded to the survey, making it one of the most in-depth examinations to date of the prevalence of abuse and misconduct in sports. While the survey was limited to being completed only by adults, the information they provided in their survey responses pertains to experiences that occurred at any point in their athletic careers, including potentially when they were minor athletes (i.e., under the age of 18).

Throughout the sections that follow, findings from the Center's 2020 Athlete Culture and Climate Survey are presented along with other literature that sheds light on the characteristics and prevalence of sexual, emotional, and physical abuse and misconduct in sports. It is important to note that, while the Center's 2020 survey offers an in-depth perspective in many ways, the majority of athletes who responded were white (87.6%), heterosexual (88.6%) women (76.1%), and were athletes without disabilities (93.1%). More research is needed to better understand the experiences of athletes of color, LGBTQ+ athletes, and athletes with disabilities when it comes to abuse and misconduct in sports.

Sexual Maltreatment

There is considerable variation when it comes to estimates of the rate at which sexual maltreatment is experienced by athletes within the context of sports. This can be attributed both to the use of differing research design and sampling methodologies (Johnson et al., 2020; Mountjoy, 2019) and the varying definitions and behaviors that are associated with sexual maltreatment throughout the literature (Koss et al., 2014). Published scientific findings include prevalence rates for sexual abuse in sports that range from 2% to 49%, while estimates for sexual harassment in sports range even further, from 19% to 92% (Mountjoy et al., 2016). A recent report on the experiences of Canadian Olympic and Paralympic national team members found that 20% of current and 21% of retired athletes had experienced at least one form of sexual maltreatment—from unwanted comments or looks to sexual assault (Kerr, Wilson, & Stirling, 2019). Results from the Center's 2020 Athlete Culture and Climate Survey revealed rates of sexual maltreatment that are comparable to those cited in previous research, but tending toward the lower ends, as summarized below.

Of the athletes who responded to the Center's 2020 survey, 9% indicated an experience with non-consensual sexual contact, such as being touched or kissed without consent. Approximately 3.2% of athletes indicated that someone had sexually assaulted them (defined as committing sexual intercourse without consent) or attempted to sexually assault them during their sports involvement. According to the survey, perpetrators of these acts were most often (1) coaches, trainers, or other sports administrators, and (2) athlete peers. Sexual maltreatment that involved unwanted comments or looks was experienced by nearly 34% of the athletes surveyed.

Of athletes who experienced sexual maltreatment, according to the Center's 2020 survey, a small fraction—less than 7%—reported the unwelcome behavior(s) to either law enforcement, their sport organization, or the Center. The survey also revealed that experiencing sexual maltreatment in sports contexts was highly associated with experiencing negative mental health symptoms, including depression, anxiety, suicidality, disordered eating, and self-harming behaviors (U.S. Center for SafeSport, 2021b). Additionally, most athletes (68%) indicated that they did not feel they had a supportive, confidential place within their sport national governing body to talk about their experiences with sexual maltreatment.

While the Center's 2020 survey did not include minor athletes, it did ask athletes whether any of the sexual maltreatment behaviors they experienced occurred when they were under 18 years of age. More than half of athletes who had unwanted sexual experiences in sports said that some or all of those experiences took place when they were minor athletes. This finding aligns with prior research which suggests that child and adolescent athletes, in addition to more elite athletes, are at a higher risk for experiencing sexual maltreatment in sports (Mountjoy, 2019). There is also evidence to suggest that racial and gender minority athletes, as well as athletes with disabilities, are more at risk for experiencing sexual maltreatment in sports (U.S. Center for SafeSport, 2021b).

Physical Maltreatment

Few empirical studies have examined the prevalence of physical maltreatment in sports environments. Kerr, Willson, and Stirling's (2019) survey of current and former Canadian Olympic and Paralympic national team members found prevalence rates for physical maltreatment between 12% (for current athletes) and 19% (for retired athletes). The difference between current and retired athletes' experiences may be due to the normalization of physically abusive practices in sports, and the shift in perspective that athletes gain after stepping away from the sports environment (Kerr & Stirling, 2019; McMahon et al., 2018).

The Center's 2020 survey revealed rates of physical maltreatment that were comparable to, yet slightly higher than, those found in the Canadian study. Approximately 22% of athletes who responded to the Center's survey indicated that they had experienced acts that could be classified as physical misconduct (U.S. Center for SafeSport, 2021b). According to the survey report, the most commonly experienced indicator of physical misconduct was being punished with excessive exercise. Athletes also experienced being physically hit, having objects thrown at them, being physically threatened, and being denied water (U.S. Center for SafeSport, 2021b). While limited in nature due to the homogeneity of the sample, the Center's survey findings indicate that athletes of color experience higher rates of physical misconduct.

Emotional Maltreatment

A growing body of research suggests that emotional maltreatment is pervasive in sports. One study from the United Kingdom found that 75% of youth sport participants had experienced emotional maltreatment within the context of sport before the age of 17 (Stafford et al., 2015). While the study found athlete peers to be the most frequent perpetrators of potentially emotionally harmful behaviors overall, perpetration by coaches became increasingly common at more elite levels of play (Stafford et al., 2015). Kerr, Willson, and

Stirling's (2019) survey of Canadian national team athletes found that 59% of current athletes and 62% of retired athletes had experienced emotional maltreatment.

Similar to the findings listed above, results from the Center's 2020 Athlete Culture and Climate Survey indicate that emotional maltreatment is widespread, with approximately 80% of athletes who responded to the survey having experienced this type of behavior (U.S. Center for SafeSport, 2021b). While more research is needed to shed light on the experiences of minority athletes, the Center's 2020 survey suggests that women, gender non-conforming athletes, and athletes with disabilities may experience elevated rates of emotional abuse and misconduct.

There is no denying the existence of abuse and misconduct in sports, nor the need for systemic culture change. It is apparent that prevention is highly necessary, and that athletic communities need more trusted resources where they can turn to report abuse or misconduct and to receive support. Since opening its doors in 2017, the Center has endeavored to lay a strong foundation of policies and practices, as summarized below, to help meet these critical needs, while at the same time acknowledging that there is much more work to be done.

The Policies and Practices of the U.S. Center for SafeSport

The Center has exclusive congressional authority to provide education and training, investigate and resolve allegations of abuse and misconduct, and ensure athlete safety policy adherence within the Movement (Johnson et al., 2020). Through preventative measures like the Center's Minor Athlete Abuse Prevention Policies (MAAPP), requiring annual abuse prevention training for certain adult participants[2] who have regular contact with or authority over minor athletes across the Movement, and safeguarding to limit one-on-one interactions between adult participants and minor athletes in certain high-risk settings, the Center seeks to mitigate the risk of abuse and misconduct before athlete harm occurs (U.S. Center for SafeSport, 2020).

The Center has jurisdiction over more than 11 million sport participants in the Movement, from grassroots coaches, athletes, and administrators to elite Olympic, and Paralympic-level teams (USOPC, 2019). The Center is therefore in a unique position to positively shift the safety culture and environment of sports across the U.S. through the policies, training, and resources it provides while simultaneously collecting primary data on the characteristics of abuse and misconduct to inform future prevention mechanisms.

Keep in mind that both the MAAPP and the SafeSport Code apply to specific organizations and individuals who fall under the Center's jurisdiction. Both are nuanced and updated periodically, and the MAAPP includes specific exceptions that are explained within the policy. Additionally, the MAAPP contains both required and recommended policies for keeping young athletes safe. For a full explanation of the MAAPP and the SafeSport Code, refer to the most current versions that can be found on the Center's website (uscenterforsafesport.org).

Policy Development and Application

The existing literature on sexual abuse prevention in athletics points to the importance of policy application from the national organization down to their local affiliates (Parent & Demers, 2011). In the United States, policies focused on limiting abuse and misconduct were sparse and inconsistent across different sport organizations until the last decade (Brackenridge et al., 2008; Donnelly et al., 2016; Parent, 2011). The Center's MAAPP, first published in 2019, establishes a baseline level of protection for all minor athletes across the 50+ National Governing Bodies (NGBs) of sport in the United States and the USOPC.

The MAAPP includes requirements for limiting one-on-one interactions between minor athletes and adult participants (with certain exceptions specified in the policies) in many situations where the literature cited below suggests an increased likelihood of abuse. These include social media and other electronic communications (Henry & Powell, 2018; Sanderson & Weathers, 2020); massages and other athletic training modalities (Brackenridge et al., 2008; Stirling & Kerr, 2009; Toftegaard-Nielsen, 2001); locker rooms and changing areas (Brackenridge et al., 2008; Kirby & Greaves, 1996); and team travel environments (Cense & Brackenridge, 2001; Massey & Whitley, 2016). When athletes who indicated experiencing sexual maltreatment in their sports careers in the Center's 2020 Athlete Culture and Climate Survey were asked to identify the location of the experience that had the most impact on them, many chose locations now covered under the scope of the MAAPP, reinforcing the importance of policy adherence throughout the Movement.

The Center audits NGBs and the USOPC annually on their implementation of required athlete safety policies. If the Center finds that an NGB is out of compliance, the audit team specifies one or more corrective actions and works with the organization until those actions have been carried out. In addition to MAAPP adherence, compliance audits include quality control assessments regarding how well the NGB does at enforcing sanctions that individuals suspended or permanently ineligible cannot participate in any capacity at sanctioned activities (e.g., events, competitions, or camps). Audits also assess whether policies are being adequately communicated, and check to see that education and training requirements, discussed in the section below, are being met.

The MAAPP represents a key feature of the Center's model to protect athletes; understanding how these policies are being implemented and the impact they are having is essential to establishing the effectiveness of that model. For this reason, the Center has contracted with an external research partner to conduct an evaluation of the MAAPP in 2022, the results of which will inform future policy enhancements and implementation strategies.

Education and Training

Education on the signs of abuse and misconduct and how to respond to suspected abuse is a hallmark not just of the literature on abuse in sport (Brackenridge et al., 2010; Parent & Demers, 2011) but the literature on abuse prevention at large (Centers for Disease Control and Prevention, 2019). Bystander intervention education and training has shown especially positive signs in mobilization among participants (Baynard et al., 2007; Finklehor, 2009). Education and mobilization around abuse prevention is of particular importance given the reporting obligations which adult participants of NGBs are held to under federal law, including making a mandatory report immediately of child abuse, including child sexual abuse, to both law enforcement and the Center (The Protecting Young Victims from Sexual Abuse and Safe Sport Authorization Act of 2017, 2018).

Certain adult participants under the jurisdiction of U.S. NGBs and the USOPC must complete abuse prevention training provided by the Center every year. Rather than repeat the same course annually, however, participants complete a series of refresher trainings in their second, third, and fourth years. These trainings build on one another in such a way that key messages are repeated while new topics are introduced and incorporate elements of abuse prevention education best practices (such as those cited in Scholes et al., 2012). In line with the literature on continuing education for attitudinal change (Coté & Gilbert, 2009; Falcão et al., 2012) and abuse awareness in sports (Brackenridge et al., 2010), the Center's training is required for adult participants who have regular contact with or authority over minor athletes. Additionally, and in line with literature on the important role of sport organizational leadership when it comes to prevention (Carska-Sheppard & Ammons, 2021), employees and board members of applicable sport organizations are also required to complete the Center's training annually. As of July 2021, the Center has delivered more than 2 million online training courses. In a 2020 survey, 90% of individuals who completed the Center's core training course reported that because of the training they felt better prepared to protect athletes from misconduct (U.S. Center for SafeSport, 2021c).

The Center has developed more than ten online education courses and numerous custom in-person or virtual trainings for different participation audiences, including coaches, administrators, adult athletes, minor athletes, and parents; training for healthcare professionals and individuals who work with athletes with disabilities; training on mandatory reporting; and training for volunteers at Olympic and Paralympic Games. Many of these trainings are available in English, Spanish, French, and a number of other languages.

Response and Resolution

Historically, amateur sports organizations have had limited financial or technical resources to investigate claims of abuse or misconduct (Cense & Brackenridge, 2001; Parent, 2011; Rhind et al., 2015). From elite levels to grassroots sports, there were few formal mechanisms to report misconduct or intervene in situations with the potential to progress into more serious harm, few resources outside of law enforcement where organizations could turn to for help, and a lack of training regarding what to do should misconduct arise (Tschan, 2014). Without appropriate training and resources for sport organization administrators, research (such as that cited below) suggests that they may have ineffective responses to reports of abuse or misconduct in their sport. These responses could range from downplaying the severity of cases of abuse in their sport (Lang & Hartill, 2015), to the inability to devote the appropriate amount of time to complex cases (Rhind et al., 2015), to the belief that creating effective mechanisms to respond to abuse and misconduct gives their sport a reputation for abuse (Brackenridge, 1997; Parent & Demers, 2011). Furthermore, there is potential for conflicting interests to influence how sport organizations internally respond to and resolve cases of abuse or misconduct involving their own members (Kerr et al., 2020). The establishment of the Center as the independent body responsible for investigating and responding to abuse allegations across the Movement has begun to provide some relief to these issues in the United States.

The Center has exclusive jurisdiction to investigate and resolve reports of sexual abuse and misconduct in the Movement, and discretionary jurisdiction over reports of emotional and physical abuse and misconduct. The Center's process does not supplant or replace other forms of accountability (such as civil or criminal law, or Title IX), and all Center employees are mandatory reporters required to immediately report any known or suspected child abuse or neglect to legal authorities. Rather, the Center's response and resolution process focuses on evaluating the fitness of individuals to participate in sport (as athletes, coaches, volunteers, or otherwise) within the Movement. There are no time bars of any kind that prevent the Center from responding to reports, and the Center can investigate reports even if law enforcement has declined to investigate or file charges. Reports to the Center can be made through its online reporting system and 24-hour phone line for reporting (for more information, visit: https://uscenterforsafesport.org/report-a-concern/).

As of November 2021, the Center has received over 10,000 reports and sanctioned more than 1,100 participants. Sanctions imposed by the Center have reciprocal enforcement across all Olympic and Paralympic NGBs of sport in the United States. The purpose of sanctioning is threefold. First, sanctions provide feedback to individuals found to have violated the SafeSport Code that their actions were inconsistent with the standards of the Movement. Second, sanctions are imposed to mitigate risk to others within the sports community. Third and finally, sanctions serve the purpose of upholding the Code and all relevant policies. A number of considerations are taken into account in the Center's determination of appropriate sanctions, such as the age of the involved individuals, whether there is a pattern of misconduct, as well as other factors. The Center may issue several different types of sanctions depending on the facts and circumstances established in particular cases; these can include written warnings, probation, suspension and other eligibility restrictions, and other discretionary sanctions.

The Center maintains a Centralized Disciplinary Database (CDD) that is intended to inform the public when adult participants have engaged in, or are alleged to have engaged in, forms of misconduct that present a potential risk to other members of the sport community. The Center does not publish all of its decisions to the CDD; decisions about sanctions and temporary restrictions imposed on minors are not included, nor those imposed on individuals when a potential risk to the broader sport community has not been established (U.S. Center for SafeSport, 2021d).

FUTURE DIRECTIONS

As noted above, studies on abuse in sport suggest that while sexual abuse and misconduct are pervasive issues, emotional and physical abuse together are likely more prevalent (Stirling & Kerr, 2013). This is in line with the Center's findings from the 2020 Culture and Climate Survey, where prevalence rates of emotional and physical maltreatment (approximately 80% and 22%, respectively) were together much higher than survey participants' experiences of sexual maltreatment. Nevertheless, the full scope of emotional and physical maltreatment in American sport has not yet been well documented.

The Center exercises discretionary authority over reports of emotional and physical abuse and misconduct. However, most reported cases are still handled by NGBs or their affiliated organizations. This can be problematic, given that many sport organizations lack the appropriate resources, knowledge, or technical experience to effectively respond to allegations of emotional and physical abuse and misconduct (Kerr, Battaglia, & Stirling, 2019; Parent & Demers, 2011; Rhind et al., 2015). With this understanding, the Center has committed to exercising discretionary jurisdiction over additional emotional and physical misconduct matters in the future. The Center will also continue to provide training and resources aimed at helping NGBs respond to those allegations that the Center does not exercise jurisdiction over. These measures will allow for a more standardized approach for addressing all forms of misconduct across the Movement and will provide valuable data points to inform future policies and prevention education. Many cases will continue to be addressed by sport organizations themselves; but there is hope that, increasingly, they will be investigated and resolved in a more consistent manner.

Also, by 2023, the Center plans to carry out a number of additional steps based on the needs of athletes that were identified through the 2020 Culture and Climate Survey. These include establishing a web resource to help connect athletes with mental health supports, gathering feedback on the Center's response and resolution process, and developing educational materials aimed at combating retaliation, abuses of power, and barriers to reporting (U.S. Center for SafeSport, 2021b). The Culture and Climate Survey will be repeated in 2023, with the goal of hearing from a more diverse array of athletes to better understand their unique experiences in sports, as well as to evaluate change in the culture and climate of sports over time.

Abuse in sports is, of course, not limited to the United States. The need for independent mechanisms to report abuse and misconduct in sports were identified in policy documents as early as the late 1990s in Canada and the United Kingdom (Kerr et al., 2020; Lang & Hartill, 2015) and have been echoed in subsequent publications (Coaching Association of Canada, 2019; International Olympic Committee, 2017; Kerr et al., 2020; Rhind et al., 2015). Recent reports of abuse and misconduct out of Japan and a review of failed safeguarding reforms from the United Kingdom have exemplified the need for formal reporting systems and independent investigation structures in other countries (Sheldon, 2021; Tofte et al., 2020). In recent years, several countries have made strides to establish their own independent mechanisms for reporting abuse in sports. Examples include Sport Singapore, which has released a unified, cross-sport organization code of conduct and introduced an independent mechanism for reports (Safe Sport Commission Singapore, 2021), and Canada, which after years of activism from athletes and researchers has granted funding to pursue the formation of an independent safe sport agency (Kerr et al., 2020). Continued international collaboration and information sharing will help to advance the global collective understanding of best practices for athlete safety and what works in prevention.

The Center strives to use evidence-informed and athlete-centered approaches in preventing and responding to abuse in sports and looks to both scientific and athletic communities as key informants for these efforts. Future research on the nature of emotional and physical abuse in sports, with particular attention paid to the representativeness of the sample, could help the field of prevention develop stronger and more holistic approaches to athlete protection. Additionally, research and evaluation are needed to shed more light on outcomes associated with prevention education programs, the impact of governance strategies in grassroots sports, and the types of sanctions that work best with minor athletes at reducing maltreatment in sports settings. More efforts need to be made to lift athlete voices, and to empower athletes to influence the directions in which the culture of sports changes (Mountjoy, 2019). Qualitative research with athletes—as well as research conducted and driven in a participatory manner by and with athletes—will be particularly valuable when it comes to understanding and advocating for the needs of participants across sports.

A safe sport environment is one with a prevailing culture of respect, where well-being and safety are prioritized, and where athletes can realize the many benefits of sports participation. The U.S. Center for SafeSport plays an important role in moving the needle toward a more positive sports culture, but to achieve lasting change we must take collective, collaborative action.

REFERENCES

Baynard, V. L., Moynihan, M. M., & Plante, E. G. (2007). Sexual violence prevention through bystander education: An experimental evaluation. *Journal of Community Psychology*, *35*(4), 463–481. doi:10.1002/jcop.20159.

Brackenridge, C. H. (1997). "He owned me basically . . . ": Women's experience of sexual abuse in sport. *International Review for the Sociology of Sport*, *32*(2), 115–130. doi:10.1177/101269097032002001.

Brackenridge, C. H., Bishopp, D., Moussalli, S., & Tapp, J. (2008). The characteristics of sexual abuse in sport: A multidimensional scaling analysis of events described in media reports. *International Journal of Sport and Exercise Psychology*, *6*(4), 385–406. doi:10.1080/1612197x.2008.9671881.

Brackenridge, C. H., Fasting, K., Kirby, S., & Leahy, T. (2010). *Protecting children from violence in sport: A review with a focus on industrialized countries.* Florence: United Nations Children's Fund. Retrieved from: https://www.unicef-irc.org/publications/pdf/violence_in_sport.pdf.

Carska-Sheppard, A., & Ammons, S. (2021). Tone from the top: The role of the general counsel in the prevention of harassment and abuse in international sports. *Frontiers in Sports and Active Living*, *3*, 18. doi:10.3389/fspor.2021.625684.

Cense, M., & Brackenridge, C. (2001). Temporal and developmental risk factors for sexual harassment and abuse in sport. *European Physical Education Review*, *7*(1), 61–79. doi:10.1177/1356336x010071006.

Centers for Disease Control and Prevention. (2019). DHHS Report to Congress on Child Sexual Abuse Prevention. Retrieved from: https://www.jhsph.edu/research/centers-and-institutes/moore-center-for-the-prevention-of-child-sexual-abuse/policy-and-advocacy/FY_2019_CDC-Report-to-Congress-Child-Sexual-Abuse-Prevention%20copy.pdf.

Coaching Association of Canada. (2019). National Sport Organization Safe Sport Working Group Presents Consensus Statements on Pan-Canadian Safe Sport on the Prevention of Abuse and Harassment. *National Safe Sport Summit*. Ottawa: Coaching Association of Canada. Retrieved from: https://coach.ca/national-sport-organization-safe-sport-working-group-presents-consensus-statements-pan-canadian-0.

Coté, J., & Gilbert, W. (2009). An integrative definition of coaching effectiveness and expertise. *International Journal of Sports Science & Coaching, 4*(3), 307–323. doi:10.1260/174795409789623892.

Donnelly, P., Kerr, G., Heron, A., & DiCarlo, D. (2016). Protecting youth in sport: An examination of harassment policies. *International Journal of Sport Policy and Politics, 8*(1), 33–50. doi:10.1080/19406940.2014.958180.

Doré, I., O'Loughlin, J. L., Schnitzer, M. E., Datta, G. D., & Fournier, L. (2018). The longitudinal association between the context of physical activity and mental health in early adulthood. *Mental Health and Physical Activity, 14*, 121–130. doi:10,1016/j.mhpa.2018.04.001.

Eime, R., Young, J., Harvey, J., Charity, M., & Payne, W. (2013). A systematic review of the psychological and social benefits of participation in sport for children and adolescents: Informing development of a conceptual model of health through sport. *International Journal of Behavioral Nutrition and Physical Activity, 10*(1), 98. doi:10.1186/1479-5868-10-98.

Empowering Olympic, Paralympic, and Amateur Athletes Act of 2020. (2020). S.2330, 116th Cong. Retrieved from: https://www.congress.gov/bill/116th-congress/senate-bill/2330.

Falcão, W. R., Bloom, G. A., & Gilbert, W. D. (2012). Coaches' perceptions of a coach training program designed to promote youth developmental outcomes. *Journal of Applied Sport Psychology, 24*(4), 429–444. doi:10.1080/10413200.2012.692452.

Finklehor, D. (2009). The prevention of child sexual abuse. *The Future of Children, 19*(2), 169–194. doi:10.1353/foc.0.0035.

Ford, B., Roenigk, A., & Pomeroy, L. (2020). The gymnastics factory: The rise and fall of the Karolyi Ranch. A *30 for 30 Podcasts* and *EspnW* collaboration. Retrieved from: https://www.espn.com/espn/feature/story/_/id/29235446/the-karolyi-ranch-where-us-women-gymnastics-gold-was-forged-price.

Henry, N., & Powell, A. (2018). Technology-facilitated sexual violence: A literature review of empirical research. *Trauma, Violence, & Abuse, 19*(2), 195–208.

International Olympic Committee. (2017). *Safeguarding athletes from harassment and abuse in sport: IOC Toolkit for IFs and NOCs*. Lausanne: International Olympic Committee. Retrieved from: https://d2g8uwgn11fzhj.cloudfront.net/wp-content/uploads/2017/10/18105952/IOC_Safeguarding_Toolkit_ENG_Screen_Full1.pdf.

Johnson, N., Hanna, K., Novak, J., & Giardino, A. P. (2020). U.S. Center for SafeSport: Preventing abuse in sports. *Women in Sport and Physical Activity Journal, 28*(1), 66–71. doi:10.1123/wspaj.2019–0049.

Kirby, S., & Greaves, L. (1996, July). Foul play: Sexual abuse and harassment in sport. In *Pre-Olympic Scientific Congress, Dallas, USA* (pp. 11–14).

Kerr, G., Battaglia, A., & Stirling, A. (2019). Maltreatment in youth sport: A systemic issue. *Kinesiology Review, 8*(3), 237–243. doi:10.1123/kr.2019–0016.

Kerr, G., Kidd, B., & Donnelly, P. (2020). One step forward, two steps back: The struggle for child protection in Canadian sport. *Social Sciences, 9*(5), 68. doi:10.3390/socsci9050068.

Kerr, G., & Stirling, A. (2019). Where is safeguarding in sport psychology research and practice? *Journal of Applied Sport Psychology, 31*(4), 367–384. doi:10.1080/10413200.2018.1559255.

Kerr, G., Willson, E., & Stirling, A. (2019). Prevalence of maltreatment among current and former national team athletes (pp. 1–51). Retrieved from: https://athletescan.com/sites/default/files/images/prevalence_of_maltreatment_reporteng.pdf.

Koss, M. P., Wiglus, J. K., & Williamsen, K. M. (2014). Campus sexual misconduct: Restorative justice approaches to enhance compliance with Title IX guidance. *Trauma, Violence, & Abuse, 15*(3), 242–257. doi: 10.1177/1524838014521500.

Lang, M., & Hartill, M. (2015). *Safeguarding, Child Protection and Abuse in Sport— International Perspectives in Research, Policy and Practice.* London: Routledge.

Lastuka, A., & Cottingham, M. (2015). The effect of adaptive sports on employment among people with disabilities. *Disability and Rehabilitation, 38*(8), 742–748. doi:10.3109/09638288.2015.1059497.

Lechner, M. (2009). Long-run labour market and health effects of individual sports activities. *Journal of Health Economics, 28*(4), 839–854. doi:10.1016/j.jhealeco.2009.05.003.

Logan, K., & Cuff, S. (2019). Organized sports for children, preadolescents, and adolescents. *Pediatrics, 143*(6), e20190997. doi:10.1542/peds.2019–0997.

Massey, W. V., & Whitley, M. A. (2016). The role of sport for youth amidst trauma and chaos. *Qualitative Research in Sport, Exercise and Health, 8*(5), 487–504. doi:10.1080/2159676x.2016.1204351.

McMahon, J., Knight, C. J., & McGannon, K. R. (2018). Educating parents of children in sport about abuse using narrative pedagogy. *Sociology of Sport Journal, 35*(4), 314–323. doi:10.1123/ssj.2017–0186.

Mountjoy, M. (2019). "Only by speaking out can we create lasting change": What can we learn from the Dr. Larry Nassar tragedy? *British Journal of Sports Medicine, 53*(1), 57–60. doi:10.1136/bjsports-2018–099403.

Mountjoy, M., Brackenridge, C., Arrington, M., Blauwet, C., Carska-Sheppard, A., Fasting, K., . . . & Budgett, R. (2016). International Olympic Committee consensus statement: Harassment and abuse (non-accidental violence) in sport. *British Journal of Sports Medicine, 50*(17), 1019–1029. doi:10.1136/bjsports-2016–096121.

Noble, J., & Vermillion, M. (2014). Youth sport administrators' perceptions and knowledge of organizational policies on child maltreatment. *Children and Youth Services Review, 38*, 52–57. doi: 10.1016/j.childyouth.2014.01.011.

Parent, S. (2011). Disclosure of sexual abuse in sport organizations: A case study. *Journal of Child Sexual Abuse, 20*(3), 322–337. doi:10.1080/10538712.2011.573459.

Parent, S., & Demers, G. (2011). Sexual abuse in sport: A model to prevent and protect athletes. *Child Abuse Review, 20*(2), 120–133. doi:10.1002/car.1135.

Protecting Young Victims from Sexual Abuse and Safe Sport Authorization Act of 2017. (2018). S. 534, 155th Cong. Retrieved from: https://www.congress.gov/bill/115th-congress/senate-bill/534.

Rhind, D., McDermott, J., Lambert, E., & Koleva, I. (2015). A review of safeguarding cases in sport. *Child Abuse Review, 24*(6), 418–426. doi:10.1002/car.2306.

Safe Sport Commission Singapore (2021). Safe Sport Unified Code. Retrieved from: https://www.safesport.sg/files/Safe%20Sport%20Unified%20Code.pdf.

Sanderson, J., & Weathers, M. R. (2020). Snapchat and child sexual abuse in sport: Protecting child athletes in the social media age. *Sport Management Review, 23*(1), 81–94. doi:10.1016/j.smr.2019.04.006.

Scholes, L., Jones, C., Stieler-Hunt, C., Rolfe, B., & Pozzebon, K. (2012). The teachers' role in child sexual abuse prevention programs: Implications for teacher education. *Australian Journal of Teacher Education (Online), 37*(11), 109–136. doi:10.14221/ajte.2012v37n11.5.

Sheldon, C. (2021). *Independent review into child sexual abuse in football 1970–2005.* London: The Football Association. Retrieved from: https://www.thefa.com/-/media/thefacom-new/files/about-the-fa/sheldon-report/independent-review-into-child-sexual-abuse-in-football-1970-2005.ashx.

Stafford, A., Alexander, K., & Fry, D. (2015). "There was something that wasn't right because that was the only place I ever got treated like that": Children and young people's experiences of emotional harm in sport. *Childhood, 22*(1), 121–137. doi:10.1177/0907568213505625.

Stirling, A., & Kerr, G. (2013). The perceived effects of elite athletes' experiences of emotional abuse in the coach-athlete relationship. *International Journal of Sport and Exercise Psychology, 11*(1), 87–100. doi:10.1080/1612197x.2013.752173.

Stirling, A., & Kerr, G. (2009). Abused athletes' perceptions of the coach-athlete relationship. *Sport in Society, 12*(2), 227–239. doi:10.1080/17430430802591019.

Tofte, S., Husain, N., & Worden, M. (2020). *"I was hit so many times I can't count": Abuse of child athletes in Japan.* New York: Human Rights Watch. Retrieved from: https://www.hrw.org/sites/default/files/media_2020/07/Japan0720_web.pdf.

Toftegaard-Nielsen, J. (2001). The forbidden zone: Intimacy, sexual relations and misconduct in the relationship between coaches and athletes. *International Review for the Sociology of Sport, 36*(2), 165–182. doi:10.1177/101269001036002003.

Tschan, W. (2014). *Professional sexual misconduct in institutions: Causes and consequences, prevention and intervention.* Boston: Hogrefe Publishing.

U.S. Census Bureau. (2020). Population division, estimates. Retrieved from: https://www.childstats.gov/AMERICASCHILDREN/tables/pop1.asp.

U.S. Center for SafeSport. (2020). 2022 Minor Athlete Abuse Prevention Policies (Published September 2020; Effective January 2022). Retrieved from: https://

uscenterforsafesport.org/wp-content/uploads/2020/09/FINAL-2022-MAAPP-9.21.pdf.

U.S. Center for SafeSport. (2021a). SafeSport Code for the U.S. Olympic and Paralympic Movement. Retrieved from: https://uscenterforsafesport.org/wp-content/uploads/2021/04/SafeSportCode2021_040121_V3.pdf.

U.S. Center for SafeSport. (2021b). 2020 Athlete Culture & Climate Survey. Retrieved from: https://uscenterforsafesport.org/wp-content/uploads/2021/07/CultureClimateSurvey_ExternalReport_071421_Final.pdf.

U.S. Center for SafeSport. (2021c). We are all champions: 2020 annual report. Retrieved from: https://www.flipsnack.com/safesport/u-s-center-for-safesport-2020-annual-report/full-view.html.

U.S. Center for SafeSport. (2021d). *Centralized disciplinary database*. Retrieved from: https://uscenterforsafesport.org/response-and-resolution/centralized-disciplinary-database/.

U.S. Department of Health and Human Services. (2019). National youth sports strategy. Washington, DC. U.S. Department of Health and Human Services. Retrieved from: https://health.gov/sites/default/files/2019-10/National_Youth_Sports_Strategy.pdf.

U.S. Olympic & Paralympic Committee. (2019). Team USA NGB activation reference guide: 2019. Retrieved from: https://www.teamusa.org/-/media/USA_Rollersports/Documents/2019/2019-NGB-activation-guide/2019-NGB-Activation-Reference-Guide.pdf?la=en&hash=CB7266DC899AFE5361E595883386DB86300C969E.

NOTES

1. For the purposes of this chapter, the term *maltreatment* is encompassing of both abuse and misconduct, and includes non-accidental acts of both commission and omission that result in, or have the potential to result in, harm (sexual, physical, or emotional). For a discussion on this choice of terminology, see Kerr & Stirling, 2019.

2. The term *adult participants* in this context includes individuals (18 years of age and over) who are members, license holders, employees, or board members of NGBs, the USOPC and other applicable organizations. It also includes anyone appointed by those organizations to have regular contact with or authority over minor athletes. Examples may include adult athletes, coaches, volunteers, staff, medical personnel, van/bus drivers, trainers, officials, and other individuals who meet the definition provided within the MAAPP.

Chapter Eleven

Athletes, Social Media, and Health

Ellen MacPherson, Erin Willson, and Gretchen Kerr

Social media use has become ubiquitous for athletes and sport fans alike. For instance, social media may be used in the sport realm to enhance a sense of connectedness with others, build a personal brand, share interests and sport-related information, and discuss important topics (e.g., athlete rights). Sport fans, specifically, may also use social media to communicate supportive and encouraging, as well as hostile and discriminatory messages. This chapter will address the intersections of social media and athletes' health and well-being. To frame this chapter and to illustrate these intersections, we will draw on the experiences and social media activities related to Simone Biles, Olympic champion in artistic gymnastics.

A Case Study of Simone Biles

Simone Biles has a strong social media presence and uses her platform to communicate thoughts and feelings on a wide range of topics, promote products, highlight sponsors, and share interests outside of sport. Most recently, Simone used her social media accounts to document her experiences at the Tokyo 2020 Summer Olympic Games. In the midst of the Games, Simone withdrew from the team final event after her first vault (Maine, 2021). Following her withdrawal from the team event, she subsequently opted out of the all-around individual final, as well as vault, uneven bars, and the floor exercise finals. At the time, Simone cited the reason for opting out was to focus on her mental health and cope with the emotional toll of the Games (Maine, 2021). As the competition proceeded, Simone used social media to communicate further information about her well-being through a series of posts and videos (Maine, 2021), including her experience with the "twisties" and that her "mind and body [were] simply not in sync." Simone's social media activities and subsequent responses from fans will be shared throughout this chapter to explore the potential benefits and detriments of social media to athletes' health and well-being.

SPORT AND ATHLETE HEALTH AND WELL-BEING

According to the World Health Organization (2021), "health" is defined as the existence of complete physical, psychological, and social well-being, not simply by a lack of disease or illness. In this context, a person's well-being refers to "psychological, physical, and social states that are distinctly positive" (Huppert et al., 2004, p. 1331). An individual's general well-being is integral to one's ability to thrive and attain optimal health, personal development, productivity, performance excellence, longevity and quality of life (e.g., De Neve et al., 2018; Diener et al., 2018; Huppert et al., 2004). There are a number of determinants of one's general well-being, including the social and economic environment (e.g., income, social status, social connections, education); the physical environment (e.g., employment conditions, safe communities); as well as the personal qualities or characteristics (e.g., personality traits, genetics, gender) and other contextual factors unique to the individual (e.g., personal stressors) (WHO, 2021).

One of the contextual factors often assumed to positively contribute to overall health and well-being is participation in sport. Indeed, researchers have demonstrated the potential for sport participation at all levels to foster key physical, psychological, social, and academic outcomes important to overall well-being including increased intrinsic motivation, self-concept, empowerment, emotion regulation, setting and achieving goals, resilience, relational skills, and improved academic grades (e.g., Barber et al., 2001; Eccles et al., 2003; Gould et al., 2002). Yet, there is also evidence to suggest that features of the sport environment, such as the coaching climate, presence of maltreatment, early sport specialization, substance use, retirement transition, and a win-at-all-costs mentality may negatively influence participants' health and well-being (e.g., Cho et al., 2019; Kerr et al., 2020; Stirling & Kerr, 2013; Willson et al., 2021; Xanthopoulos et al., 2020). Specifically, these features of the sport environment may influence health and well-being through the manifestation of burnout, injury, overtraining, and mental health challenges such as disordered eating behaviors, depression, and performance anxiety, among others (e.g., Appaneal et al., 2009; Goodger et al., 2007; Gulliver et al., 2015; Kerr et al., 2020; Schaal et al., 2011).

In particular, the contemporary nature of high-performance sport, marked by the increased commodification, professionalization, and globalization of athletes, has become an important context for well-being research

(Barker-Ruchti, 2019; Brady, 2022). In this environment, athletes are required to adhere to expanded training, performance, health, and lifestyle expectations, while balancing contracts, sponsorship, politics of the sport, public interest, and the development of a personal brand (Barker-Ruchti, 2019; Brady, 2022; Purcell et al., 2019). Cumulatively, these factors may facilitate, challenge, or threaten the health and well-being of high-performance athletes (Brady, 2022).

SPORT AND SOCIAL MEDIA

One of the most significant influences in the evolution of sport in the last decade is the growth of social media (Sanderson et al., 2015). While the use of social media is impactful on the sport industry as a whole (e.g., enhanced communication, consumption, marketing), it has been particularly influential in the lives of athletes in the public sphere (i.e., professional or elite amateur) as it provides opportunities for more direct interactions with fans, personal brand or sponsored promotions, sharing interests or sport-related information, and may serve as a platform for public relations (Hambrick, 2012; Hambrick et al., 2010). To date, much of the research attention related to social media and sport has focused on what the platforms offer and the ways in which they are used in the sport context, with little attention dedicated to the potential influence of social media on the health and well-being of sport's key stakeholders: athletes. Drawing from scholarship outside of the sport context, preliminary research suggests social media use may be associated with a variety of positive health and well-being outcomes, including enabling peer support (Naslund et al., 2020); increased happiness and self-esteem (e.g., Kim & Lee, 2011; Lian et al., 2018); strengthening existing relationships (Subrahmanyam & Greenfield, 2008); and increased social connections (Naslund et al., 2020; Moreno et al., 2009).

In contrast, extensive research suggests social media may also be used to engage in hostile interactions (e.g., cyberbullying, public shaming) (Wolak et al., 2006; Ybarra & Mitchell, 2007), risk-taking behavior (Hinduja & Patchin, 2008), and increased social comparison (Rosenthal-von der Pütten et al., 2019). As a result, social media may contribute to mental health challenges and poor well-being (Woods & Scott, 2016), including feelings of social isolation, rumination, anxiety, and depression (Feinstein et al., 2013; Rideout & Fox, 2018). Importantly, there is a recent push for research related to the intersections of social media, health, and well-being to address contextual nuances influencing social media experiences, as the connections between social media, health, and well-being are neither inherently good or bad, but complex and influenced by an individual's activities (e.g., interactions with others, "liking" or following, posting), motives (e.g., uses and gratifications), and communications online (Best et al., 2014; Beyens et al., 2020). To advance our understanding of the intersections of social media and athletes' health and well-being, this chapter will explore some of the contextual factors that contribute to athletes' experiences online.

Social Media as a Potential Facilitator of Athlete Health and Well-being

In the sport context, social media has evolved to become an integrated part of athletes' lives and may be viewed as an extension of the self (Geurin, 2017) as it enables athletes to become more active in the production of stories and public representations of themselves (Sanderson & Kassing, 2011). Specifically, social media allows athletes to have a direct connection with fans and the public, the power to create and shape their own brands, and an enhanced platform for advocacy (Filo et al., 2015; Sanderson & Kassing, 2011; Schmittel & Sanderson, 2015). This section will explore each of these benefits in detail and suggest connections between these constructs and athlete health and well-being.

Direct Communication to Fans and Public

A key benefit that social media facilitates for athletes is the ability to directly communicate with the public openly and honestly (Pegoraro, 2010). Prior to the advent of social media, this degree of direct communication between athletes and fans was not possible. As a result, social media breaks down the barriers of access and fundamentally changes the landscape of fan-athlete relationships (Kassing & Sanderson, 2010). In this context, research shows athletes use social media for a variety of reasons, including to promote and share information, interact with and receive feedback from fans, and provide a behind-the-scenes perspective of their sport (Geurin, 2017; Lebel & Danylchuk, 2014; Sanderson & Truax, 2014). Athletes may also use social media to demonstrate a more nuanced personal identity (Sanderson, 2013), such as sharing unique personality traits, home life, personal thoughts, hobbies, and other interests (Geurin, 2017; Pegoraro, 2010; Sanderson, 2013).

The case of Simone Biles from the 2020 Olympic Games provides a helpful example of the ways in which athletes may use social media to directly communicate with the public, as well as share personal thoughts and feelings. For instance, during the competition, Simone posted a message to Instagram stating, "It wasn't an easy day or my best but I got through it. I truly do feel like I have the weight of the world on my shoulders at times." Shortly after posting this message, Simone withdrew from the team competition due to health challenges. Upon withdrawal from the competition, Simone received numerous positive comments from fans, including, "she did the right thing and handled it with grace and poise," "you're even more of a real hero for your choices. I'm honored to have you representing our country," and "few understand what you went through and what a very difficult decision you had to make. Congratulations to you. Safety first." In response to these positive messages, Simone posted a statement that expressed gratitude and reflected the meaningful nature of the public's support: "The outpouring of love & support I've received has made me realize I'm more than my accomplishments and gymnastics which I never truly believed before." This statement underscores the potential benefits of social media for athlete health and well-being through the reception of public support and encouragement during a challenging personal experience.

Building a Brand

Social media may also be used to help athletes build and maintain their personal brand. Parmentier and Fischer (2012) suggest that an athlete's personal brand can be considered "the set of associations identified with a particular person" (p. 107), including personal perspectives, interests, connections, consumer behaviors, and sponsorships. For athletes, social media has become an avenue to construct ways they are perceived by others and manage their self-presentation (Geurin-Eagleman & Burch, 2016). Arai and colleagues (2014) noted three aspects of successful branding via athletes' social media channels: athletic performance (e.g., win rates), attractive appearance (e.g., physical fitness), and a marketable lifestyle (e.g., life story, fan interaction, romantic relationships). Possessing a strong personal brand on social media may provide increased opportunities for revenue generation for athletes within and outside of sport, such as increased financial support, sponsorships or partnerships with businesses, and educational opportunities (Bigsby et al., 2019; Geurin, 2017). For example, Simone Biles showcases the value of her personal brand on social media through the promotion of clothing line Athleta (e.g., targeted advertisements, launch of exclusive clothing lines), partnerships with VISA and Oreo (e.g., virtual vision board sessions, contest promotions), and advertisement of her post-Olympics sponsored gymnastics tour, Gold Over America.

Sanderson (2013) suggests that diversifying revenue sources for athletes is important, particularly due to the unpredictable nature of sport, where athletes may experience sudden withdrawal from sport because of injury, illness, or team de-selections. A successful athlete brand may impact an athlete's health and well-being by providing increased financial security and facilitating the expansion of athletes' perceived identities beyond their sport (e.g., exploring new interests, business opportunities).

Platform for Advocacy

Another potential facilitator for athlete health and well-being through social media is the use of social media as a platform for advocacy, wherein athletes participate in discussions and coalesce with other like-minded individuals to spark change related to contemporary issues (Sanderson, 2018), including social justice issues and athletes' rights. As Coombs and Cassilo (2017) observed, athletes have historically supported social justice issues publicly, dating back to the civil rights movement. More recent examples of athletes' use of social media to advocate for social justice issues include commentary following George Zimmerman's acquittal in the Trayvon Martin death (e.g., outrage of the verdict, critiques of the justice system, links to broader racial discrimination) (Schmittel & Sanderson, 2015), encouragement of and participation in the Black Lives Matter protests following a series of murders of Black citizens by police officers, and support for gender equity and ending the pay gap (e.g., Equal Play, Equal Pay Campaign).

In addition to broader societal issues, athletes also use social media to share personal experiences in sport and promote sport-specific causes important to them (e.g., athlete well-being, eradicating maltreatment in sport). Although there is limited empirical research to date, recent anecdotal evidence demonstrates the use of social media to initiate and/or elevate the conversation related to the importance of prioritizing health and well-being of athletes over performance, such as public statements from Women's Tennis Association player Naomi Osaka (i.e., withdrawal from French Open due to negative effect of press conferences on mental health) and Angela Price, wife of National Hockey League goalie Carey Price (i.e., entered NHL/NHLPA player assistance program for mental health challenges) (Carayol, 2021). Further, Simone Biles' withdrawal from several Olympic Games events and subsequent social media activities (e.g., sharing thoughts, feelings, and challenges) helped the public see the individual beyond the athlete, with fans sending comments such as: "you have to take care of yourself first ALWAYS," "your actions have been a tremendous example of how to honour yourself. That is something most people struggle with. I am in awe," "I'm happy you chose yourself over the performance," and "your bravery is going to show [people] that it's okay to walk away from things that aren't working for them and that is a bigger legacy than any sport."

Finally, anecdotal evidence also suggests that athletes have recently started using social media as an avenue to share experiences of maltreatment in sport. To date, revelations of maltreatment have been particularly salient in gymnastics, with many athletes speaking out about their experiences on social media in the wake of the Larry Nassar trial, such as Olympians Aly Raisman and Gabby Douglas (Fouriezos, 2018). In addition, following the release of the Netflix documentary *Athlete A*, gymnasts worldwide shared experiences of psychological, physical, and sexual maltreatment on social media through the hashtag #gymnastalliance (Gymnasts for Change, n.d.). Simone Biles also contributed her personal experiences with the #MeToo movement and Larry Nassar on Twitter, stating:

> *Feelings . . . #MeToo. Most of you know me as a happy, giggly, and energetic girl. But lately . . . I've felt a bit broken and the more I try to shut off the voice in my head the louder it screams. I am not afraid to tell my story anymore. I too am one of the many survivors that was sexually abused by Larry Nassar. Please believe me when I say it was a lot harder to first speak those words out loud than it is now to put them on paper. There are many reasons that I have been reluctant to share my story, but I know now it is not my fault. It is not normal to receive any type of treatment from a trusted team physician and refer to it horrifyingly as the "special" treatment. This behavior is completely unacceptable, disgusting, and abusive, especially coming from someone whom I was TOLD to trust. For too long I've asked myself, "Was I too naïve? Was it my fault?" . . . I know that this horrific experience does not define me . . . I have promised myself that my story will be much greater than this and I promise you I will never give up . . . I won't let one man and the others that enabled him, to steal my love and joy . . . we need to know why this was able to take place for so long and to so many of us. We need to make sure something like this never happens again.*

In response to Simone's message, she received supportive comments via social media from the public, including "bursting with pride that you have the courage to speak your truth," "I hope you can find peace and healing," and "[you are] helping countless others feel brave enough to do the same or seek help."

Social Media as a Potential Detriment to Athlete Health and Well-being

In addition to the potential facilitators of social media for athlete health and well-being, research demonstrates the potential ways in which social media may harm or be detrimental to health and well-being.

Hostile Fan-Athlete Interactions on Social Media

Although direct communications between fans and athletes may have benefits for the athletes, there is also a potential for these interactions to be hostile and pose a risk to athletes' health and well-being. Specifically, a growing body of research exploring fan-athlete interactions online demonstrates that fans may use social media to criticize, disparage, and/or deliver confrontational, threatening, or misogynistic comments directly to athletes (e.g., Kavanagh et al., 2016; MacPherson & Kerr, 2019; Sanderson & Emmons, 2014; Sanderson & Truax, 2014). These interactions are often of a sexual, psychosocial, physical, or discriminatory nature (Kavanagh et al., 2016; MacPherson & Kerr, 2019, 2020; Sanderson & Emmons, 2014; Sanderson & Truax, 2014), with comments directed at athletes such as "please just die," "no one will ever respect you anymore," and "stop tennis and go for modelling" (MacPherson & Kerr, 2019, 2020). Fans' comments of this nature may be delivered in response to various behaviors, including poor athletic performance and behavior within and outside of the sport context, such as substance abuse, public advocacy (e.g., standing up for social justice issues), or personal scandals (MacPherson & Kerr, 2019; Sanderson & Emmons, 2014; Sanderson & Truax, 2014). As Browning and Sanderson (2012) note, social media amplifies the visibility—and therefore potential scrutiny—of athletes based on their performance and personal choices.

Researchers have also demonstrated that fans may deliver derogatory messages towards or about athletes based on their social identities, including gender and race (Dickerson, 2016; Litchfield et al., 2018; Kavanagh et al., 2019; MacPherson & Kerr, 2019, 2020). For instance, Kavanagh and colleagues (2019) and MacPherson and Kerr (2020) found that women professional athletes received social media comments that were gendered, sexualized, or misogynistic, threatened sexual violence, and/or suggested that women do not belong as athletes in professional sport. Comments directed at women athletes included "you should retire from tennis and do porn. I bet people will start to enjoy watching you then," "I always thought you could just be a model anyway," "keep stuffing that [food] down your fat face," "[athlete] is a massive whore," and "I want to shove a sock down [athlete]'s throat so she can stop howling like an animal on the court," among others. In another example, Stick et al. (2021) examined Reddit forums of fans discussing a professional Black male athlete's physical altercation with a woman in a hotel and found fans' determinations of guilt of the athlete drew on racialized assumptions, including attributing the athlete's aggressive behavior to a lack of intelligence, morality, and self-control, as well as likening the athlete's behavior to other Black athletes who have broken the law. Further, a study conducted by Litchfield and colleagues (2018) highlighted disparaging gendered and racialized messages directed at Serena Williams, including gender questioning (e.g., "has [athlete] ever been tested for being a man?"). For Simone Biles, examples of hostile fan comments directed to her on social media following her withdrawal from several Olympic events included "you're selfish, weak and no girls should look up to you," "wonder how much money and what else this traitor and sellout got for quitting on her country and teammates," "couldn't handle the pressure," and "you quit on your team to save face with fans and sponsors cuz you knew you'd take a [loss] in gold," among others.

Taken together, it is clear that athletes are subject to harmful messages of a sexual, physical, psychosocial, or discriminatory nature. Although research connecting the reception of these messages to specific health and well-being outcomes for athletes is scant, preliminary findings suggest that messages of a harmful nature directed at athletes on social media may be associated with negative mental health outcomes for athletes, including somatic complaints and social dysfunction (Walton et al., 2021). Future research should explore the intersections between hostile interactions on social media and associated outcomes for athlete health and well-being.

Organizational Conflict

Another factor that may pose a potential threat to the health and well-being of athletes is the organizational conflict that can emerge based on the athletes' online behavior, especially due to the instantaneous nature of social media (Sanderson, 2018). As noted above, social media is used by athletes as a platform for advocacy (Yan et al., 2018), as well as a space to post content in the midst of experiencing heightened emotions related to their sport or personal life, such as issues with their coach, amount of playing time, or circumstances outside of sport (Bhattacharya, 2017). It is often content of the latter nature that attracts uptake from the public (Sanderson, 2018). Given the immediacy of social media and the fact that the content posted by athletes is outside of the control of the sport organization, conflicts may arise (Sanderson, 2018). We suggest that an athlete's well-being or health may be at risk due to the potential organizational conflict that may result from social media activities. Specifically, the increased visibility of moments of heightened emotion, pressures to use social media strategically, and/or expectations to conform to certain public or organizational standards may have implications for the health and well-being of athletes, particularly as they relate to their perceptions of agency, autonomy, and self-expression.

CONCLUSION

The use of social media is widespread in sport, serving to enhance communications with fans and the public, increase marketing of the sport and athletes for financial gain, and to meet the needs of sponsors. For high-performance athletes specifically, social media serves to enable direct interactions with fans, develop a personal brand, engage in public advocacy, or to share information. Although previous researchers have suggested that social media can be associated with several positive benefits and various harms for health and well-being, limited research to date has explored these potential associations in athletes.

For optimal well-being to be experienced, basic human needs such as feeling a sense of connectedness and belonging, being recognized and valued as an individual, having meaning, purpose, and autonomy in life, must be met (e.g., Ryan & Deci, 2001; Todres et al., 2009). When such needs are not met, individuals may feel unworthy, devalued, disconnected, and dehumanized, thus placing well-being at risk. High-performance athletes are at risk of being dehumanized given that they are often viewed as commodities—as tools or means to an end—and that end is one of winning. When performance excellence is prioritized, valued, and rewarded, the personal well-being of athletes may become secondary and compromised (Kavanagh & Brady, 2014), as athletes get lost in the process (Ingham et al., 2002).

The over-emphasis and often singular focus on winning in sport is also reflected in social media. When athletes are meeting expectations, performing well and winning, social media messages tend to be positive and reinforcing; however, when athletic performance is subpar and/or results in losing, messages on social media can become hostile. Moreover, the nature of the social media messages can turn on a dime—supportive one day and insulting the next—depending upon performance outcomes. If an athlete's well-being is tied to performance, their well-being will be unstable and variable. Future research will benefit from studying athletes' lived experiences with social media and the conditions by which athlete well-being is directly facilitated or hindered by these online spaces (Poucher et al., 2021).

REFERENCES

Appaneal, R. N., Levine, B. R., Perna, F. M., & Roh, J. L. (2009). Measuring postinjury depression among male and female competitive athletes. *Journal of Sport and Exercise Psychology, 31*, 60–76.

Arai, A., Ko, Y. J., & Ross, S. (2014). Branding athletes: Exploration and conceptualization of athlete brand image. *Sport Management Review*, *17*(2), 97–106. https://doi.org/10.1016/j.smr.2013.04.003.

Barber, B. L., Eccles, J. S., & Stone, M. R. (2001). Whatever happened to the "jock," the "brain," and the "princess"? Young adult pathways linked to adolescent activity involvement and social identity. *Journal of Adolescent Research, 16*, 429–455.

Barker-Ruchti, N. (2019). *Athlete learning in elite sport: A cultural framework*. Abingdon, UK: Routledge.

Best, P., Manktelow, R., & Taylor, B. (2014). Online communication, social media and adolescent well-being: A systematic narrative review. *Children and Youth Services Review, 41*, 27–36.

Beyens, I., Pouwels, J. L., van Driel, I. I., Keijsers, L., & Valkenburg, P. M. (2020). The effect of social media on well-being differs from adolescent to adolescent. *Scientific Reports, 10*(1), 1–11.

Bhattacharya, S. (2017, August 29). Why venting work-related anger via social media can ruin your career. Retrieved from https://blogs.economictimes.indiatimes.com/careerlounge/why-venting-work-related-anger-via-social-media-can-ruin-yourcareer/.

Bigsby, K. G., Ohlmann, J. W., & Zhao, K. (2019). Keeping it 100: Social media and self-presentation in college football recruiting. *Big Data, 7*(1), 3–20. https://doi.org/10.1089/big.2018.0094.

Brady, A. (2022). Introducing holistic well-being within the athlete journey. In N. Campbell, A. Brady, & A. Tincknell-Smith (Eds.), *Developing and supporting athlete well-being: Person first, athlete second*. Abingdon, UK: Routledge.

Browning, B., & Sanderson, J. (2012). The positives and negatives of Twitter: Exploring how student-athletes use Twitter and respond to critical tweets. *International Journal of Sport Communication, 5*(4), 503–521.

Carayol, T. (2021, May 31). Naomi Osaka withdraws from French open amid row over press conferences. *The Guardian*. https://www.theguardian.com/sport/2021/may/31/naomi-osaka-withdraws-french-open-press-conference-fines-tennis.

Cho, S., Choi, H., & Kim, Y. (2019). The relationship between perceived coaching behaviors, competitive trait anxiety, and athlete burnout: A cross-sectional study. *International Journal of Environmental Research and Public Health, 16*(8), 1424.

Coombs, D. S., & Cassilo, D. (2017). Athletes and/or activists: LeBron James and Black Lives Matter. *Journal of Sport and Social Issues, 41*(5), 425–444.

De Neve, J. E., Krekel, C. M. & Ward, G. (2018). Work and well-being: A global perspective. In J. D. Sachs, A. Bin Banshir, J. E. De Neve, M. Durand, E. Diener, J. F. Helliwell, R. Layard, & M. Seligman (Eds.), *Global happiness: Policy report* (pp.74–128). New York, NY: Sustainable Development Solutions.

Dickerson, N. (2016). Constructing the digitalized sporting body: Black and white masculinity in NBA/NHL internet memes. *Communication & Sport, 4*(3), 303–330.

Diener, E., Lucas, R. E., & Oishi, S. (2018). Advances and open questions in the science of subjective well-being. *Collabra: Psychology, 4*(1), 1–49.

Eccles, J. S., Barber, B. L., Stone, M., & Hunt, J. (2003). Extracurricular activities and adolescent development. *Journal of Social Issues, 59*, 865–889.

Feinstein, B. A., Hershenberg, R., Bhatia, V., Latack, J. A., Meuwly, N., & Davila, J. (2013). Negative social comparison on Facebook and depressive symptoms: Rumination as a mechanism. *Psychology of Popular Media Culture, 2*(3), 161–170.

Filo, K., Lock, D., & Karg, A. (2015). Sport and social media research: A review. *Sport Management Review, 18*(2), 166–181. https://doi.org/10.1016/j.smr.2014.11.001.

Fouriezos, N. (2018, January 25). Aly Raisman is the #MeToo hero that American sports needed. *Ozy.* https://www.ozy.com/news-and-politics/aly-raisman-is-the-metoo-hero-that-american-sports-needed/83485/.

Geurin, A. N. (2017). Elite female athletes' perceptions of new media use relating to their careers: A qualitative analysis. *Journal of Sport Management, 31*(4), 345–359. https://doi.org/10.1123/jsm.2016-0157.

Geurin-Eagleman, A. N., & Burch, L. M. (2016). Communicating via photographs: A gendered analysis of Olympic athletes' visual self-presentation on Instagram. *Sport Management Review, 19*(2), 133–145.

Goodger, K., Gorely, T., Lavallee, D., & Harwood, C. (2007). Burnout in sport: A systematic review. *The Sport Psychologist, 21*, 127–151.

Gould, D., Dieffenbach, K., & Moffett, A. (2002). Psychological characteristics and their development in Olympic champions. *Journal of Applied Sport Psychology, 14,* 172–204.

Gulliver, A., Griffiths, K. M., Mackinnon, A., Batterham, P. J., & Stanimirovic, R. (2015). The mental health of Australian elite athletes. *Journal of Science and Medicine in Sport, 18*(3), 255–261.

Gymnasts for Change (n.d.) *A brighter future.* https://www.gymnastsforchange.com/.

Hambrick, M. E. (2012). Six degrees of information: Using social network analysis to explore the spread of information within sport social networks. *International Journal of Sport Communication, 5*(1), 16–34.

Hambrick, M. E., Simmons, J. M., Greenhalgh, G. P., & Greenwell, T. C. (2010). Understanding professional athletes' use of Twitter: A content analysis of athlete tweets. *International Journal of Sport Communication, 3*(4), 454–471.

Hinduja, S., & Patchin, J. W. (2008). Personal information of adolescents on the Internet: A quantitative content analysis of MySpace. *Journal of Adolescence, 31,* 125–146.

Huppert, F. A., Baylis, N., & Keverne, B. (2004). Introduction: Why do we need a science of well-being. *Philosophical Transactions of the Royal Society of London, Biological Sciences, 259,* 1331–1332.

Ingham, A., Chase, M., & Butt, J. (2002). From the performance principle to the developmental principle: Every kid a winner? *Quest, 54*(4), 308–331.

Kassing, J. W., & Sanderson, J. (2010). Fan–athlete interaction and Twitter tweeting through the Giro: A case study. *International Journal of Sport Communication, 3*(1), 113–128. https://doi.org/10.1123/ijsc.3.1.113.

Kavanagh, E., & Brady, A. (2014). Humanisation in high performance sport. In C. H. Brackenridge & D. Rhind (Eds.), *Athlete welfare: International perspectives.* London, UK: Brunel University Press.

Kavanagh, E., Jones, I., & Sheppard-Marks, L. (2016). Towards typologies of virtual maltreatment: Sport, digital cultures, & dark leisure. *Leisure Studies, 35,* 783–796.

Kavanagh, E., Litchfield, C., & Osborne, J. (2019). Sporting women and social media: Sexualization, misogyny, and gender-based violence in online spaces. *International Journal of Sport Communication, 12*(4), 552–572.

Kerr, G., Willson, E., & Stirling, A. (2020). "It was the worst time in my life": The effects of emotionally abusive coaching on female Canadian National Team athletes. *Women in Sport and Physical Activity Journal, 28*(1), 81–89.

Kim, J., & Lee, J.E.R. (2011). The Facebook paths to happiness: Effects of the number of Facebook friends and self-presentation on subjective well-being. *Cyberpsychology, Behavior, and Social Networking, 14*(6), 359–364.

Lebel, K., & Danylchuk, K. (2014). Facing off on Twitter: A generation Y interpretation of professional athlete profile pictures. *International Journal of Sport Communication, 7*(3), 317–336. https://doi.org/10.1123/IJSC.2014-0004.

Lian, S.-L., Sun, X.-J., Yang, X.-J, & Zhou, Z.-K. (2018). The effect of adolescents' active social networking site use on life satisfaction: The sequential mediating roles of positive feedback and relational certainty. *Current Psychology, 39*, 2087–2095.

Litchfield, C., Kavanagh, E., Osborne, J., & Jones, I. (2018). Social media and the politics of gender, race, and identity: The case of Serena Williams. *European Journal for Sport and Society, 15*(2), 154–170.

MacPherson, E., & Kerr, G. (2019). Sport fans' responses on social media to professional athletes' norm violations. *International Journal of Sport and Exercise Psychology, 19*(1), 1–18.

MacPherson, E., & Kerr, G. (2020). Online public shaming of professional athletes: Gender matters. *Psychology of Sport and Exercise, 51*, 101782.

Maine, D. (2021, July 30). Simone Biles withdraws from vault, uneven bars at the 2021 Olympics; status for last two individual events to be determined. *ESPN.com.* https://www.espn.com/olympics/story/_/id/31924094/simone-biles-withdraws-vault-uneven-bars-summer-olympics.

Moreno, M. A., Parks, M. R., Zimmerman, F. J., Brito, T. E., & Christakis, D. A. (2009). Display of health risk behaviors on MySpace by adolescents: Prevalence and associations. *Archives of Pediatric and Adolescent Medicine, 163*, 27–34.

Naslund, J. A., Bondre, A., Torous, J., & Aschbrenner, K. A. (2020). Social media and mental health: benefits, risks, and opportunities for research and practice. *Journal of Technology in Behavioral Science, 5*(3), 245–257.

Parmentier, M. A., & Fischer, E. (2012). How athletes build their brands. *International Journal of Sport Management and Marketing, 11*(1–2), 106–124.

Pegoraro, A. (2010). Look who's talking—Athletes on Twitter: A case study. *International Journal of Sport Communication, 3*(4), 501–514. https://doi.org/10.1123/ijsc.3.4.501.

Poucher, Z. A., Tamminen, K. A., Kerr, G., & Cairney, J. (2021). A commentary on mental health research in elite sport. *Journal of Applied Sport Psychology, 33*(1), 60–82.

Purcell, R., Gwyther, K., & Rice, S. M. (2019). Mental health in elite athletes: increased awareness requires an early intervention framework to respond to athlete needs. *Sports Medicine-Open, 5*(1), 1–8.

Rideout, V., & Fox, S. (2018). *Digital health practices, social media use, and mental well-being among teens and young adults in the U.S.* Retrieved from San Francisco, CA: https://www.hopelab.org/reports/pdf/a-national-survey-by-hopelab-and-well-being-trust-2018.pdf. Accessed 26 October 2021.

Rosenthal-von der Pütten, A. M., Hastall, M. R., Köcher, S., Meske, C., Heinrich, T., Labrenz, F., & Ocklenburg, S. (2019). "Likes" as social rewards: Their role in online social comparison and decisions to like other People's selfies. *Computers in Human Behavior, 92*, 76–86.

Ryan, R., & Deci, E. (2001). On happiness and human potentials: A review of research on hedonic and eudaimonic well-being. *Annual Review of Psychology, 52*, 141–166.

Sanderson, J. (2013). Stepping into the (social media) game: Building athlete identity via Twitter. In R. Luppicini (Ed.), *Handbook of research on technoself: Identity in a technological society* (pp. 419–438). Hershey, PA: IGI Global.

Sanderson, J. (2018). Thinking twice before you post: Issues student-athletes face on social media. *New Directions for Student Services, 2018*(163), 81–92.

Sanderson, J., & Emmons, B. (2014). Extending and withholding forgiveness to Josh Hamilton: Exploring forgiveness within parasocial interaction. *Communication & Sport, 2*(1), 24–47.

Sanderson, J., & Kassing, J. W. (2011). Tweets and blogs: Transformative, adversarial, and integrative developments in sports media. In A. C. Billings (Ed.), *Sports media: Transformation, integration, consumption* (pp. 114–127). New York: Routledge.

Sanderson, J., & Truax, C. (2014). "I hate you man!": Exploring maladaptive parasocial interaction expressions to college athletes via Twitter. *Journal of Issues in Intercollegiate Athletics, 7*, 333–351.

Sanderson, J., Snyder, E., Hull, D., & Gramlich, K. (2015). Social media policies within NCAA member institutions: Evolving technology and its impact on policy. *Journal of Issues in Intercollegiate Athletics, 8*, 50–73.

Schaal, K., Tafflet, M., Nassif, H., Thibault, V., Pichard, C., et al. (2011). Psychological balance in high level athletes: Gender-based differences and sport-specific patterns. *PLoS One, 6*(5), e19007.

Schmittel, A., & Sanderson, J. (2015). Talking about Trayvon in 140 characters: Exploring NFL players' tweets about the George Zimmerman verdict. *Journal of Sport and Social Issues, 39*(4), 332–345. https://doi.org/10.1177/0193723514557821.

Stick, M., Scheibling, C., & Norman, M. (2021). "Kareem Hunt cut by the Chiefs for brutalizing woman on video": Online framings of racialized and gendered violence by a professional athlete. *Sport in Society,* 1–16.

Stirling, A. E., & Kerr, G. A. (2013). The perceived effects of elite athletes' experiences of emotional abuse in the coach–athlete relationship. *International Journal of Sport and Exercise Psychology, 11*(1), 87–100.

Subrahmanyam, K., & Greenfield, P. (2008). Virtual worlds in development: Implications of social networking sites. *Journal of Applied Developmental Psychology, 26*, 407–417.

Todres, L., Galvin, K., & Holloway, I. (2009). The humanization of healthcare: A value framework for qualitative research. *International Journal of Qualitative Studies on Health and Well-being, 4*(2), 68–77.

Walton, C., Rice, S., Gao, C., Butterworth, M., Clements, M., & Purcell, R. (2021). Gender differences in mental health symptoms and risk factors in Australian elite athletes. *BMJ Open Sport & Exercise Medicine, 7*, 1–6.

Williams, C. A. (2018). Elite youth sports—the year that was 2017. *Pediatric Exercise Science, 30*(1), 25–7.

Willson, E., Kerr, G., Stirling, A., & Buono, S. (2021). Prevalence of maltreatment among Canadian National Team athletes. *Journal of Interpersonal Violence*, 1–23.

Wolak, J., Mitchell, K., & Finkelhor, D. (2006). Online victimization of youth: Five years later. Durham, NH: Crimes Against Children Research Center. Retrieved October 26, 2021 from www.unh.edu/ccrc/pdf/CV138.pdf.

Woods, H. C., & Scott, H. (2016). #Sleepyteens: Social media use in adolescence is associated with poor sleep quality, anxiety, depression and low self-esteem. *Journal of Adolescence, 51*, 41–49.

World Health Organization. (2021). WHO remains firmly committed to the principles set out in the preamble to the Constitution. https://www.who.int/about/governance/constitution.

Xanthopoulos, M. S., Benton, T., Lewis, J., Case, J. A., & Master, C. L. (2020). Mental Health in the Young Athlete. *Current Psychiatry Reports, 22*(11), 1–15.

Yan, G., Pegoraro, A., & Watanabe, N. M. (2018). Student-athletes' organization of activism at the University of Missouri: Resource mobilization on Twitter. *Journal of Sport Management, 32*(1), 24–37.

Ybarra, M. L., & Mitchell, K. J. (2007). How risky are social networking sites? A comparison of places online where youth sexual solicitation and harassment occurs. *Pediatrics, 121*, e350–e357.

Chapter Twelve

Athletes, Mental Health, and the COVID-19 Pandemic

Carly Perry, Ali Bowes, and Alex Culvin

In recent years, athletes, researchers, practitioners, and sporting organizations have highlighted the importance of both physical and mental health for improving sports performance, life satisfaction, and positive well-being. As such, it is well accepted that good mental health is a key part of success for elite athletes (Henriksen et al., 2020). Across the sporting literature, "mental health" has been defined in many ways; therefore when discussing this topic, it is critical that researchers and practitioners alike provide a definition to avoid confusion (Vella et al., 2021). Here, we use the definition of mental health presented in the International Society of Sport Psychology consensus statement: "a state of well-being in which every individual realizes his or her own potential, can cope with the normal stresses of life, can work productively and fruitfully, and is able to make a contribution to his or her community" (WHO, 2014; Henriksen et al., 2020, p. 555). In using this definition, "mental health" and "mental ill-health" will be presented as two distinct concepts throughout this chapter (Henriksen et al., 2020). Further, "mental health" will be discussed as a component of a person's overall well-being and "mental ill-health" will be discussed as a diagnosable "condition" or "disorder" (e.g., depression and anxiety) (Centers for Disease Control and Prevention, 2021). Therefore, an athlete can encounter poor mental health, yet not meet the criteria for mental ill-health, and an athlete with a diagnosable mental illness can have good mental health.

During the 2020 COVID-19 pandemic, there were heightened concerns over the mental health of athletes from researchers, practitioners, and athletes themselves (Haan et al., 2021; Southern et al., 2021). The pandemic and consequent world-wide lockdowns resulted in sporting activities and competitions being cancelled around the globe. While there were some variations in state responses to COVID-19, the pandemic created a myriad of challenges for all athletes such as financial stress, eligibility concerns, isolation from teammates, lack of motivation, and homesickness (Haan et al., 2021; Souter et al., 2021). At the elite level, unique stressors occurred for high-level athletes due to the postponement of competitions, such as the Tokyo 2020 Olympics and the UEFA European Championship 2020 events, which are the pinnacle of athletes' careers, resulting in disappointments, uncertainty, lack of motivation, and heightened mental health symptoms (Reardon et al., 2021). Accordingly, drawing from research in the fields of sport psychology, sport sociology, and sport management, this chapter will

a. discuss the relationship between athletes and mental health
b. consider the implications the COVID-19 pandemic had on that relationship, and
c. propose specific directions for future research in this space.

Athletes and Mental Health

In recent years, "athlete welfare" has emerged as a priority for researchers and major sporting organizations. As Kavanagh et al. (2021) note, sport can be seen to have a moral duty to protect its participants, although there have been questions about whether athlete welfare and safety have been given the priority they deserve in elite sport. "Athlete welfare" is most often defined as one's holistic wellness and satisfaction across various domains, including "physical, emotional, psychological, sexual, financial, social, behavioural and intellectual" wellness (Lang, 2020, p. 2). In line with the increasing concern over athlete welfare, there has been increased concern regarding the mental health of elite athletes from practitioners, researchers, and sporting organizations (see, e.g., Henriksen et al., 2020). For decades, the physical health of athletes has received substantial attention from the media, sport scholars, and athletes themselves. In contrast, far less attention has been given to the mental health of athletes. There are a multitude of reasons for this imbalance, one being the persistent belief that athletes are exempt or immune from poor mental health due to their superior "mental toughness" (Gucciardi et al., 2017). In recent years, however, this narrative has been challenged by athletes who have shared their experiences with mental ill-health (see, e.g., Michael Phelps and Simone Biles).

Further challenging the narrative is the substantial increase in research and subsequent findings over the last decade (Kuettel & Larsen, 2020). Research concerning mental health and elite athletes has highlighted: (1) mental health is a resource for coping with predicted and unpredicted career transitions (e.g., injury) (Champ et al., 2020; Henrikson et al. 2020), and (2) athletes, like the general population, encounter poor mental health and mental ill-health, with 5–35% experiencing mental ill-health annually (Castaldelli-Maia et al., 2019; Goutterbarge et al., 2019).

To date, the majority of research concerning mental health and athletes has focused on identifying prevalence and incidence rates of mental ill-health (e.g., depression, anxiety, eating disorders), particularly amongst elite athletes (Goutterbarge et al., 2019). Findings from recent meta-analyses, which included 2,895 to 5,555 current elite athletes, evidenced that the prevalence of mental health symptoms and disorders ranged from 19% for alcohol misuse to 34% for anxiety/depression for current elite athletes, and for retired athletes it ranged from 16% for distress to 26% for anxiety/depression (Gouttebarge et al., 2019). Further, their analysis showed high sleep disturbance prevalence amongst current elite athletes (26%) and retired athletes (21%) (Gouttebarge et al., 2019).

Research shows athletes competing at the elite level (e.g. professional, international, Olympic, or NCAA collegiate) are exposed to unique stressors that may impact mental health (Henriksen et al., 2020; Rice et al., 2016). More specifically, Goutterbarge et al. (2019) stated that an elite sport career is characterized by more than 640 stressors that could heighten mental health symptoms. These stressors include both sport stressors (e.g., intense performance demands, intense training schedules, contract renewal, social media abuse, heightened media attention, injury, and de-selection) and personal stressors (e.g., living away from home, relationship problems, death of a family member, financial instability) (see Champ et al., 2020; Kuettel & Larsen, 2020; Rice et al., 2016; Sarkar & Fletcher, 2014). Together, the research indicates elite athletes require support during and after their sporting careers given the unique and challenging demands they experience.

Much like research in the sport sciences generally (Elliot-Sale et al., 2021), there has been a disproportionate focus on elite male athletes across this research area (Kuettel & Larsen, 2020). However, emerging research has shown that elite female athletes, compared to male athletes, are at an increased risk for anxiety, depression, and disordered eating (Kuettel & Larsen, 2020). Body image concerns and disordered eating are the most frequently studied and identified of the mental disorders for elite female athletes (Perry et al., 2021). More specifically, the majority of research into elite female athletes has focused on those competing in "lean-physique" sports (e.g., distance running) where the focus tends to be on appearance and thinness as opposed to strength and muscularity (Perry et al., 2021). This focus on elite female athletes in "lean-physique" sports is due to researchers identifying this population to be at risk for body image concerns (Perry et al., 2021). Athletes in such sports are thought to experience sport-specific pressures around body, weight, eating, and performance from those in the sporting environment (e.g., coaches, teammates, and media) (Kong & Harris, 2015). Moreover, research indicates such athletes are at a higher risk for disordered eating than those competing in power sports (e.g., football) (see Kong & Harris, 2015). However, as argued by Perry et al. (2021), research concerning the mental health experiences of elite female athletes competing in power sports is warranted as this population will face their own unique stressors and they too must balance societal and sport-specific pressures.

Together, the literature surrounding elite athletes has heavily focused on prevalence studies which do not account for the social and cultural factors that influence poor mental health (Papathomas, 2018; Perry et al., 2021). Of the literature that has focused on the sociocultural context, researchers have found that the elite athlete environment perpetuates excessive pressures to perform (Hughes & Coakley, 1991), alongside toxic norms around body image and exercise behaviors (e.g., over training) (McMahon & Dinan-Thompson, 2012; McGannon & McMahon, 2019). Moreover, it's been found that 20–60% of youth athletes have reported overtraining (Hughes & Leavey, 2012), which is suggested to be a way that athletes embody the win-at-all-costs approach in sport and show their dedication, legitimizing their position as an elite athlete. These behaviors are often admired and accepted as acts of commitment by those in the elite sporting environment (McMahon & Penney, 2013). Consequently, affirmation of these types of behaviors further encourages and perpetuates obsessive behaviors around exercise, disordered eating, and body image concerns (McMahon & Penney, 2013).

Further, the sporting culture is believed to negatively impact athletes' decision to seek help for their mental health due to the fear of being perceived as "weak" by those in the sporting environment (Gulliver et al. 2012). In a study exploring barriers to help-seeking for athletes, stigma was unanimously expressed by athletes as the largest barrier for seeking help (Gulliver et al. 2021). Aside from the stigma around mental health in sport, other factors also contribute to athletes neglecting to seek help, such as socio-economic factors, cultural factors, gender differences, religious factors, other lifestyle factors, previous poor experience, and misinformation about mental health (Gulliver et al. 2012).

FACTORS INFLUENCING MENTAL HEALTH IN ATHLETES

In addition to gathering prevalence data around mental ill-health in athletes, researchers have suggested numerous factors that might serve as protective or risk factors for mental health and mental ill-health (see Kuettel & Larsen,

2020). While there are many factors that may potentially impact mental health, we discuss several factors below that are commonly cited across the literature, including: gender, sport-type (e.g., early specialization sports) and sport-level (e.g., professional, collegiate), in-career transitions (e.g., injury), out-of-career transitions (e.g., retirement), and help-seeking behaviors. It is important to note here that these issues are intersectional and as such there may be overlap in how each aspect serves as a risk factor for mental ill-health.

Gender. In a recent review by Kuettel and Larsen (2020), gender emerged as a risk factor for poor mental health. Specifically, as mentioned above, elite female athletes are at an increased risk for anxiety, depression, and disordered eating when compared to elite male athletes. While there are various reasons for their heightened rates of mental ill-health, Castaldelli-Maia et al. (2019) hypothesized that female athletes are at an increased risk for poor mental health due to the lack of acceptance of female athletes in certain cultures, unequal training opportunities, limited financial support, sexuality stereotypes, and societal and personal expectations around traditional gender roles, all which could negatively impact the mental health of women in sport. Recently work by Walton et al. (2021) found that elite female athletes in Australia experience adverse life events at higher rates than men (e.g., interpersonal conflict, financial hardship, and discrimination), which again can contribute to poor mental health. Despite their recent findings, there is a lack of research into this population (Perry et al. 2021).

Sport-type & Sport-level. Research has indicated that certain sports (e.g., individual vs. team sports) place athletes at a heightened risk for poor mental health (Pluhar et al., 2019). For example, sport scholars have indicated those in team sports (e.g., football) are less likely to suffer from anxiety and depression than those in individual sports (e.g., running) (Pluhar et al., 2019). More specifically, there are certain sports, such as gymnastics, that place athletes at an increased risk for poor mental health due to the nature of their chosen sport: early specialization, body image concerns, spectator sport, high rates of injury, and early retirement (Kong & Harris, 2015; Myer et al. 2015). Early specialization can be harmful for athletes as it often requires excess training during childhood or adolescence which can have detrimental impacts to biological development (e.g., injury, delayed maturation) while also causing numerous negative psychological effects, including burnout, overdependence, identity conflict, and increased risk for depression (Myer et al. 2015; Warriner & Lavalle, 2008).

Involvement in elite sport brings many challenges. The reality for many professional athletes, especially in team sports, is that they lack control over their lives, and are regulated by a schedule, controlled by organizations and/or clubs (Culvin, 2019). This disempowerment and a perceived loss of autonomy has been established as a key factor in athletes developing depression and anxiety (Hughes & Leavey, 2012). The win-at-all-costs approach seen in elite sport (Hughes & Coakley, 1991) shapes most sports organizations' performance measurements and philosophy of practice (Relvas et al., 2010). Thus, it is fair to say that athletes operating in this controlled environment may find themselves in uncertain and precarious circumstances (Culvin, 2019). This environment has the potential to produce feelings of a loss of control and a lack of autonomy in an athletes' career (Culvin, 2019). Such feelings, paired with the numerous stressors inherent to the sporting environment, place elite athletes at an increased risk for poor mental health, particularly if they are not properly supported in the elite environment.

Professionalization. Sport is a contingent form of employment in the sense that athletes recognize a surplus of labor and the inevitability of aging and the ever-present risk of injury (Culvin, 2021; Roderick, 2006). For example, injury presents a significant risk factor for mental ill-health in elite athletes. Athletes possess a market value based on performances at work, and the value of an athlete can drop dramatically if they obtain an injury or loss of form. Meaning there are unique stressors at work for professional athletes. These unique stressors are exacerbated for athletes as they accept an intense approach to accountability, surveillance, measurement, and quantification in their work-life (Roderick et al. 2017). This all-encompassing experience at work leaves athletes unable to switch off (Culvin, 2021). Previous research characterizes taking-your-work-home as work spill (Patricia et al., 2003). Such work spills are highly problematic, as athletes are unable to switch off, often resulting in poor well-being and ill-health (Michie &Williams, 2003). It must be noted work spill may be common within other professions. However, unlike other professions, professional and/or elite athletes encounter intense training schedules, sponsorship commitments, living away from home, and high surveillance of their lifestyles outside of working hours.

It is worth considering here the differences between elite men's and women's sport (Bowes & Culvin, 2021). The growth of professional opportunities for elite female athletes have resulted in heightened sport-specific and personal pressures, often without appropriate mental health support. For example, research by Culvin (2019) suggests such support is not there for certain elite female athlete populations (e.g., professional female footballers in England). At the elite level, athletes face pressures to improve performance, attain results in the short-term, prove themselves as legitimate athletes, and balance societal and personal expectations (Bowes & Culvin, 2021).

In-career Transitions. All athletes, independent of sporting level or sport type, will encounter a transition at some point during their sporting career, with some transitions serving as protective factors for mental health and other transitions heightening the risk for poor mental health (Kuettel & Larsen, 2019). While transitions impact all athletes differently, there are several in-career transitions (e.g., a new team, new level, moving to a new country, injury, de-selection) that have received increased research attention and are well-documented to impact elite athletes' mental health (Kuettel & Larsen, 2020). Injury, for example, can negatively influence an athlete's mental health, especially at the elite level where their sporting body and performance is critical to their identity (Kuettel & Larsen, 2020). Additionally, at the elite level, there are increased pressures to push through injury from the sporting culture and athletes themselves (Roderick, 2006).

Out-of-career Transitions. Transitions out of sport (e.g., retirement, career-ending injury) is inevitable and results in athletes encountering numerous financial, social, psychological, physical, and emotional changes. For some athletes, transitioning out of sport can enhance their mental health as they, for example, are able to spend more time with their family. However, for most athletes this transition can be very challenging and, in some cases, lead to poor mental health (Kuettel & Larsen, 2019). For example, upon retirement athletes often see changes to their body as they no longer exercise in the same way as they once did. As a result, athletes often struggle to navigate their food and exercise behaviors and often encounter increased body image concerns (Papathomas et al., 2018; Plateau et al., 2017). Additionally, research has shown that professional athletes encounter an increased rate of poor mental health and mental ill-health upon retirement (Kuettel & Larsen, 2021; van Ramele et al., 2017). For example, male professional footballers in Europe showed high rates of sleep disturbance (28%), anxiety/depression symptoms (29%), and adverse alcohol use (15%) upon retirement (van Ramele et al., 2017).

There are many factors that influence the heightened rates of poor mental health amongst professional athletes. One example being that professional athletes are expected to fully dedicate themselves to achieving performance excellence during their sporting career and therefore they have little time to develop themselves outside of sport (e.g., educationally, vocationally, or holistically) (McCormack & Walseth, 2013). As a consequence they are tasked with the challenge of finding a new identity and purpose upon retirement (Papathomas et al. 2018; Rice et al. 2016). Thus, education is often cited as a potential solution to prepare and ease this transition out of sport. In fact, several sporting organizations have now created education policies allowing for athletes in education to be better supported during their career (see F. A. education policy *In Pursuit of Progress, 2018*).

THE IMPACT OF COVID-19 ON THE MENTAL HEALTH OF ATHLETES

As Evans et al. (2020) noted, during COVID-19 there was "little doubt that the everyday lives and practices of sports participants, not least athletes, have had to change, pause or even cease as a result of the pandemic" (p. 90). Schinke et al. (2018) describe non-normative sports career transitions as unpredictable circumstances (e.g., an injury) that are difficult to prepare for in advance and are therefore more difficult for athletes to cope with. In this case, we can consider COVID-19 as a significant, non-normative transition that athletes unexpectedly had to manage. Facer-Childs et al. (2021) identify that mitigation strategies to control the pandemic had significant impacts on athletes, as athletes rely on regular access to training facilities, practitioners, and coaches. Significant challenges during this time, specific to elite athletes, included

- Immediate closure of training facilities and competition facilities
- Implications of rehabilitation for injured athletes as facilities closed and health care providers sought to deal with emergencies only
- Lack of certainty about competition schedules, with many postponed or cancelled indefinitely
- Given the short nature of athlete's careers, many experienced issues around time, including eligibility issues in the American collegiate system, and delayed and/or enforced retirements for athletes nearing the end of their careers
- Financial implications of reduced and/or no competition, fixtures, or races for many athletes
- Effects of isolation and travel restrictions on athletes, especially those living abroad and away from families, due to imposed government restrictions
- Risk of testing positive for COVID-19, with the associated short- and long-term physical risks including, in the worst case, potential of fatality.

Subsequently, during the COVID-19 pandemic, it has been claimed that rates of mental ill-health in athletes were heightened, and that COVID-19 had a significant negative impact on the mental health of elite athletes (Facer-Childs, 2021; Han, 2021). Based in the United Kingdom (UK), the Professional Football Association (PFA) reported an increase in football players seeking support during the pandemic. In the first couple of months of the pandemic, the PFA spoke to 262 current and former professionals and found that 22% felt depressed and had considered self-harm, 69% were worried about their future career, and 72% were regularly aware of feelings of nervousness or anxiety (Fisher, 2020). The PFA's director of player welfare, Michael Bennett, was quoted as saying:

> For the current players it's been the fact of [having] no structure.... They don't know if they're going to go back to football, they don't know if the football season will start again, they're not sure what's going on. There are financial situations with clubs furloughing players, there is deferral of wages. We have got a number of players who are living from pay cheque to pay cheque and this is having a real impact on them emotionally. (Fisher, 2020)

The example from English football is just one of many. Mehrsafar et al. (2020) noted that psychologists were reporting higher demand for online psychological counselling and diagnosis of psychological disorders among athletes during the pandemic. Athletes' concerns included fear of being infected, anxiety of physical recovery if infected, lack of access to fitness centers, disturbed sleep, eating disorders, obsessive-compulsive disorder, and family conflicts.

In considering a specific athlete population that might be considered more "at risk" for mental ill-health (Bowes et al., 2020), into the experiences of elite female athletes during the pandemic was insightful in understanding the realities of elite sport at this time with respect to mental health. During initial lockdowns, with most sports concerned for athlete welfare, two-thirds of female athletes felt that coaches were cognizant of providing mental health support, with many elite athletes accessing sport psychology sessions, mindfulness sessions, and online calls virtually. One netballer stated:

> Support from the staff have been really good. They've been able to adapt training, keeping things as fun and upbeat as possible, regular meetups and check ins for mental health and general health. They've been supportive in making sure that they're keeping in contact and close eyes on my well-being as they're not seeing me most days of the week like usual. (Bowes et al., 2020, p. 8)

This was a similar experience to a hockey player, who reported:

> We can speak to our psych when we want/need. I speak to her every 2 weeks. We also have nutritional support and a lifestyle manager. All contactable on zoom or by phone. (Bowes et al., 2020, p. 8)

For some athletes, some levels of support were provided, although mainly in a virtual format. Not all athletes were able to report supportive experiences during the initial lockdown regarding their mental health. Instead, almost one-third of participants in the study did not feel the support for their mental health and well-being was wholly adequate. From the sport of archery, one elite athlete stated:

> No, our discipline is underfunded so mental health support is not offered but if we need help with sport psych we could be offered an online session. (Bowes et al., 2020, p. 9)

Other athletes reported that some sports were slow to offer support. In the case of cricket, one athlete stated:

> Initially no there was not enough check-ups and contact however it has stepped up towards week 5–7 of lockdown. (Bowes et al., 2020, p. 9)

During COVID-19, both male and female athletes had varied experiences of mental health support and navigated a host of challenges that acted as stressors on their mental health and well-being. However, some research was contradictory. Broader research into the effect of isolation on athletes' mental health during COVID-19 found sport and physical activity could help protect mental health, with rates of depression and anxiety lower in professional athletes in Turkey than in non-athletes (Şenışık et al., 2020). Likewise, Souter et al. (2021) concluded that challenging times can be used to garner positive experiences and that the pandemic had provided unexpected opportunities for growth (Bowes et al., 2021).

MANAGEMENT OF MENTAL HEALTH DURING COVID-19 AND BEYOND

Writing about athletes during COVID-19, Schinke et al. (2020) explain that

> Discussions have varied from the challenges that athletes are encountering to issues associated with social isolation, career disruption, qualification process uncertainty, and unconventional and limited access to effective training environments and training partners. Underpinning these considerations is the health and well-being of athletes in their pursuits toward excellence. (p. 269)

As Henriksen et al. (2020) note, mental health is a core component of a culture of excellence, noting that much research has found significant levels of ill health among athlete populations. The British Psychological Society highlighted that the transition for athletes during COVID-19 would be overwhelming for some, and they provided guidance for elite athletes regarding psychological health during COVID-19 (Breslin et al., 2020). They concluded that focusing on three priority areas can support athletes: mental health and dealing with uncertainty; maintaining social connections; and motivation and goal setting.

Reardon et al.'s (2021) comprehensive review of literature on the impact of the pandemic on the management of mental health symptoms of athletes provided clear recommendations to guide management. This included a consideration of the challenges of in-person management and support, recommendations for both psychotherapy, such as crisis counselling, and pharmacotherapy, and new methods of providing mental health care that could continue post-pandemic. Significantly, during this time, care for mental health symptoms was often provided virtually, instead of in person.

FUTURE RESEARCH DIRECTIONS

In simple terms, Mehrsafar et al. (2020) summarize that in critical situations, such as the pandemic, sports organizations need to identify their priorities and make plans to support athlete mental health. This, however, is easier said than done in the world of elite sport. Nonetheless, in recent years increased attention has been placed on supporting athlete mental health and well-being, which is evidenced by the formation of mental health position statements and the increase in published mental health interventions for athletes (Breslin et al., 2017; Vella et al., 2021). While this is a step in the right direction, most mental health interventions in sport are neither evidence-based nor theory-based and do not consider important sociocultural factors in the design, such as sporting level and gender (Breslin et al., 2017). Consequently, many interventions are not effective across different sporting populations.

While the increased attention in this area is positive, there are more questions than answers that surround the impact of the culture of sport on mental health, sources of mental ill-health, the role of parents and support staff, the role of mental health officers, and mental health literacy (Vella et al., 2021). In fact, Vella et al. (2021) make 35 research recommendations for research in this area, including a call for robust data into mental health diagnosis, symptoms, risk factors, and treatments. In addition to the need for more research into athlete-specific diagnosis and symptomology, Kavanagh et al. (2021) highlighted the importance of changing the sociocultural context to promote better mental health. To do this, researchers have called for sporting organizations to better the sporting environment by adopting a more holistic approach to caring for its athletes (Henriksen et al., 2020; Kavanagh et al., 2021). Simply put, sporting organizations must find a way to better support both athletic performance and athlete welfare. We, as the larger sporting community, believe we can help facilitate this change through both education and research.

REFERENCES

Bowes, A., & Culvin, A. (Eds.). (2021). *The professionalisation of women's sport: Issues and debates*. Bingley, UK: Emerald Group Publishing.

Bowes, A., Lomax, L., & Piasecki, J. (2020). The impact of COVID-19 lockdown on elite sportswomen. Advance online publication. *Managing Sport and Leisure*. doi: 10.1080/23750472.2020.1825988.

Bowes, A., Lomax, L., & Piasecki, J. (2021). A losing battle? Women's sport pre- and post-COVID-19. *European Sport Management Quarterly*, *21*(3), 443–461. doi:10.1080/16184742.2021.1904267.

Breslin, G., Lowry, R., Lafferty, M., Britton, D., Morris, R., Barker, J., Slater, M., & Eubank, M. (2020). Advice for athletes during COVID-19. *British Psychological Society*. https://www.bps.org.uk/sites/www.bps.org.uk/files/Policy/Policy%20-%20Files/Advice%20for%20athletes%20during%20Covid-19.pdf.

Breslin, G., Shannon, S., Haughey, T., Donnelly, P., & Leavey G. (2017). A systematic review of interventions to increase awareness of mental health and well-being in athletes, coaches, and officials. *Systematic Reviews*, *6* (1), 1–15. doi:10.1186/s13643-017-0568-6.

Castaldelli-Maia, J. M., Gallinaro, J. G. M. E, Falcão, R. S., Gouttebarge, V., Hitchcock, M. E., Hainline, B., Reardon, C., & Stull, T. (2019). Mental health symptoms and disorders in elite athletes: a systematic review on cultural influencers and barriers to athletes seeking treatment. *British Journal of Sports Medicine*, *53*(11), 707–721. doi: 10.1136/bjsports-2019–100710.

Centers for Disease Control and Prevention (2021). About mental health. https://www.cdc.gov/mentalhealth/learn/index.htm.

Champ F., Nesti M., Ronkainen N., Todd, D., & Littlewood, M. (2020). An exploration of the experiences of elite youth footballers: The impact of organisational culture. *Journal of Applied Sport Psychology*, *32*(4), 1–43. doi:10.1080/10413200.2018.1514429.

Culvin, A. (2019). *Football as work: The new realities of professional women footballers in England* (Doctoral dissertation, University of Central Lancashire).

Culvin, A. (2021). Football as work: the lived realities of professional women footballers in England. *Managing Sport and Leisure*, 1–14. doi:10.1080/23750472.2021.1959384.

Elliott-Sale, K. J., Minahan, C. L., de Jonge, X. A. K. J., Ackerman, K. E., Sipila, S., Constantini, N. W., Lebrun, C. M., & Hackney, A. C. (2021). Methodological considerations for studies in sport and exercise science with women as participants: A working guide for standards of practice for research on women. *Sports Med 51*, 843–861. doi:10.1007/s40279-021–01435–8.

Evans, A. B., Blackwell, J., Dolan, P., Fahlén, J., Hoekman, R., Lenneis, V., McNarry, G., Smith, M., & Wilcock, L. (2020). Sport in the face of the COVID-19 pandemic: Towards an agenda for research in the sociology of sport. *European Journal for Sport and Society 17*(2), 85–95. doi: 10.1080/16138171.2020.1765100.

The Football Association (2018). *In pursuit of progress*. London: The Football Association.

Facer-Childs, E. R., Hoffman, D., Tran, J. N., Drummond, S. P., & Rajaratnam, S. M. (2021). Sleep and mental health in athletes during COVID-19 lockdown. *Sleep*, *44*(5), 1–9. Doi: 10.1093/sleep/zsaa261.

Fisher, B. (2020, May 19). PFA study reveals 22% of members depressed or considered self-harm. *The Guardian.* https://www.theguardian.com/football/2020/may/19/22-of-footballers-depressed-or-considered-self-harm-during-pandemic.

Gorczynski, P. F., Coyle, M., & Gibson K. (2017) Depressive symptoms in high-performance athletes and non-athletes: a comparative meta-analysis. *British Journal of Sports Medicine, 51*(18): 1348–1354. doi:10.1136/bjsports-2016–096455.

Gouttebarge, V., Castaldelli-Maia, J. M., Gorczynski, P., Hainline, B., Hitchcock, M. E., Kerkhoffs, G. M., Rice, S. M., & Reardon, C. L. (2019). Occurrence of mental health symptoms and disorders in current and former elite athletes: A systematic review and meta-analysis. *British Journal of Sports Medicine*, *53*(11), 700–706. doi:10.1136/bjsports-2019-100671.

Gucciardi, D., Hanton, S., & Fleming, S. (2017). Are mental toughness and mental health contradictory concepts in elite sport? A narrative review of theory and evidence. *Journal of Science and Medicine in Sport*, *20*(3), 307–311.

Gulliver, A., Griffiths, K. M., & Christensen, H. (2012). Barriers and facilitators to mental health help-seeking for young elite athletes: A qualitative study. *BMC Psychiatry*, *12*(1), 1–14. doi:10.1186/1471-244X-12-157.

Haan, R., Alblooshi, M. E. A., Syed, D. H., Dougman, K. K., Al Tunaiji, H., Campos, L. A. & Baltatu, O. C. (2021) Health and well-being of athletes during the coronavirus pandemic: A scoping review. *Frontiers in Public Health*, *9*, 641392. doi:10.3389/fpubh.2021.641392.

Henriksen, K., Schinke, R., Moesch, K., McCann, S., Parham, W., Larsen, C., & Terry, P. (2019). Consensus statement on improving the mental health of high performance athletes. *International Journal of Sport and Exercise Psychology*, *18*(5), 553–560. Doi:10.1080/1612197X.2019.1570473.

Hughes, R., & Coakley, J. (1991). Positive deviance among athletes: The implications of overconformity to the sport ethic. *Sociology of Sport Journal*, *8*(4), 307–325.

Hughes, L., & Leavey, G. (2012). Setting the bar: athletes and vulnerability to mental illness. *The British Journal of Psychiatry*, *200*(2), 95–96. doi:10.1192/bjp.bp.111.095976.

Kavanagh, E., Rhind, D., & Gordon-Thomson, G. (2021). Duties of care and athlete welfare. In R. Arnold & D. Fletcher (Eds). *Stress, Well-Being, and Performance in Sport*. New York: Routledge. 313–331.

Kong, P., & Harris, L. (2015). The sporting body: Body image and eating disorder symptomatology among female athletes from leanness focused and non-leanness focused sports. *Journal of Psychology*, *149*(2), 141–160. doi:10.1080/00223980.2013.846291.

Kuettel, A., & Larsen, C. (2020). Risk and protective factors for mental health in elite athletes: A scoping review. *International Review of Sport and Exercise Psychology*, *13*(1): 231–265. doi:10.1080/1750984X.2019.1689574.

Lang, M. (2020). Introduction to athlete welfare. In M. Lang (Ed.). *The Routledge Handbook of Athlete Welfare*, London: Routledge. 1–11.

Michie, S., & Williams, S. (2003). Reducing work related psychological ill health and sickness absence: A systematic literature review. *Occupational and Environmental Medicine, 60*(1), 3–9. doi:10.1136/oem.60.1.3.

McCormack, C., & Walseth, K. (2013). Combining elite women's soccer and education: Norway and the NCAA. *Soccer & Society, 14*(6), 887–897. doi:10.1080/14660970.2013.843927.

McGannon, K. R., & McMahon, J. (2019). Understanding female athlete disordered eating and recovery through narrative turning points in autobiographies. *Psychology of Sport and Exercise, 40*, 42–50.

McMahon, J., & Dinan-Thompson, M. (2012). "Body work—regulation of a swimmer body": An autoethnography from an Australian elite swimmer. *Sport, Education and Society, 16*(1), 35–50. doi:10.1080/13573322.2011.531960.

McMahon, J. A., & Penney, D. (2013). (Self-)surveillance and (self-)regulation: Living by fat numbers within and beyond a sporting culture. *Qualitative Research in Sport, Exercise and Health, 5*, 157–178. doi:10.1080/2159676X.2012.712998.

Mehrsafar, A. H., Gazerani, P., Zadeh, A. M., & Sánchez, J. C. J. (2020). Addressing potential impact of COVID-19 pandemic on physical and mental health of elite athletes. *Brain, Behavior, and Immunity, 87*, 147–148. doi: 10.1016/j.bbi.2020.05.011.

Mohr, M., Nassis, G. P., Brito, J., Randers, M. B., Castagna, C., Parnell, D., & Krustrup, P. (2020). Return to elite football after the COVID-19 lockdown. *Managing Sport and Leisure*, 1–9. doi:10.1080/23750472.2020.1768635.

Myer, G., Jayanthi, N., Difiori, J., Faigenbaum, A., Kiefer, A., Logerstedt, D., & Micheli, M. (2015). Sport specialization, part I: Does early sports specialization increase negative outcomes and reduced the opportunity for success in young athletes? *Sports Health, 7*(5), 437–442. doi:10.1177/1941738115598747.

Papathomas, A. (2018). Disordered eating in sport: Legitimized and stigmatized. In M. Atkinson (Ed.). *Sport, Mental Illness, and Sociology* (pp. 97–109). Bingley, UK: Emerald.

Papathomas, A., Petrie, T. A., & Plateau, C. R. (2018). Changes in body image perceptions upon leaving elite sport: The retired female athlete paradox. *Sport, Exercise, and Performance Psychology, 7*(1), 30–45. doi:10.1037/spy0000111.

Perry, C., Champ, F., Macbeth, J., Spandler, H. (2021). Mental Health and Elite Female Athletes: A Scoping Review. *Psychology of Sport and Exercise, 56*, 101961. doi:10.1016/j.psychsport.2021.101961.

Plateau, C. R., Petrie, T. A., & Papathomas, A. (2017). Exercise attitudes and behaviors among retired female collegiate athletes. *Psychology of Sport and Exercise, 29*(1), 111–115. doi:10.1016/j.psychsport.2017.01.001.

Pluhar, E., McCracken, C., Griffith, K. L. Christino, M., Sugimoto, D., & Meehan, P. (2019). Team sport athletes may be less likely to suffer anxiety or depression than individual sport athletes. *Journal of Sports Science and Medicine, 18*, 490–496.

Poucher, A., Tamminen, K., Kerr, G., & Cairney, J. (2021). A commentary on mental health research in elite sport. *Journal of Applied Sport Psychology, 33*(1), 60–82. doi:10.1080/10413200.2019.1668496.

Reardon, C. L., Bindra, A., Blauwet, C., Budgett, R., Campriani, N., Currie, A., Gouttebarge, V., McDuff, D., Mountjoy, M., Purcell, R., Putukian, M., Rice, S., &

Hainline, B. (2021). Mental health management of elite athletes during COVID-19: A narrative review and recommendations. *British Journal of Sports Medicine*, 55(11), 608–615. doi:10.1136/bjsports-2020–102884.

Relvas, H., Littlewood, M., Nesti, M., Gilbourne, D., & Richardson, D. (2010). Organizational structures and working practices in elite European professional football clubs: Understanding the relationship between youth and professional domains. *European Sport Management Quarterly*, 10(2), 165–187. doi:10.1080/16184740903559891.

Rice S. M., Purcell R., De Silva S., Mawren D., McGorry P. D., Parker A. G. (2016). The mental health of elite athletes: A narrative systematic review. *Sports Med*, 46(9),1333–1353. doi:10.1007/s40279-016-0492-2.

Roderick, M. (2006). *The work of professional football*. London: Routledge.

Roderick, M., Smith, A., & Potrac, P. (2017). The sociology of sports work, emotions and mental health: scoping the field and future directions. *Sociology of Sport Journal*, 34(2), 99–107. doi:10.1123/ssj.2017–0082.

Roehling, P. V., Moen, P., and Batt, R. (2003). When work spills over into the home and home spills over into work. In P. Moen (Ed.), *It's About Time: Couples and Careers* (pp. 101-122). Ithaca, NY: Cornell University Press.

Sarkar M., & Fletcher D. (2014). Psychological resilience in sport performers: a review of stressors and protective factors. *J Sports Sci.*, 32(15), 1419–1434. doi:10.1080/02640414.2014.901551.

Şenışık, S., Denerel, N., Köyağasıoğlu, O., & Tunç, S. (2021). The effect of isolation on athletes' mental health during the COVID-19 pandemic. *The Physician and Sports Medicine*, 49(2), 187–193. doi:10.1080/00913847.2020.1807297.

Schinke, R., Papaioannou, A., Henriksen, K., Si, G., Zhang, L., & Haberl, P. (2020). Sport psychology services to high performance athletes during COVID-19. *International Journal of Sport and Exercise Psychology*, 18(3), 269–272. doi:10.1080/1612197X.2020.1754616.

Schinke, R., Stambulova, N., Si, G., & Moore, Z. (2018) International society of sport psychology position stand: Athletes' mental health, performance, and development, *International Journal of Sport and Exercise Psychology*, 16(6), 622–639. doi:10.1080/1612197X.2017.1295557.

Souter, G., Tonge, A., & Culvin, A. (2021). The impact of Covid-19 on the mental health of professional footballers. *Managing Sport and Leisure*, 1–4. doi:10.1080/23750472.2021.1877569.

van Ramele, S., Aoki, H., Kerkhoffs, G., Gouttebarge, V., (2017). Mental health in retired professional football players: 12-month incidence, adverse life events and support. *Psychology of Sport and Exercise*, 28, 85–90. doi:10.1016/j.psychsport.2016.10.009.

Vella, S. A., Schweickle, M. J., Sutcliffe, J. T., & Swann, C. (2021). A systematic review and meta-synthesis of mental health position statements in sport: Scope, quality, and future directions. *Psychology of Sport and Exercise*, 55, 101946. doi:10.1016/j.psychsport.2021.101946.

Walton C. C., Rice S., Gao C. X., Butterworth, M., Clements, M., & Purcell, R. (2021) Gender differences in mental health symptoms and risk factors in Australian elite athletes. *BMJ Open Sport & Exercise Medicine, 7:e000984.* doi:10.1136/bmjsem-2020–000984.

Warriner, K. & Lavallee, D. (2008). The retirement experiences of elite female gymnasts: Self identity and the physical self. *Journal of Applied Sport Psychology, 20,* 301–317. doi:10.1080/10413200801998564.

Chapter Thirteen

Athletes, Wearable Technology, and Health

Roth Smith

Smartwatches, skin patches, biomechanical shoe insoles, pedometers, augmented reality, sunglasses, smartphone applications, and even smart clothing are but a few examples of the continually advancing wearable sport technology segment. These devices capture and report data related to heart rate, breathing patterns, movement patterns, step frequency, sleep quality, eye movement, hydration, calories burned, stress levels, fatigue levels, and even cognitive function. Wearables are studied in a variety of academic disciplines and subfields including social psychology, kinematics, human-computer interaction, health informatics, behavioral science, education, media studies, health, critical sociology, leisure studies, and communication studies. A dizzying array of acronyms, such as Online Social Fitness Networks (OSFNs), Online Fitness Community (OFC), Sports and Mobile Fitness Applications (SFMAs), Internet of Things (IoT), Wearable Health Technologies (wHealth), Digital Health Technologies (DHTs), Health Information Technology (HIT), and Wearable Fitness Device (WFD), are used throughout these literatures. The boundaries of what constitutes a wearable device vary across academic disciplines. Most definitions describe wearables as the use of an electronic technology or microcomputer worn on the body, equipment, or in clothing, that is enabled with sensors that capture, transmit, display, or provide haptic feedback related to the wearer's activity.

These definitions usually do not encompass other forms of wearable technology. For instance, as far back as 1994 the NFL has allowed teams to equip the quarterback with a one-way (sideline coach to quarterback) wireless headset mounted inside the player's helmet. The film and television branch of the NFL, NFL Films, has also "Mic'd up" several players to capture novel interactions for later film productions and social media content. Portable music devices (e.g., cassette players, MP3 players, smartphones) also have a lengthy history in individual sports and exercise. Although these are all forms of wearable technology in sport, they are not often included in existing research on wearable devices, especially from health and sport communication. Yet, given the convergence of technologies, these entertainment or media production technologies that are often not classified as wearables are often controlled through a wearable device. For instance, an athlete can control their music streaming service through a smartwatch—a clear form of wearable technology. Although headphones, microphones, or other entertainment streaming devices could be considered forms of wearable technology, this chapter primarily discusses wearables as devices that capture and display data related to athlete *health and performance* in both team and individualized leisure sport settings. This chapter begins by providing a brief overview of wearables and detailing their prevalence in various sport contexts. The chapter also reviews some of the existing areas of research on wearables and highlights places where sport and health communication can inform one another. The chapter then discusses some of the emerging applications of wearables and concludes with directions for future research.

Contemporary Settings and Connections to Health

Professional sports teams, Olympic hopefuls, and ordinary consumers interested in monitoring their fitness and endurance are increasingly adopting wearable technologies. With about one in five Americans utilizing a smartwatch or wearable fitness tracker (Vogels, 2020), the global end-user purchase of wearable devices has continually grown and is projected to reach $93 billion in 2022 (Rimol, 2021). Although the first consumer-available pedometer was released in Japan in 1965 (Lewis, 2016), wirelessly connected digital pedometers only recently started gaining mass popularity in the early 2010s. Fitbit, a wirelessly enabled pedometer, Apple Watch, and Samsung are some of the more popular wearable device makers among ordinary consumers. Apple computers announced in October 2021 that they will expand their Fitness+ service, Apple's exercise tracking application that pairs with the Apple Watch wearable, to 15 new countries including France, Germany, Saudi Arabia, and the United Arab Emirates, among others (Adorno, 2021). Indeed, wearable use has quickly spread across the globe. Market research companies have suggested that 2020 was a record year for wearable device sales due in part to the COVID-19 pandemic. During the pandemic, individuals reallocated disposable spending from group-based or indoor recreational activities (e.g., gym memberships, group yoga) to more socially distant individual sports that are often amenable to wearables (Fortune Business Insights, 2021; International Data Corporation, 2021).

For professional team sports, wearable devices were initially used in laboratory settings for research (e.g., motion capture suits). However, wearables are now also used for research beyond laboratory settings to study the kinematics of athletes and athletic equipment on the actual playing field. With sensors shrinking to increasingly smaller and non-invasive sizes, wearables can assist researchers in monitoring athletic performance, improving training, assessing risk of injury, and analyzing equipment function from in-the-field settings. Both professional and collegiate coaching staffs are utilizing wearable technologies to gain a competitive edge. In a 2020 study of 113 NCAA Division I athletic trainers and strength and conditioning coaches, over 72% indicated actively using wearable technologies in their facilities (Luczak et al., 2020). Several Major League Baseball (MLB) teams have adopted a sensor-laden compression arm sleeve to monitor pitch count, arm speed, release point, elbow height at release, and shoulder rotation of pitchers. Overall, the wearable sleeve helps to improve pitching mechanics and curb ulnar collateral ligament injuries that are common to professional pitchers.

Some NFL teams have embedded small nickel-sized radio-frequency identification (RFID) transmitters into player shoulder pads, the referee's clothing, the game ball, and pylons. The RFID transmitters provide data on player position, speed, passing rate, rushing attempt yards, and speed and rotation of the football. In addition to allowing coaches to fine-tune player performance, the data provided by wearables can help prevent injury and/or overtraining. The Philadelphia Eagles NFL team were early adopters of the Zebra Technologies player tracking system. The small RFID transmitters allowed coaches to determine if their quarterback, who recently underwent surgery for an ACL injury, was back at full playing strength (McManus, 2018). Beyond the NFL, the governing body for world football, FIFA, approved the use of wearable tracking technology during the 2018 World Cup in Russia. Regulations over in-game use of wearables vary and are slowly evolving across the MLB, NBA, NHL, and PGA Tour.

Wearable devices are also increasingly used by spectators of professional sport. Miah (2017) notes that, in addition to second screen effects, augmented and virtual reality (VR) experiences are changing spectator experiences. For instance, virtual reality headset technologies (e.g., Oculus Rift, Samsung Gear VR, Microsoft Hololens) provide a totally immersive event for spectators. In one case, a VR headset paired with a motion-sensing tennis racquet allowed ordinary fans to experience what it's like to return a serve from a professional tennis player. In other cases, augmented reality is used to overlay virtual mascots onto live camera feeds of real-world sporting arenas (Miah, 2017).

The rise of wearable technologies poses an interesting area of study for scholars at the nexus of sport and health communication. The most closely aligned field of study from health communication is mobile health or mHealth. The World Health Organization (WHO, 2011) defines mHealth as "medical and public health practice supported by mobile devices, such as mobile phones, patient monitoring devices, personal digital assistants (PDAs), and other wireless devices" (p. 6). Typically, studies of mHealth are focused on managing or treating health conditions and do not center on sport. However, mHealth studies that have focused on sport tend to investigate the use of smartphone applications or pedometers during individualized fitness or leisure pursuits (e.g., cycling, running) that may or may not incorporate an additional wearable device beyond the actual smartphone. The quantified self and "datafication" (Cukier & Mayer-Schoenberger, 2014) movements are also closely aligned to mHealth. Quantified self, also sometimes described as self-tracking, lifelogging, personal analytics, or personal informatics, refers to any self-tracking or collection of data about the self, but typically includes recording biological, physical, and behavioral data (Lupton, 2013, 2014). Many quantified self and wearable devices incorporate gamification aspects, or the process of using game principles, such as rewards, penalties, competition, and goal-setting, in non-game contexts (Hamari et al., 2014; Seaborn & Fels, 2015).

Much of the mHealth research has focused on adoption of technologies, motivation, or behavior change and employs a wide range of theories including the theory of reasoned action, self-determination theory, diffusion of innovation, technology acceptance model (TAM), unified theory of acceptance and use of technology, self-determination theory, health belief model, theory of planned behavior, and uses and gratifications theory. Niknejad et al.'s (2020) comprehensive review of 244 peer-reviewed wearable research articles revealed that most studies focus on the technological aspects of the devices rather than users' perceptions and preferences and TAM is the most commonly used theory. In sum, the mHealth research to date has centered on individualized forms of sport or exercise and has not examined team sports as extensively.

SOCIAL COMMUNITY ASPECTS

Whereas mHealth, information science, and human-computer interaction studies often focus on technical aspects of wearables, the broader humanities and social sciences explores the social aspects of wearables and their associated online communities. A persistent problem with wearable device use is that many individuals discontinue use after a short time period. One report even notes that 50% of new users of wearable devices and 74% of new health app users discontinue using them after only two weeks (Endeavour Partners, 2014). Stragier et al. (2016) found that the key to sustained use of wearable devices in sport is that they are integrated into daily habits. While many individuals initially adopt wearables for self-tracking reasons, research is beginning to find that often the online community and accompanying social benefits lead to habit formation and sustained use of the device. Thus, the social and community aspects often associated with wearable devices provide one method to increase sustained use and are deserving of further study.

For instance, Kreitzberg et al. (2016) employ a sociomateriality perspective in revealing that it is not only technical features of fitness tracking apps that promote physical activity, but communication in online communities also plays a vital role in motivation. Relatedly, health communication research has already explored the benefits of online health communities particularly for providing support for health conditions. Individuals often turn to online communities seeking social support for chronic illnesses (Rains et al., 2015), cancer diagnoses (Sharf, 1997), disabilities (Braithwaite et al., 1999), weight loss (Hwang et al., 2010), and injuries. Despite the plethora of existing health communication research into online communities, most are focused on health and illness to the neglect of sport.

The data provided by wearable devices, and the online communities related to the devices, are also an opportunity for health communication scholars to study information seeking. Much research has documented the processes of health information seeking online (Cline & Haynes, 2001; Lemire et al., 2008). Considering about one in three adults in the U.S. use the Internet to seek information or diagnose health conditions (Fox & Duggan, 2013), it seems logical that online communities related to wearable devices might increase or alter information seeking behaviors. Investigating online sporting communities through a health communication lens seems a nice point of overlap.

Despite the potential benefits of online communities, not all who use wearables for sport participate in online communities. Some wearables may not offer an online community, or as found in Smith and Treem's (2017) study of Strava, a fitness tracking application focused primarily on cycling, some users may simply wish to individually use the technology to track their own performance and do not desire to participate in the larger social community. Therefore, health communication researchers could tease apart whether individualistic wearable users differ from community-oriented users in terms of health information seeking or understanding. Further, recent research on the co-constructed meanings of wearable use has even found that some individuals wear the device but do not take advantage of the health data provided. Blaszka and Rascon's (2021) study of college students' use of wearable fitness devices revealed that some students simply wore devices as a fashion statement, and in one case, continued to wear a broken device because it was "a cool thing to have" (p. 16). Much like individualistic users do not engage in online communities, it will be important not to assume that mere possession of a sport wearable means the device is actually used for sport or health reasons. Researchers should aim to understand what wearable device users actually do, or do not do, with the technology.

SPECIFIC DIRECTIONS FOR FUTURE RESEARCH

Many of the existing studies of self-tracking and wearables have examined smartphone applications, Fitbits, or pedometers. Health communication scholars interested in wearables for sport should consider investigating a wider variety of wearable technologies as they develop. As sensors become smaller and smaller they will likely be increasingly integrated into various sport contexts. Sensors hidden or sewn into clothing, or "smart" textiles, are still in early developmental stages but will likely advance in the coming years. If smart clothing becomes more mainstream, then scholars could investigate those technologies in both organized team sports and individualized recreation.

Noting the shrinking sensor sizes and increasing prevalence of technological devices into every aspect of life, Rich and Miah (2016) even speculate that "the end point of this trend seems likely to be the emergence of ingestible sensors" (p. 86). Indeed, the authors point to the United States Food and Drug Administration's recent approval of the Proteus Technologies sensor-laden ingestible pill designed to measure medication adherence as evidence of such a trend. Ingestibles for sport may not be too far in the future. In fact, in 2005 the University of South Florida Sports Medicine Department used an ingestible pill, originally designed by NASA to monitor astronaut core body temperature, to monitor for heatstroke in football players during practice (NASA, 2006). While the encroachment of ingestible sensors into sport contexts may be a hard pill to swallow (quite literally), it seems the advances in technology and reductions in sensor sizes means we will continue to see more devices like this in the future.

Much of the extant academic research, and even the very classification offered at the start of this chapter, excludes helmet or body mounted action sports cameras, such as GoPro Hero, Garmin VIRB, or Sony Action Cam. At first glance, these cameras may not seemingly fit the category of traditional wearable devices for sport or health because they are media capture devices. However, in the case of Garmin VIRB, the camera is equipped with built-in sensors and GPS to capture distance traveled, speed, altitude, and even heart rate when paired with extra sensors. All of these cameras are technically wearable in that they can be strapped to the body or helmet of the user. Whereas helmet camera use has been examined from a media creation and consumption standpoint (Evers, 2015; Ferrell et al., 2001), these technologies are not as often studied as wearable health devices. Health communication scholars could pay more attention to the impact of wearable sports cameras on health outcomes, specifically by investigating voluntary risk-taking behaviors. For example, does the average rock climber wearing a helmet camera feel more inclined to attempt a risky route, especially if the route would provide captivating footage for sharing to social media? In sum, the helmet camera is an under-researched wearable device from a health communication standpoint.

Scholars have also critiqued the privacy considerations and potential "dataveillance" (Van Dijck, 2014) of wearable technologies. Workplaces often incentivize employees to adopt wearable technologies to track steps or record other sports activities (Lupton, 2016; Moore & Robinson, 2016). The wearables can be subtly, and not so subtly, pushed onto employees under the guise of contributing to team spirit, boosting productivity, or contributing to workplace wellness. Corporations that pay for their employees' health insurance have a clear financial interest to make sure workers are healthy. Healthy workers miss fewer work days and keep health insurance premiums low (Lupton, 2016). These programs raise concerns over privacy if employers are now able to monitor employees' steps and activities outside of the workplace.

Team sports also raise concerns over surveillance. College athletes in particular are often heavily monitored across both academic and athletic domains to be sure they stay eligible to compete and are capable of performing at an elite level (Hatteberg, 2018). Many college athletic programs require players to pass hydration tests as a way to monitor that their off-field activities (e.g., nutrition habits) are in line with program expectations. With wearable devices now able to remotely monitor hydration status, the wearables may usher in an age of around-the-clock totalitarian surveillance for the already heavily surveilled student athlete. Privacy concerns are also relevant at the amateur and professional team sports levels. For example, Waltz (2015) detailed how some minor league baseball players are concerned about the repercussions of biometric data generated by a wearable sleeve that monitors pitching mechanics.

For both minor league players seeking competitive big league positions through the draft system and professional baseball players renegotiating contracts, biometric data that reveals red flags of injury potential "could cost a player his career for an injury that hasn't yet occurred—or may never occur" (Waltz, 2015, p. 2). Fitbit, a wearable pedometer popular with corporate wellness programs, became Health Insurance Portability and Accountability Act (HIPAA) compliant in 2015 providing some semblance of data security. However, future research should continue to analyze and critique the collection, storage, security, and possible dissemination of private health information—whether shared with corporate wellness programs or stored individually.

For individualized sports, others have critiqued that wearables encourage a "panoptic self-care" wherein the user, now afforded access to myriad personal health data, views themselves as both the doctor and as a perpetual subject in need of care (Gilmore, 2016). In some cases, wearable users experience psychological discomfort if denied access to their data. In a study of self-tracking women runners, Esmonde (2019) found that the self-trackers experienced "feelings of loss" or anxiety when tracked data became corrupted or they forgot to turn on the wearable device to start recording. Studies into Strava found that the Strava community developed the pithy saying of "if it's not on Strava, it didn't happen" (Couture, 2021, p. 22; Pink et al., 2017), which ultimately "reflects a normalization of data (over)reliance" (Couture, 2021, p. 22). Some Strava users felt that the exercise was not fully accomplished until it was shared online and externally validated by others (Pink et al., 2017).

Other exercise groups outright resist use of the technologies. Zimdars (2021) sought a sample of individuals who specifically quit using Fitbit to explore their "discourse of discontinuance." After analyzing blogs written by those who discontinued use, Zimdars (2021) claims the blogs exemplify "a failure of self-surveillance and of wearable communication for comporting one's body or behaviors to socially idealized notions of health and fitness" (p. 38). Fitbit users discontinued use because they began obsessing over data or felt that they were exercising out of guilt or shame rather than enjoyment of the activity. Although Luczak et al.'s (2020) study revealed the prevalence of wearables in NCAA Division I athletic programs, athletic trainers and strength and conditioning coaches were "surprisingly very negative about all wearables used in athletics in general" (p. 27). The coaches and trainers expressed frustration with the technologies due to inaccurate data, a lack of meaning surrounding the data collected, and issues with getting the wearables to operate consistently. Thus, it will be important to investigate if wearable devices communicate about the data in such a way that individuals can interpret and make health decisions based on the information presented.

Goodyear et al.'s (2019) study of schoolchildren's use of Fitbit as part of an educational program found that, while the tracking of steps, peer-comparison, and goal-setting features of the wearable did initially increase physical activity, most children did not engage with the device longer than a few weeks. Further, some children viewed the device as another layer of teacher-imposed surveillance and ultimately resisted use of the wearable. Perhaps most worrying from a health communication standpoint is that some children experienced "negative feelings of self" (Goodyear et al., 2019, p. 220) if they did not reach their step target and actively resisted using the device. Similarly, at the other end of the age spectrum, Copelton (2010) investigated the introduction of pedometers to a senior citizen walking club. The walking club members largely rejected the wearables because they "symbolise competition and a potential for hierarchy that is contrary to both sociable group relations and women walkers' sense of self" (p. 314). In other words, the walking club feared that the datafication of their leisure time would possibly introduce unwanted competition and comparison that would violate the social norms of the club.

These fears are not entirely unfounded. For instance, Smith's (2017) study of the Strava cycling community found that, while some digital features of the online community allowed for exhibiting sportsmanship, the competitive nature of Strava use facilitated various forms of cheating or other ethically ambiguous action. Although embedding wearable use into daily habits and interacting with an online community are methods to increase engagement, scholars should continue to investigate reasons for rejection of wearables and the character of associated online communities. Moving forward, scholars interested in sport, health communication, and wearables should be sure to consider both on- and offline forms of communication. Many studies, especially into online health communities associated with wearables, focus primarily on the online interactions of the community. While many online social support groups for health (e.g., a breast cancer support forum) exist entirely online, wearables blend real world activity with online representation and interaction. This hybrid of both online and offline communication represents an interesting, and somewhat understudied, area for health communication research.

Another critical concern over the use of wearables and their associated online communities is how the idea of "being healthy" or "being fit" is discursively constructed. For instance, Elman (2018) critiqued that, although Fitbit advertisements appeal to inclusive ideals by featuring wheelchair users in advertisements, the device ultimately only records steps. Elman argues that more research on wearables should explore "how able-bodied bias affects how exercise and movement are quantified and interpreted" (p. 3763). Although advances in tactile and haptic feedback mechanisms can help adapt wearable technologies for individuals with disabilities, Goggin et al. (2019) argue that there "is a lack of systematic participation of people with disabilities in design, implementation, or consideration of emerging digital inclusion issues" (p. 295). Indeed, extant studies of wearable use in adaptive or Paralympic sports focus mainly on performance assessment for wheelchair sports (Rum et al., 2021); thus future research could further parse out the design and use of wearables for adaptive forms of sport. Relatedly, health communication scholars are well positioned to further investigate the sociocultural issues of wearable devices. For example, the data tracked and displayed by wearable devices may privilege certain cultural understandings of health and fitness while disregarding others.

Little research from sport or health communication has explored wearables with an eye toward digital inequalities. Research on the digital divide has revealed that more advantaged socioeconomic groups are better poised to take advantage of digital health technologies (Arcaya & Figueroa, 2017; Phelan et al., 2010; Timmermans & Kaufman, 2020). Although smartphones, a common platform that links with wearable devices, are ubiquitous, it is important to keep in mind that not all who participate in sport have access to technologies or wearables. Further, if one does have access to a smartphone they may still be limited by data caps and resist using the devices so as not to use up data limits. Bol et al. (2018) even caution that differences in mobile health app use could expand the digital divide. They call for researchers, device manufacturers, and health practitioners to not only focus on the most typical adopters, but to also "invest in informing and addressing the concerns of those parts of the population, such as older and less educated individuals, that have shown lesser propensity to use mobile apps" (p. 190). More work remains to be done that explores differences in access, use, skills, and beliefs among various socioeconomic groups, specifically in relation to sports wearables.

Beyond issues of access to wearables, health communication scholars are well positioned to explore how individuals with varying levels of health literacy process information displayed by wearables and online communities. For example, in a combined study of fitness apps, nutrition apps, activity trackers, and patient portals, Mackert et al. (2016) found that individuals with low health literacy are less likely to use the technologies or to perceive them as useful. Further, a number of studies provide evidence that individuals with low health literacy struggle to use or mistrust technologies (Irizarry et al., 2015; Neter & Brainin, 2012; Sarkar et al., 2010), yet, more research could focus exclusively on health literacy and sport wearables. It will also be important to understand if the communication and advertising around these products influences individuals' attitudes and knowledge of their own health.

For team sports, scholars could take an ethical angle to examine how these devices are deployed and untangle the intersecting agency of the players, officials, coaches, and devices. Studies into the philosophy of sport have already questioned how digitally enhanced "third eye" refereeing technologies could undermine human judgement in sport (Collins, 2010). Similarly, the rise of wearable devices prompts new questions about human and technological agency. For instance, if a football player feels concussed, yet the wearable head impact sensor mounted in their helmet does not register a heavy hit, will the coaches sideline the player based on the player's verbal feedback or accept the data provided by the sensor and leave them in the game?

In sum, although there are demonstrated health benefits associated with wearable use, excesses in self-monitoring and tracking may cause individuals to obsess over their personal health, develop a dependence on the technology, or experience psychological discomfort due to narrow definitions of health or feelings of surveillance. As wearable use continues to grow and spread throughout the various domains of sport there will be increasing avenues of research and critical questions for scholars of health and sport communication to pursue.

REFERENCES

Adorno, J. (2021, October 25). *Apple Fitness+ to launch in 15 new countries on November 3rd*. 9TO5Mac.com. https://9to5mac.com/2021/10/25/apple-fitness-to-launch-in-15-new-countries-on-november-3/.

Arcaya, M. C., & Figueroa, J. F. (2017). Emerging trends could exacerbate health inequities in the United States. *Health Affairs, 36*, 992–998.

Blaszka, M., & Rascon, N. A. (2021). Wearable fitness devices: An investigation into co-constructed meaning of use. *Communication & Sport*, doi: 21674795211033332.

Bol, N., Helberger, N., & Weert, J. C. (2018). Differences in mobile health app use: A source of new digital inequalities? *The Information Society, 34*(3), 183–193.

Braithwaite, D. O., Waldron, V. R., & Finn, J. (1999). Communication of social support in computer-mediated groups for people with disabilities. *Health Communication, 11*(2), 123–151.

Cline, R. J., & Haynes, K. M. (2001). Consumer health information seeking on the Internet: The state of the art. *Health Education Research, 16*(6), 671–692.

Collins, H. (2010). The philosophy of umpiring and the introduction of decision-aid technology. *Journal of the Philosophy of Sport, 37*(2), 135–146.

Copelton, D. A. (2010). Output that counts: Pedometers, sociability and the contested terrain of older adult fitness walking. *Sociology of Health & Illness, 32*(2), 304–318.

Couture, J. (2021). Reflections from the "Strava-sphere": Kudos, community, and (self-)surveillance on a social network for athletes. *Qualitative Research in Sport, Exercise and Health, 13*(1), 184–200.

Cukier, K., & Mayer-Schoenberger, V. (2014). The rise of big data: How it's changing the way we think about the world. In Mircea Pitici (Ed.), *The Best Writing on Mathematics 2014* (pp. 20–32). Princeton, NJ: Princeton University Press.

Elman, J. P. (2018). "Find Your Fit": Wearable technology and the cultural politics of disability. *New Media & Society, 20*(10), 3760–3777. https://doi.org/10.1177/1461444818760312.

Endeavour Partners. (2014). *Inside wearables Part 1: How behavior change unlocks long-term engagement.* Retrieved from https://medium.com/@endeavourprtnrs/

inside-wearable-how-the-science-of-human-behavior-change-offers-the-secret-to-long-term-engagement-a15b3c7d4cf3.

Esmonde, K. (2019). Training, tracking, and traversing: Digital materiality and the production of bodies and/in space in runners' fitness tracking practices. *Leisure Studies*, *38*(6), 804–817.

Evers, C. (2015). Researching action sport with a GoPro camera: An embodied and emotional mobile video tale of the sea, masculinity, and men-who-surf. In I. Wellard (Ed.), *Researching embodied sport: Exploring movement cultures* (pp. 145–162). Routledge.

Ferrell, J., Milovanovic, D., & Lyng, S. (2001). Edgework, media practices, and the elongation of meaning: A theoretical ethnography of the Bridge Day event. *Theoretical Criminology*, *5*(2), 177–202. doi:10.1177/1362480601005002003.

Fortune Business Insights (2021). *Fitness tracker market*. https://www.fortunebusinessinsights.com/fitness-tracker-market-103358.

Fox, S., & Duggan, M. (2013). Health online 2013. *Health*, *2013*, 1–55.

Gilmore, J. N. (2016). Everywear: The quantified self and wearable fitness technologies. *New Media & Society*, *18*(11), 2524–2539.

Goggin, G., Ellis, K., & Hawkins, W. (2019). Disability at the centre of digital inclusion: Assessing a new moment in technology and rights. *Communication Research and Practice*, *5*(3), 290–303.

Goodyear, V. A., Kerner, C., & Quennerstedt, M. (2019). Young people's uses of wearable healthy lifestyle technologies; surveillance, self-surveillance and resistance. *Sport, Education and Society*, *24*(3), 212–225.

Hamari, J., Koivisto, J., & Sarsa, H. (2014, January). Does gamification work?—a literature review of empirical studies on gamification. In *2014 47th Hawaii international conference on system sciences* (pp. 3025–3034). IEEE.

Hatteberg, S. J. (2018). Under Surveillance: Collegiate athletics as a total institution. *Sociology of Sport Journal*, *35*(2), 149–158. https://doi.org/10.1123/ssj.2017-0096.

Hwang, K. O., Ottenbacher, A. J., Green, A. P., Cannon-Diehl, M. R., Richardson, O., Bernstam, E. V., & Thomas, E. J. (2010). Social support in an Internet weight loss community. *International Journal of Medical Informatics*, *79*(1), 5–13.

International Data Corporation (2021). *Consumer enthusiasm for wearable devices drives the market to 28.4% growth in 2020, according to the IDC*. https://www.idc.com/getdoc.jsp?containerId=prUS47534521.

Irizarry, T., Dabbs, A. D., & Curran, C. R. (2015). Patient portals and patient engagement: A state of the science review. *Journal of Medical Internet Research*, *17*(6), e148.

Kreitzberg, D. S. C., Dailey, S. L., Vogt, T. M., Robinson, D., & Zhu, Y. (2016). What is your fitness tracker communicating?: Exploring messages and effects of wearable fitness devices. *Qualitative Research Reports in Communication*, *17*(1), 93–101.

Lemire, M., Paré, G., Sicotte, C., & Harvey, C. (2008). Determinants of Internet use as a preferred source of information on personal health. *International Journal of Medical Informatics*, *77*(11), 723–734.

Lewis, L. (2016, April 6). *A Japanese first-mover in the fitness wearables race. Financial Times.* https://www.ft.com/content/2b146d46-f274-11e5-9f20-c3a047354386.

Luczak, T., Burch, R., Lewis, E., Chander, H., & Ball, J. (2020). State-of-the-art review of athletic wearable technology: What 113 strength and conditioning coaches and athletic trainers from the USA said about technology in sports. *International Journal of Sports Science & Coaching, 15*(1), 26–40. https://doi.org/10.1177/1747954119885244.

Lupton, D. (2013). Quantifying the body: Monitoring and measuring health in the age of mHealth technologies. *Critical Public Health, 23*(4), 393–403.

Lupton, D. (2014, December). Self-tracking cultures: Towards a sociology of personal informatics. In *Proceedings of the 26th Australian computer-human interaction conference on designing futures: The future of design* (pp. 77–86).

Lupton, D. (2016). The diverse domains of quantified selves: Self-tracking modes and dataveillance. *Economy and Society, 45*(1), 101–122.

Mackert, M., Mabry-Flynn, A., Champlin, S., Donovan, E. E., & Pounders, K. (2016). Health literacy and health information technology adoption: The potential for a new digital divide. *Journal of Medical Internet Research, 18*(10), e264.

McManus, T. (2018, August 23). *How nickel-sized tech helps Eagles track Wentz's recovery.* ESPN. https://www.espn.com/blog/philadelphia-eagles/post/_/id/25698/technology-helps-eagles-track-recovery-of-players-like-carson-wentz.

Miah, A. (2017). *Sport 2.0: Transforming sports for a digital world.* Cambridge, MA: MIT Press.

Moore, P., & Robinson, A. (2016). The quantified self: What counts in the neoliberal workplace. *New Media & Society, 18*(11), 2774–2792.

NASA. (2006). *Spinoff.* https://www.nasa.gov/topics/nasalife/thermometer_pill.html.

Navarro, J., Peña, J., Cebolla, A., & Baños, R. (2020). Can Avatar Appearance Influence Physical Activity? User-Avatar Similarity and Proteus Effects on Cardiac Frequency and Step Counts. *Health Communication,* 1–8. https://doi.org/10.1080/10410236.2020.1834194.

Neter, E., & Brainin, E. (2012). eHealth literacy: Extending the digital divide to the realm of health information. *Journal of Medical Internet Research, 14*(1), e19.

Niknejad, N., Ismail, W. B., Mardani, A., Liao, H., & Ghani, I. (2020). A comprehensive overview of smart wearables: The state of the art literature, recent advances, and future challenges. *Engineering Applications of Artificial Intelligence, 90,* 103529.

Phelan, J. C., Link, B. G., & Tehranifar, P. (2010). Social conditions as fundamental causes of health inequalities: Theory, evidence, and policy implications. *Journal of Health and Social Behavior, 5*(1), S28–S40. https://doi.org/10.1177/0022146510383498.

Pink, S., Sumartojo, S., Lupton, D., & Heyes La Bond, C. (2017). Mundane data: The routines, contingencies and accomplishments of digital living. *Big Data & Society, 4*(1), 1–12.

Rains, S. A., Peterson, E. B., & Wright, K. B. (2015). Communicating social support in computer-mediated contexts: A meta-analytic review of content analyses examining support messages shared online among individuals coping with illness. *Communication Monographs*, *82*(4), 403–430.

Rich, E., & Miah, A. (2017). Mobile, wearable and ingestible health technologies: Towards a critical research agenda. *Health Sociology Review*, *26*(1), 84–97. https://doi.org/10.1080/14461242.2016.1211486.

Rimol, M. (2021). *Gartner forecasts global spending on wearable devices to total $81.5 billion in 2021*. Gartner. https://www.gartner.com/en/newsroom/press-releases/2021-01-11-gartner-forecasts-global-spending-on-wearable-devices-to-total-81-5-billion-in-2021.

Rum, L., Sten, O., Vendrame, E., Belluscio, V., Camomilla, V., Vannozzi, G., . . . & Bergamini, E. (2021). Wearable sensors in sports for persons with disability: A systematic review. *Sensors*, *21*(5), 1858.

Sarkar, U., Karter, A. J., Liu, J. Y., Adler, N. E., Nguyen, R., Lopez, A., & Schillinger, D. (2010). The literacy divide: Health literacy and the use of an internet-based patient portal in an integrated health system—results from the Diabetes Study of Northern California (DISTANCE). *Journal of Health Communication*, *15*(S2), 183–196.

Seaborn, K., & Fels, D. I. (2015). Gamification in theory and action: A survey. *International Journal of Human-Computer Studies*, *74*, 14–31.

Sharf, B. F. (1997). Communicating breast cancer on-line: Support and empowerment on the Internet. *Women & Health*, *26*(1), 65–84.

Smith, W. R. (2017). Communication, sportsmanship, and negotiating ethical conduct on the digital playing field. *Communication & Sport*, *5*(2), 160–185.

Smith, W. R., & Treem, J. (2017). Striving to be king of mobile mountains: Communication and organizing through digital fitness technology. *Communication Studies*, *68*(2), 135–151. https://doi.org/10.1080/10510974.2016.1269818.

Stragier, J., Vanden Abeele, M., Mechant, P., & De Marez, L. (2016). Understanding persistence in the use of Online Fitness Communities: Comparing novice and experienced users. *Computers in Human Behavior*, *64*(12), 34–42. https://doi.org/10.1016/j.chb.2016.06.013.

Timmermans, S., & Kaufman, R. (2020). Technologies and health inequities. *Annual Review of Sociology*, *46*, 583–602.

Van Dijck, J. (2014). Datafication, dataism and dataveillance: Big Data between scientific paradigm and ideology. *Surveillance & Society*, *12*(2), 197–208.

Vogels, E. (2020). About one-in-five Americans use a smart watch or fitness tracker. *Pew Research Center*. https://www.pewresearch.org/fact-tank/2020/01/09/about-one-in-five-americans-use-a-smart-watch-or-fitness-tracker/.

Waltz, E. (2015). A wearable turns baseball pitching into a science [News]. *IEEE Spectrum*, *52*(9), 16–17.

World Health Organization. (2011). *mHealth: New horizons for health through mobile technologies*. https://www.who.int/goe/publications/goe_mhealth_web.pdf.

Zimdars, M. (2021). The self-surveillance failures of wearable communication. *Journal of Communication Inquiry*, *45*(1), 24–44.

Index

abuse and maltreatment: athletes with disabilities and, 143–44; Biles, Simone, 86, 132, 161; body shaming and weight surveillance, 127–32; Cain, Mary, 127–28; coaches' role in, 83–84, 86, 127–29, 130, 133, 142–43; depression and, 142, 156; doctors and, 131–32, 161; Douglas, Gabby, 161; emotional abuse, 127—30, 141, 143–44; gender and, 143–44; #gymnastalliance, 161; in gymnastics, 129–30, 132–33, 140, 160–61; health and, 125–26; IOC Consensus Statement on harassment, 125, 127, 133; laws for athletic safety, 140; long-term consequences, 126–27, 130, 132–33; #MeToo, 161; Nassar, Larry, 132, 161; negative health consequences, 126–28, 130, 142; neglect rates, 126; nutritionists/dieticians and, 131; outside the United States, 149; physical abuse, 126, 127, 129, 130, 141, 143; post-sport life consequences, 130–31; preventative education and training, 146–47; prohibited conduct under SafeSport Code, 140–41; psychological abuse, 126, 130; race and, 143–44; Raisman, Aly, 161; reporting of, 127, 142, 148; response and resolution, 147–48; self-injury as coping mechanism, 132–33, 142; sexual abuse and harm, 126, 132–33, 141–43; shared on social media, 160–61; in swimming and diving, 128–29, 130–31; in track and field, 127–28, 131; US Center for SafeSport, 140–41, 144–48; verbal aggressions, 84. *See also* eating disorders and disordered eating

activism and advocacy, athletes': abuse reporting, 127; ascendancy of, 55; Biles, Simone, 32, 160–61; Black Lives Matter protests, 40–41, 53, 160; concerning health and well-being, 160; death of Trayvon Martin, 160; Douglas, Gabby, 161; Equal Pay Campaign, 160; Equal Play, 160; #gymnastalliance, 161; James, Lebron, 56; Kaepernick, Colin, 53; Love, Kevin, 55–56; Mahomes, Patrick, 56; #MeToo, 161; More Than A Vote advocacy group, 56; Osaka, Naomi, 160; player-led vs league-approved campaigns, 56; race and, 40–41, 56–57, 160; Raisman, Aly, 161; Rashford, Marcus, 56; social justice, 40–41,

95–99, 160; social media for, 55, 160–61, 163; spousal activism, 160; Wilson, A'ja, 56

alcohol misuse, 173, 177

American Academy of Pediatrics, 139

anxiety: Cain, Mary, 127; elite sports and, 175–76; increased risk in female athletes, 173, 175; individual sports vs team sports, 175; Kevin Love Fund, 55–56; Love, Kevin, 35–36; Osaka, Naomi, 6–7, 21, 32; rates of, 173, 177, 179–80; sexual abuse and, 142

Applequist, Janelle: author bio, 201; chapter abstract, ix; chapter by, 15–30

Arai, A., 159

archery, 180

Armstrong, C. G., 56

ASCD (Association for Supervision and Curriculum Development), 99, 102

Ashe, Arthur, 17

Association for Supervision and Curriculum Development (ASCD), 99, 102

athletes: coach-athlete communication, 80–86; commodification of, 5–6, 33–34, 156–57; cyclists, 17; golfers, 24; hockey players, 160, 179; personal brand, xii, 155, 157–60, 164; professional vs college athletes, 5; track and field athletes, 17, 22, 127–28, 131. *See also* abuse and maltreatment; baseball players; basketball players; coaches; college athletes; football players; gender; gymnasts; health; mental health; race; soccer players; social media and online communities; sport organizations and leagues; swimmers and divers; tennis players; youth sport

Athletes Connected, 8

Baker, J., 125

Bandhauler, D., 99

Basch, Charles, 100

baseball players: biometric data and privacy, 193; Harnisch, Pete, 35; injuries among youth, 85; mental health concerns and MLB, 35; Piersall, Jimmy, 1, 6, 35; steroid use, 17; wearable technology and, 189, 193. *See also* Major League Baseball (MLB); National Collegiate Athletic Association (NCAA)

basketball players: Brown, Sterling, 40–41; Cambage, Liz, 39; Carton, D. J., 5–6, 35; coaching abuse by Rice Jr., 86; Curry, Steph, 22, 55; DeRozan, DeMar, 4–5, 9, 21, 35–36; Gobert, Rudy, 51; HIV/AIDS, 17; House, Danuel, 112; Irving, Kyrie, 22, 24; James, Lebron, 56; Johnson, Magic, 17; Love, Kevin, 4–5, 9, 21, 35–36, 38, 55–56; McGee-Stafford, Imani, 39; mental health disclosures, 4, 5, 21, 35–36, 39; police brutality and, 40–41; proximity tracking devices for COVID-19, 113; racism in tournaments, 97; Sefolosha, Thabo, 40–41; White, Royce, 5, 21, 31–32, 36–37, 40; Wilson, A'ja, 39, 56. *See also* National Basketball Association (NBA); National Collegiate Athletic Association (NCAA); Women's National Basketball Association (WNBA)

Beauboeuf-LaFontant, T., 39

Bell, Lee Anne, 95–96

Bell, Travis R.: author bio, 201; chapter abstract, ix; chapter by, 15–30

Bennett, Michael, 179

Berg, B. K., 88

Bettman, Gary, 117

Biles, Simone: abuse, 86, 132, 161; activism of, 32, 160–61; fan response to, 9, 22, 32, 160, 162–63; mental health of, 1, 22–23, 155, 172; Nassar and, 161; Olympic Summer Games

Tokyo 2020/2021, 1, 7, 15, 22, 32, 155, 158–59; personal brand, 159; social media and, 22–23, 155, 158–59, 160–62
bipolar disorder, 1, 6
Bishop, R., 6, 35
Black Women's Health Imperative (BWHI), 53
Blaszka, M., 191–92
BNP Paribas Open tennis tournament, 2021, 114–15
borderline personality disorder, 31
Bol, N., 196
Bolt, Usain, 22
Borland, Chris, 2
Bowes, Ali: author bio, 202; chapter abstract, xiii; chapter by, 171–86
Brady, Tom, 19–20
Brown, Sterling, 40–41
Browning, Blair: author bio, 202; chapter abstract, xi–xii; chapter by, 107–23; referenced, 162
bulimia, 129, 130–33. *See also* eating disorders and disordered eating
Bündchen, Gisele, 19–20
Burke, Kenneth, 33, 37
Butterbaugh, Nicole: author bio, 202; chapter abstract, xi–xii; chapter by, 107–23
Butterworth, M. L., 53

Cain, Mary, 127–28
Cambridge, Liz, 39
cancer, 16
Carly (11-year-old swimmer), 130
Carton, D. J., 5–6, 35
Casper, J., 51–52
Cassilo, David: author bio, 202; chapter abstract, ix; chapter by, 1–14; referenced, 2, 5–6, 24, 35–36, 160
Castaldelli-Maia, J. M., 175
the Center. *See* US Center for SafeSport
Chen, M., 3
chronic traumatic encephalopathy (CTE), 18–20. *See also* concussions

coaches: athlete abuse and, 83–84, 86, 127–29, 130, 133, 142–43; athlete mental well-being and, 84–85; coach-athlete communication, 80–86; concussions and, 86; Court, Rich, 86; COVID-19 and recruitment, 116–17; eating disorders and, 83–84, 127–28; injuries and, 80–83, 86; Knight, Bobby, 84; Martin, Petra, 86; Rolovich, Nick, 24; Salazar, Alberto, 127; social support from, 82–83; Winslow, Greg, 86
college athletes: abusive coaches, 86; Carton, D. J., 5–6, 35; COVID-19 and, 7, 109, 116–17; holistic approach to health, 105; Holistic Kinesiology-Athletic Model, 105; masculinity and mental health, 8; mental health awareness, 8, 35, 40; mental health challenges of, 8, 40, 117; playing through injury, 81; student-athletes, 105; wearable technology and, 191–93; willingness to seek help, 7
communication: around eating disorders, 83–84; autoethnographic approaches, 9; coach-athlete communication, 80–86; family and, 63, 65–70; first-person accounts, 9, 21, 23; health communication's stakes, vii–viii; health information seeking, 191–92; mHealth, viii, 190; obituaries of athletes, 35; online support communities, 191; pro-social means of, 85; rhetoric, 32–33, 37–41, 53–54; timing and conditions of athlete communication, 35; use of humor, 35; verbal aggression in coaching, 84–85; wearable technology and, 190. *See also* activism and advocacy, athletes'; media framing and traditional media; social media and online communities
concussions: chronic traumatic encephalopathy, 18–20; coaches' role

in addressing, 86; depression and, 34; gendered identity and, 18–19; media framing of, 2, 18, 19–20; parental management of, 65–68; rates of, 81; reporting of, 9, 81; social isolation and, 34; technological and equipment advances, 67, 86; youth sport and, 20, 66–68, 81
Coombs, D. S., 160
Cooper, J. N., 55
Cooper Institute, 50, 55
Copelton, D. A., 195
corporate social responsibility (CSR) in sport, 45–57; as branding and marketing, 53; campaigns as public relations strategy, 48–49; children's health, 49; COVID-19 and, 51–54; CSR campaigns in sports leagues, 47–57; CSR defined, 47; intersectional lens on, 57; player-led initiatives and, 56
Court, Rick, 86
COVID-19: athletes testing positive, 51, 115–16; breakthrough cases, 115–16; bubble and hub approaches, 109–13, 118; cancellations due to, 108–10, 178; career transitions due to, 178, 180; collegiate-level responses, 109; contact tracing, 113–14; COVID-19 Testing and Surveillance Program, 109; CSR campaigns and platforms, 50–54; disparate impact of, 54; economic impact of, 23, 117–18; fan attendance and spectator policies, 110; health vs economics and fandom, 23, 54; heterogenous sports policies for, 109; hockey players and, 179; Join the Team, Get the Vaccine, 52; media framing of, 2, 23–24, 112, 119; mental health impacts, 112, 117–18, 171–72, 178–81; as mental health stressor, 7, 40; mitigation efforts, 178; MLS Unites, 53–54; NBA Together, 53–54; NFL and NFLPA and, 109; Olympic Summer Games Tokyo 2020/2021, 108, 110, 115, 172; partisan divide over, 54; PGA and, 114; psychological counselling during, 179; race and, 54; recruitment of college athletes, 116–17; retirement from sport and, 178; rhetoric of unity and, 53–54; soccer players and, 114, 178–79; social media and, 23–24, 54; sports leagues and public messaging, 51; Take The Shot for the WIN, 53–55; Take Your Shot campaign, 52; Vaccinate at the Plate, 52, 115; vaccines and vaccination, 24, 51–55, 114–16; wearable technology and, 113–14, 188–89; women in sport and, 23, 54, 179
Cranmer, Gregory A.: author bio, 202; chapter abstract, xi; chapter by, 79–94; referenced, 87
cricket, 180
CSR (corporate social responsibility). *See* corporate social responsibility (CSR) in sport
CTE (chronic traumatic encephalopathy), 18–20. *See also* concussions
Culp, Brian, 96, 97
Culvin, Alex: author bio, 202; chapter abstract, xiii; chapter by, 171–86; referenced, 176
Curriculum and Instruction (C&I), 99
Curry, Steph, 22, 55
cyclists, 17

Davis, Ashley, 129–30
DeChambeau, Bryson, 24
Dennis, Tyler, 114
DePadilla, L., 81
depression: abuse and maltreatment, 84, 142; abusive sports practices and, 156; Cain, Mary, 127; DeRozan, DeMar, 35; elite sports and, 175–76; gender and, 34, 39; increased risk in female athletes, 39, 173, 175;

individual vs team sports and, 175; injury and, 34, 82; Kevin Love Fund, 55–56; Love, Kevin, 35; Osaka, Naomi, 21; Phelps, Michael, 1, 31; rates of, 173, 177–178, 180; retirement and, 40
DeRozan, DeMar, 4–5, 9, 21, 35, 36
dietary disorders. *See* eating disorders and disordered eating
dieticians, 131
Discovery Education, 50
disordered eating. *See* eating disorders and disordered eating
distress, 173
doctors, 131–32, 161
Douglas, Gabby, 161
drug use, 16–17

eating disorders and disordered eating: abusive sports practices and, 127–28, 156; bulimia, 129, 130–31, 132–33; coaches and, 83–84, 127–28; communication around, 83–84; gender and, 34, 128–29, 173–75; Kowalski, Daniel, 128–29; mental health and, 83–84, 127–29; physical health consequences, 129; Seebohm, Emily, 128; sexual abuse and, 142; slim to win, 131; weight surveillance, 127–32. *See also* abuse and maltreatment
Elman, J. P., 195
Elsey, C., 4, 33, 35, 39
emotions, 89, 127–28, 129–30, 141, 143–44
employment: bodies as commodities, 33–34; career transitions, 178, 180; contracts and, 35, 36, 40; mental health and, 31–32, 35, 40; race and, 36; recruitment, 116–17; retirement, 2, 40, 89, 177–78
Engel, S. G., 83
Entman, R. M., 2
Esmonde, K., 194

Euro 2020 Group Stage soccer matches, 114
Evans, A. B., 178
EVERFI (educational technology company), 50

Facer-Childs, E. R., 178
fans. *See* sport fans
Fauci, Anthony, 55
Fedorocsko, M., 6, 35
femininity, 38
Ferguson, T., 38
FIFA, 189. *See also* soccer players
Fischer, E., 159
FITNESSGRAM initiative, 50
football players: Borland, Chris, 2; Brady, Tom, 19–20; COVID-19 vaccine hesitancy, 116; CTE, 18–20; eating disorders and, 129; head injuries, 2; Hernandez, Aaron, 19; Kaepernick, Colin, 53; Mahomes, Patrick, 56; painkiller use, 17; public health of sport, 19; Waters, Andre, 19; wearable technology use, 113, 187–89; Webster, Mike, 19. *See also* concussions; National Collegiate Athletic Association (NCAA); National Football League (NFL)
football (soccer) players. *See* soccer players
Fortier, K., 129
French Open 2021, 1, 6–7, 21, 32
Fútbol World Cup 2022, 115

Gamson, W. A., 16
gender: abuse and, 143–44; concern over injuries and, 71; concussions and gendered identity, 18–19; depression and, 34, 128–29, 173–75; eating disorders and, 128–29, 173–75; Equal Pay Campaign, 160; Equal Play, 160; intersection with race, 23, 38–39; mental health and, 173–76; research focus on male athletes, 173; risk factor for mental

ill-health, 175; sexism of fans, 162; sport specialization and, 71. *See also* masculinity, hegemonic; women athletes
Gerald, C., 22–23
Giulianotti, R., 48
Gobert, Rudy, 51
Goggin, G., 195
golfers, 24
Goodyear, V. A., 194
Goutterbarge, V., 173
gymnasts: abuse and maltreatment of, 129–30, 132–33, 140, 160–61; activism of, 32, 160–61; Davis, Ashley, 129–30; Douglas, Gabby, 161; #gymnastalliance, 161; increased risk of poor mental health, 175; Maroney, McKayla, 132; #MeToo, 161; Raisman, Aly, 161; Strug, Kerri, 22. *See also* Biles, Simone

Hanninen, V., 34
Harnisch, Pete, 35
Harrison, C. Keith: author bio, 202; chapter abstract, xi; chapter by, 95–106
Hassan, Martha James, 97–98
health: athlete welfare, 172; Black Women's Health Imperative (BWHI), 53; body shaming and, 130; bulimia's effects on, 131; cancer, 16; children's health and CSR, 49; CSR health promotion campaigns, 47–57; defined, 156; determinants of well-being, 156; environmental factors in, 95–96, 98, 105; health equity, 95, 98, 99, 104; health policymaking, 108–18; health-related fitness and school achievement, 101; performance-enhancing drugs, 16–17; public health, 15–18, 19, 23; social media and online communities and, 157–58, 195–96; sport and abuse, 125–26; sport's negative and positive effects on, 125–28, 156–57; wearable technology and, 191–92, 193, 196; weight surveillance, 127–28; youth sport and, 50, 63–74, 100–105, 139. *See also* COVID-19; eating disorders and disordered eating; mental health
Health Education Teacher Education (HETE), 99
Henriksen, K., 180
Hernandez, Aaron, 19
Hillard, R. C., 8
HIV/AIDS, 17
hockey players, 111, 160, 179. *See also* National Collegiate Athletic Association (NCAA); National Hockey League (NHL); National Women's Hockey League (NWHL)
Hodge, Sam, 97
Holistic Kinesiology-Athletic Model, 102–3
House, Danuel, 112
Hyman, M., 79

injuries: career-ending injuries and retirement, 2, 89; coaches and, 80–81, 129–30; communication barriers about, 66–67; COVID-19 and rehabilitation, 178; depression and, 34, 82; disabled list, 35; gender and concern over, 71; mental health impacts, 82, 176–77; overuse injuries, 85, 86; painkillers, 17; parental assessment challenges, 66–69; playing through, 81; playing through pain and, 33–34, 68–69, 177; prevention and wearable technology, 189; rehabilitation and recovery, 82–83; reporting of, 68–69, 80–81; specialization and, 70–71; stigmatization around, viii, 81; youth sports and risk of, 65
International Olympic Committee (IOC), 125, 127, 133
Irving, Kyrie, 22, 24
Ivy League, 109

James, Lebron, 56
Johnson, Magic, 17
Johnson, Nicole: author bio, 202–3; chapter abstract, xii; chapter by, 139–54
Jones, R. L., 83

Kaepernick, Colin, 53
Kavanagh, E., 162, 172, 181
Kern, A., 8
Kerr, Gretchen: author bio, 203; chapter abstract, xii–xiii; chapter by, 155–69; referenced, 126, 143–44, 162
Kevin Love Fund, 55–56
kinesiology, 98–105; courses in, 98–99; existing model, 101–2; Holistic Kinesiology-Athletic Model, 102–5; new model in, 98–101, 102–5
KINEXON, 113
King, Billy Jean, 22
Kluch, Y., 5–6, 24, 35
Knight, Bobby, 84
Kowalski, Daniel, 128–29
Kreitzberg, D. S. C., 191
Kuettel, A., 175
Kuhn, A. W., 18

Larsen, C., 175
Lavelle, Katherine L.: author bio, 203; chapter abstract, ix–x; chapter by, 31–45; referenced, 5, 21, 36, 38
Lawrie, S., 3
Litchfield, C., 162
Louganis, Greg, 17
Love, Kevin, 4–5, 9, 21, 35–36, 38, 55–56
Luczak, T., 194

Mack, C. D., 113
Mackert, M., 196
MacPherson, Ellen: author bio, 204; chapter abstract, xii–xiii; chapter by, 155–69; referenced, 162
Mahomes, Patrick, 56

Major League Baseball (MLB): COVID-19 and, 51, 52, 109, 111, 115; CSR and, 48, 50, 51; Discovery Education partnership, 50; EVERFI partnership, 50; mental health support, 35; Play Ball at Home CSR campaign, 51; Play Ball CSR campaign, 50; Summer Slugger platform, 50; Vaccinate at the Plate, 52, 115; wearable technology use, 189. *See also* baseball players; National Collegiate Athletic Association (NCAA)
Major League Soccer (MLS), 50–51, 52, 53–54. *See also* National Collegiate Athletic Association (NCAA); soccer players
Maroney, McKayla, 132
Marshall, Brandon, 31
Martin, Petra, 86
Martin, Trayvon, 160
masculinity, hegemonic: concussions and, 18–19; CTE and hypermasculinity, 20; defined, 45n3; depression and, 34; limitations on male athletes, 5, 21, 32; mental health and, 8, 20, 32, 34, 38; pain valorized, 33, 68–69, 81; race and, 36; in sport, 33, 38; suicide and, 20. *See also* gender
McArdle, Danielle: author bio, 203; chapter abstract, xi; chapter by, 95–106
McCall, Kristen West, 128
McCann, Michael, 31–32, 40
McConnell, Erin: author bio, 203; chapter abstract, xii; chapter by, 139–54
McGannon, Kerry R.: author bio, 203; chapter abstract, xii; chapter by, 125–38; referenced, 131, 132–33
McGee-Stafford, Imani, 39
McGinty, E. E., 3
McGlynn, Joseph: author bio, 203; chapter abstract, x; chapter by, 63–78

McMahon, Jennifer: author bio, 204; chapter abstract, xii; chapter by, 125–38; referenced, 130, 131, 132–33

media framing and traditional media: athlete mental health and, 1–10; of athlete mental health disclosures, 2, 4–6, 21–22; citizen journalism, 3; commodification of athletes, 5–6; concussions and, 2, 18, 19–20; COVID-19 and, 2, 23–24, 112; CTE and, 19–20; defined, 2, 16; education and miseducation of public, viii, 2, 20; ESPN.com series on mental health, 35–36; HIV/AIDS, 17; performance-enhancing drugs, 16–17; public health and, 16–18; role of wives in health issues, 19–20; stigmatization of mental health and, 3–4; as tool, 10; women's sport coverage, 23

Mehrsafar, A. H., 179, 181

mental health: defined, 171; alcohol misuse, 173; athlete vulnerability, 7; Biles, Simone, 1, 22–23, 155, 172; bipolar disorder, 1, 6; borderline personality disorder, 31; career transitions and, 176–77; coaches' impact on, 84–86; commodification of athletes' bodies and, 33–34; communicative practices and, vii–viii, 9, 21, 23, 32–33, 80–86, 89; COVID-19 and, 112, 117–18, 171–72, 178–81; culture of excellence in sport, 174, 180; defined, 45n1; DeRozan, DeMar, 4–5, 21, 35, 36; destigmatization, 23; disclosures of, 4–5, 6, 21, 24, 35–39, 172; elite sports and, 175–76; emotions and emotional regulation, 39, 89, 127–30, 141, 143–44; factors and stressors of, 34, 39–41, 173–77; gender and, 173––76; injury and, 82, 176–77; lack of attention on, 1, 34, 172; Love, Kevin, 4–5, 21, 35–36; management of, 40; mental ill-health vs poor mental health, 171, 173; mental illness, 40–41, 45n2; vs mental toughness, 1, 31, 33–34, 172, 174; Osaka, Naomi, 1, 6–7, 21–22, 32; panic attacks, 21, 35–36; Phelps, Michael, 1, 31, 172; physical activity as protective of, 180; physical health and, 126–27; Piersall, Jimmy, 1, 6, 35; rates of distress, 173; retirement and, 89, 177; rhetoric of, 32–33, 36–41, 53–54; seeking help for, 7, 174; self-protection, 22–23; sleep disturbance, 173, 177; specialization and, 175; stigmatization, viii, 3–4, 20–21, 33–35, 174; supports for, 181; toxic behaviors in sport, 174; violence and, 3–4, 20; wearable technology and, 194–95; work spill and, 176; youth sport stressors on, 40. *See also* abuse and maltreatment; anxiety; depression; eating disorders and disordered eating; gender; health; media framing and traditional media; social media and online communities

mental health awareness: among college athletes, 8, 35, 40; athletes as advocates, 1, 5, 22–23, 32, 160; *Athletes Connected,* 8; ESPN.com series, 35–36

Merz, Z. C., 35

mHealth (mobile health), xiii, 190

Miah, A., 189, 192

Mikkilineni, Sai Datta: author bio, 204; chapter abstract, xi; chapter by, 79–94

Minor Athlete Abuse Prevention Policies (MAAPP), 144–45

MLB. *See* Major League Baseball (MLB)

MLS. *See* Major League Soccer (MLS)

mobile health (mHealth), xiii, 190

Molloy, C., 37

Montez de Oca, J., 49, 50

Moretton, Gilles, 22

Morgan, Piers, 22

the Movement, 140, 144–45, 147–49
Murray, C., 16

Nassar, Larry, 132, 161
National Association of Intercollegiate Basketball National Tournament, 97
National Basketball Association (NBA): COVID-19 health policies, 24, 51–52, 108–11; COVID-19 revenue impacts, 118; ESPN.com series on mental health, 35–36; Jr. NBA, 50; Jr. NBA at Home, 50–51; masculinity culture within, 21; NBA Cares CSR platform, 47; Protect Our Power campaign and, 56; societal oppression as stressor, 40–41. *See also* basketball players; National Collegiate Athletic Association (NCAA); Women's National Basketball Association (WNBA)
National Collegiate Athletic Association (NCAA): COVID-19 and, 108–9, 113, 117; healthcare services, 105; promotion of health and safety, vii; wearable technology use, 189, 194. *See also* college athletes
National Council of Negro Women (NCNW), 53
National Football League (NFL): Cooper Institute partnership, 50; COVID-19, 51, 52, 109, 113, 115, 117–18; Crucial Catch CSR initiative, 47–48; CSR and, 47–51; CTE and, 19–20; FITNESSGRAM initiative, 50; football's risks and, 49–50; Fuel up to Play 60 CSR initiative, 47, 49–50; Huddle at Home CSR campaign, 50; Inspire Change campaign, 53, 56–57; My Cleats, My Cause, 56; Play 60 CSR campaign, 49–50; promotion of health and safety, vii; protection of sport over players, 19–20; repackaging Kaepernick's activism, 53; wearable technology, 187–89; youth sport and, 50
National Football League Players Association (NFLPA), 109, 115
National Governing Bodies (NGBs), 145–46, 148–49
National Hockey League (NHL): adoption of Play 60 model, 50; COVID-19, 51–52, 109, 111, 179; CSR campaigns, 48, 51. *See also* hockey players; National Collegiate Athletic Association (NCAA); National Women's Hockey League (NWHL)
National Women's Hockey League (NWHL), 111
National Women's Soccer League (NWSL), 11, 23
NBA. *See* National Basketball Association (NBA)
NCAA. *See* National Collegiate Athletic Association (NCAA)
NFL. *See* National Football League (NFL)
NFL Alumni, 53
NHL. *See* National Hockey League (NHL)
NHL/NHLPA player assistance program, 160
Nike, 127–28
Niknejad, N., 190
nutritionists, 131

Olympic and Paralympic Movement, 140, 144–45, 147–49
Olympic Summer Games Tokyo 2020/2021: Biles, Simone, 1, 7, 15, 22, 32, 155, 158–59; COVID-19 and, 108, 110, 115, 172
Omalu, Bennet, 19
Osaka, Naomi, 1, 6–7, 9, 21–22, 32, 160

pain, 17, 33–34, 177. *See also* injuries
panic attacks, 21, 35–36
Paramio-Salcines, J. L., 49

parents and parental roles: barriers to communication, 66–67; concussions and, 9, 20, 66–68, 73; health and development double-bind, 68; involvement in youth sports, 64, 69–70; parental biases, 67–68; risk perception, 73; youth sports specialization, 85
Parmentier, M. A., 159
Parrott, S., 36
Parry, K. D., 23
performance-enhancing drugs, 16–17
Perry, Carly: author bio, 204; chapter abstract, xiii; chapter by, 171–86; referenced, 174
PFA (Professional Footballers' Association), 178–79
PGA (Professional Golfers' Association), 114
Phelps, Michael, 1, 31, 172
Physical Education Teacher Education (PETE), 99
Piersall, Jimmy, 1, 6, 35
Poucher, Z. A., 34
Price, Angela, 160
Price, Carey, 160
Proctor, Larry D.: author bio, 204; chapter abstract, xi; chapter by, 95–106
Professional Footballers' Association (PFA), 178–79. *See also* soccer players
Professional Golfers' Association (PGA), 114
public health, 15–19, 23. *See also* health
public service announcements (PSAs), 48, 52

race: abuse and, 143–44; athlete activism and, 40–41, 56–57, 160; Black Lives Matter protests, 40–41, 53, 160; Black players banned from tournament, 97; Black women athletes, 38–39; COVID-19 and, 54; employment and, 36; intersection with gender, 23, 36, 38–39; mental health advocacy and, 5, 21; racism of fans, 38–39, 162; social justice, 95–99; systemic racism, 36, 40–41; Whiteness as relatability, 38
Raisman, Aly, 161
Rascon, N. A., 191–92
Rashford, Marcus, 56
Reardon, C. L., 181
Reitz, Aaron, 22
retirement from sport, 89, 177
Rey, Rikishi T.: author bio, 204; chapter abstract, xi; chapter by, 79–94
rhetoric, 32–33, 36–41, 53–54. *See also* communication
Rice, Mike, Jr., 86
Rice, Stephanie, 125
Rice Effect, 86
Rich, E., 192
Rolovich, Nick, 24
Rovegno, I., 99
Rugg, Adam: author bio, 204–5; chapter abstract, x; chapter by, 47–61

Salazar, Alberto, 127
Sanderson, Jimmy: author bio, 201; chapter by, vii–xiv; referenced, 2, 159, 162
Satterfield, J. W., 38
Schinke, R., 178, 180
schools: academic achievement and health-related fitness, 101; community support of students, 103; coordinated school health (CSH) approach, 101; mental health of school children, 194–95; partnerships with sports leagues, 49–50; role in youth health, 100–101; wearable technology and, 194–95; Whole School, Whole Communities, Whole Child (WSCC) model, 102. *See also* kinesiology
Schuck, R. I., 35, 39
Seebohm, Emily, 128
Sefolosha, Thabo, 40–41

sleep disturbance, 173, 177
Smith, D. K., 51–52
Smith, Roth: author bio, 205; chapter abstract, xiii; chapter by, 187–200
Smith, W. R., 191, 195
Sobande, F., 54
soccer players: COVID-19 and, 114–15, 178–79; media framing of concussions, 2; Rashford, Marcus, 56; wearable technology, 189. *See also* FIFA; Major League Soccer (MLS); National Collegiate Athletic Association (NCAA); National Women's Soccer League (NWSL); Professional Footballers' Association (PFA); Women's Super League
social justice, 40–41, 95–99, 160
social media and online communities: abuse and maltreatment awareness, 160–61; athlete activism and, 55, 160–61, 163; athletes in the public sphere, 157; Biles, Simone, 22–23, 155, 158–62; brand building for athletes, 159–60; construction of being healthy/fit, 195–96; COVID-19 and, 23–24, 54; DeRozan, DeMar, 5, 21, 35–36; extension of self, 158; focus on winning in sport, 164; #gymnastalliance, 161; health outcomes, 157, 159, 161–64; Instagram, 21–22, 55; Love, Kevin, 5, 21; mental health and, 5, 20–24, 35–36, 157; #MeToo, 161; negative interactions on, 157, 161–62, 164; Osaka, Naomi, 21–22, 160; public health forum, 23; racism on, 162–63; Reddit, 162; sexism on, 162–63; as support system, 22, 191; Twitter, 6, 21–22, 35, 55; wearable technology and, 191, 194
Souter, G., 180
sport, culture of: burnout, 25; celebrity, 25; romanticization of unity, 53–54; US nationalism and, 53. *See also* athletes; gender; sport organizations and leagues
sport fans: COVID-19 and, 112, 114–15; cultivated in schools, 49–50; player-led activism causes and, 56; racism of, 38–39, 162; reactions to mental health disclosures, 9, 21–22, 36, 38, 159; sexism of, 38–39, 162; social media and, 9, 22, 155, 158–62, 164; unifying messages as league engagement, 54; wearable technology and, 189
sport organizations and leagues: abuse and maltreatment and, 125, 127, 133, 146–48; athlete activism and, 53, 56; athletes' use of social media, 163; COVID-19 and revenue decrease, 117–18; COVID-19 bubble and hub approaches, 109–13, 118; COVID-19 policies, 109–18; COVID-19 vaccine, 114–16; CSR campaigns in, 47–57; duty of care post-sport, 133–34; education policies, 146–47, 177; FIFA, 189; health policymaking in, vii, 108–18; High Reliability Organizational Theory, 118; IOC, 125, 127, 133; Ivy League, 109; MLS, 51–54; National Governing Bodies (NGBs), 145–46, 148–49; NWHL, 111; NWSL, 23, 111; organizational policy and mental health, vii, 112; PFA, 178–79; PGA, 114; public service announcements (PSAs), 48, 52; Sport Singapore, 149; supports for athlete health, 181; USA Gymnastics, 22; USOPC, 140, 145;wearable technology and, 113–14, 189; WNBA, 40–41, 48, 50–53, 114; Women's Super League, 129; Women's Tennis Association, 160. *See also* Major League Baseball (MLB); National Basketball Association (NBA); National Collegiate Athletic Association (NCAA); National Football

League (NFL); National Hockey League (NHL)
sport-related concussion (SRC). *See* concussions
Sport Singapore, 149
SCR (sport-related concussions). *See* concussions
Stafford, A., 126
Stick, M., 162
Stirling, A., 143–44
Stokowski, Sarah: author bio, 205; chapter abstract, xi; chapter by, 95–106
Stragier, J., 191
Strayhorn, Terrell, 96
Strittmatter, A.M., 108
Strug, Kerri, 22
suicidal ideation, 1, 31, 34, 127, 142
suicide, 19, 20
Sundgot-Borgen, J., 128, 130–31
swimmers and divers: abuse of athletes, 128–29, 130–31; Carly (11 years old), 130; HIV/AIDS, 17; Kowalski, Daniel, 128–29; Louganis, Greg, 17; Phelps, Michael, 1, 31, 172; Rice, Stephanie, 125; Seebohm, Emily, 128; weight surveillance, 128

TBI (traumatic brain injuries), 85–86
tennis players: athlete activism, 160; HIV/AIDS, 17; King, Billy Jean, 22; Osaka, Naomi, 1, 6–7, 21–22, 32, 160; Williams, Serena, 22, 38–39, 162; Williams, Venus, 22, 38–39. *See also* National Collegiate Athletic Association (NCAA); Women's Tennis Association
Tomas, F., 129
track and field athletes, 17, 22, 127–28, 131
traumatic brain injuries (TBI), 85–86
Treem, J., 191
Trump, Donald, 53
Turnock, B. J., 15–16

UEFA European Championship 2020, 172
USA Gymnastics, 22
US Center for SafeSport: abuse prevention, 140, 144–47; Athlete Culture and Climate Survey (2020), 141–43; Centralized Disciplinary Database (CDD), 148; Culture and Climate Survey (2020), 148; Minor Athlete Abuse Prevention Policies (MAAPP), 144–45; monitoring of National Governing Bodies, 145; monitoring of USOPC, 145; response to and resolution of abuse allegations, 147–48; SafeSport Code, 140–41
US Olympic and Paralympic Committee (USOPC), 140, 145
US Open tennis tournament 2021, 115

Valkonen, J., 34
Vella, S. A., 181

Wahl, O. F., 4
Walton, C. C., 175
Waltz, E., 193
Warner, S., 88
Waters, Andre, 19
wearable technology: ableism and, 195; Apple Watch, 188; athletic performance, 189; COVID-19 and, 188–89; defined, 187–88; digital inequalities and, 196; discontinued use of, 190–91, 194; Fitbit, 188, 193–95; gamification aspects, 190; Garmin VIRB, 192–93; health and, 189, 191–93, 196; Health Insurance Portability and Accountability Act (HIPAA), 193; increased use of, 188–90; ingestible devices, 192; privacy considerations, 193–97; Proteus technologies, 192; Samsung, 188; spectators and, 189; sports cameras, 192–93; Strava, 191, 194–95; sustained use of, 190–91;

theories around use of technology, 190; virtual reality, 189; Zebra Technologies, 189
Weathers, Melinda R.: author bio, 201; chapter by, vii–xiv
Webster, Mike, 19
weight surveillance, 127–32. *See also* abuse and maltreatment; eating disorders and disordered eating
well-being. *See* health; mental health
Wenner, L., 87
White, A. J., 2
White, Royce: criticism of, 31–32; disclosure of mental health, 5, 21, 36; employment and mental health, 31, 40; rhetorical ecology and, 37
whole child health, 99, 100–105
Whole School, Whole Communities, Whole Child (WSCC) model, 102–3
Williams, Serena, 22, 38–39, 162
Williams, Venus, 22, 38–39
Willson, Erin: author bio, 205; chapter abstract, xii–xiii; chapter by, 155–69; referenced, 143–44
Wilson, A'ja, 39, 56
Wimbledon 2021, 32
Winslow, Greg, 86
WNBA (Women's National Basketball Association), 40–41, 48, 50–53, 114. *See also* basketball players; National Collegiate Athletic Association (NCAA)
WNBA players union, 53–55
women athletes: absent from concussion conversation, 20; abuse rates and, 144; backlash against female athletes of color, 23; Black athletes' identities, 38; Black women and depression, 39; COVID-19 and, 23, 54, 179; eating disorders and, 173–74, 175; Equal Pay Campaign, 160; Equal Play, 160; fan sexism and social media, 162; hyper-femininity of Black athletes, 38; increased risk various ill-health outcomes, 139, 173–75; misogyny toward, 38–39; research focus on lean-physique sports, 173–74; role of spouses in health issues, 19–20; stressors on Black women, 39
Women's National Basketball Association (WNBA), 40–41, 48, 50–53, 114. *See also* basketball players; National Collegiate Athletic Association (NCAA)
Women's Super League, 129. *See also* soccer players
Women's Tennis Association, 160. *See also* tennis players
Wooden, John, 97
work spill, 176
World Health Organization (WHO), 15, 45, 125, 156, 171, 190
WSCC (Whole School, Whole Communities, Whole Child) model, 102–3

Yang, M., 126–27
youth sport: abuse of athletes, 86, 130, 142–45; burnout, 70; as coming-of-age bridge, 64; concussions and, 20, 66–68, 81; COVID-19 and recruitment, 116–17; CSR campaigns targeting, 49–51; family demographics and, 63–64, 74; football, 49–50, 74; health and, 63–74, 100–105, 139; Holistic Kinesiology-Athletic Model, 102–4; mental health stressors in, 40; Minor Athlete Abuse Prevention Policies (MAAPP), 144–45; NFL surveillance of youth fitness, 50; overtraining of athletes, 174; playing through injury, 68–69, 81; reliance on statistics, 74; risks in, 65–68; school partnerships with sports leagues, 49–50; socialization and, 64–65, 68; sport specialization, 70–71, 85; trends in, 79; USA Football, 49–50. *See also* parents and parental roles

Zehntner, Chris: author bio, 205; chapter abstract, xii; chapter by, 125–38

Zimdars, M., 194

About the Editors

Jimmy Sanderson (Ph.D., Arizona State University) is an Associate Professor in the Department of Kinesiology and Sport Management at Texas Tech University. His research interests center on social media and its intersection in sport along with research interests in sport and health/family communication. He is the author/editor/co-editor of 5 scholarly books and has over eighty academic journal publications.

Melinda R. Weathers (Ph.D., George Mason University) is an Associate Professor in the Department of Communication Studies at Sam Houston State University in Huntsville, Texas. Her scholarly interests include intercultural communication, gender and women's health issues, and new communication technologies. Dr. Weathers' research has encompassed a range of topics addressing issues related to messages within relational, institutional, societal, and health contexts. Her research regarding health communication, sport communication, and new communication technologies has been published in journals such as *Communication and Sport*, *Sport Management Review*, *Communication Quarterly*, and *Journal of Sports Media*.

ABOUT THE CONTRIBUTORS

Dr. Janelle Applequist (Ph.D., Penn State University) is an Associate Professor of Advertising at the University of South Florida. She is the author of *Broadcast pharmaceutical advertising in the United States: Primetime pill pushers* and co-author of *CTE, media, and the NFL: Framing a public health crisis as a football epidemic*.

Dr. Travis R. Bell (Ph.D., University of South Florida) is Associate Professor of Digital and Sports Media at the University of South Florida. His research focuses on sports media and identity, intersecting with health, gender, and race. He is lead author of *CTE, media, and the NFL*.

Dr. Ali Bowes is a Senior Lecturer in the Sociology of Sport at Nottingham Trent University. Ali is the co-editor of *The Professionalisation of Women's Sport*, on the editorial board of *Managing Sport and Leisure*, on the board of the Football Collective, and a Policy Advisor for Fair Game.

Dr. Blair W. Browning is an Associate Professor in the Communication Department at Baylor University. His research focuses on communication and sport as well as on interim/temporary leadership in organizations. He teaches courses in leadership, conflict management, and small group communication.

Nicole Butterbaugh is an M.A. Communication candidate at Baylor University expected to graduate in May 2023. She earned her B.A. Communication at the University of Oklahoma in 2021, graduating in three years. She aspires to pursue a Ph.D. in the Communication field and continue her research in Sport Communication.

Dr. David Cassilo is a former sports journalist turned academic. An assistant professor at Kennesaw State University, David's research interests largely focus on media portrayals of health issues in sport, specifically examining concussions and mental health. His work has been published in leading academic journals and presented at academic conferences.

Dr. Alex Culvin is a Senior Lecturer in Sports Business at Leeds Beckett University and works in player and union relations at FIFPro. Alex's PhD examined football as work for women in England. Alex is the chair of the Football Collective and a Policy Advisor for Fair Game.

Dr. Gregory A. Cranmer is an Associate Professor of Sport Communication in the Department of Communication at Clemson University and a research fellow for the United States Center for Mental Health and Sport. His research focuses on interpersonal, organizational, and health communication within the context of sport.

Dr. C. Keith Harrison is a professor of business, Hip Hop, and Sport at UCF. Harrison is a former scholar-baller at Cerritos College and West Texas A&M where he was a center on the football team (#51). Harrison was a Nasir Jones Hip Hop Fellow at Harvard University's Hutchins Center for African and African American Research (2020–21).

Nicole Johnson is the NGB Services Coordinator for the U.S. Center for SafeSport and an M.A. student at the University of Denver studying International Human Rights. Her research interests include sport governance and the role of the global sports regime in protecting and violating human rights.

Dr. Gretchen Kerr is a Professor and Dean of the Faculty of Kinesiology and Physical Education at the University of Toronto and a co-Director of the E-Alliance, the Canadian Gender Equity in Sport Research Hub. Gretchen's research addresses maltreatment, gender-based violence, and promoting safe, equitable sport opportunities.

Dr. Katherine L. Lavelle (Wayne State University PhD) is an Associate Professor of Communication Studies at the University of Wisconsin-La Crosse. Her previous research has explored representations of race, nationality, sex/gender, and mental health in sport. She currently serves on the Board of Directors for IACS (International Association for Communication and Sport).

Danielle H. McArdle is currently pursuing a PhD in sport management in the Isenberg School of Management at the University of Massachusetts-Amherst. She studies the intersection between diversity and inclusion and consumer behavior in sport.

Erin McConnell is the Prevention Program and Research Coordinator for the U.S. Center for SafeSport. Erin is trained in community psychology and strives to apply principles of empowerment and inclusivity to her work with athletes. Her research has focused on the prevention of abuse and maltreatment within the contexts of higher education, sports, and youth-serving organizations.

Dr. Kerry R. McGannon is a Full Professor in Sport and Exercise Psychology. Research interests include socio-cultural issues in sport and exercise, identities, and critical interpretations of topics regarding health and performance. She uses critical qualitative research methodologies (e.g., discourse analysis, narrative analysis) to explore the media as a cultural site of identity constructions.

Dr. Joseph McGlynn (Ph.D., The University of Texas at Austin) is an Assistant Professor in Communication Studies at the University of North Texas. His research focuses on health communication and risk perception in sport contexts. His work seeks to improve health communication efforts by identifying influential factors that affect risk judgments.

Dr. Jennifer McMahon is an Associate Professor in Education at University of Tasmania, Australia. Before moving into academia, she was an elite swimmer who represented Australia at an International level winning numerous medals. As a result of her own experiences as an athlete, she was motivated to do more regarding athlete welfare. Since then, her research has centered on coach education, athlete welfare, athlete experience, the legacy of abuse post-sport, and the human rights of athletes in sport.

Dr. Ellen MacPherson is a Senior Research Associate in the Faculty of Kinesiology and Physical Education at the University of Toronto. Her research addresses social relationships in sport and online contexts, athlete welfare, and fostering safe and developmentally appropriate sport environments.

Sai Datta Mikkilineni is a first-year Ph.D. student in communication at the University of Alabama. Operating primarily within the realm of media psychology, he explores the cognitive and emotional responses to sport-related content. Additionally, he investigates the processes and effects of health persuasion as a function of celebrity endorsement.

Carly Perry is a PhD student at the University of Central Lancashire where she researches mental health and professional women's football. She competed at the NCAA D1 level in soccer in the United States and her research into mental health and elite-level women's sport has received multiple conference awards internationally.

Dr. Larry D. Proctor maintains research interests examining the impact of the social determinants of health on education/health. Dr. Proctor's academic experiences are grounded in athletics, physical education, and health-related fitness. His research interests examine the impact socioeconomic status/environmental influences have on biological expression (academic, health, and athletic disparities).

Dr. Rikishi T. Rey is an Assistant Professor of Sport Communication in the Department of Communication at Clemson University. Her research focuses on health-related issues within sport, including injury reporting, concussion management, and athlete-coach relationships. She received her doctoral degree from Chapman University with a concentration in health and sport communication.

Dr. Adam Rugg is an Associate Professor in the Department of Communication at Fairfield University. His research focuses on critically interrogating how sport leagues and teams leverage pressing social issues in their philanthropic efforts and general marketing strategies in ways that reaffirm existing power structures and dominant ideologies in US society.

Dr. Roth Smith is an assistant professor in the School of Communication Studies at the University of Tennessee. Roth researches how communication facilitates or constrains organizing processes in fluid, emergent, or partially formed organizational settings.

Dr. Sarah Stokowski currently serves as an Assistant Professor in the Department of Educational and Organizational Leadership Development at Clemson University. She studies college athlete development specializing in the personal development literacies.

Erin Willson, MSc., is currently a PhD student in the Faculty of Kinesiology and Physical Education at the University of Toronto. Her areas of research interest include maltreatment in sport, athlete empowerment and advocacy. As a former Olympian, Erin brings a unique perspective to her research endeavors.

Dr. Chris Zehntner is a lecturer in physical education at Southern Cross University, Australia. He teaches physical education pedagogy and sports coaching. Dr. Zehntner researches in the field of sociology of sport. His research centers on coach education, mentoring in coaching, and the barriers marginalized groups face in sport participation.

www.ingramcontent.com/pod-product-compliance
Lightning Source LLC
Chambersburg PA
CBHW020117010526
44115CB00008B/871